Alison Lurie

COSTERUS NEW SERIES 127

Alison Lurie

A Critical Study

Judie Newman

 Amsterdam-Atlanta, GA 2000

ISBN 90-420-1222-6

© Editions Rodopi B.V.
   Amsterdam - Atlanta, GA 2000

Printed in The Netherlands

For James

Contents

Preface   1

Acknowledgements   2

Chapter One.   Biographical Introduction   4

Chapter Two.   Hell Week with Emerson and Thoreau:
Love and Friendship   28

Chapter Three.   Walter Benjamin Goes to Hollywood:
The Nowhere City   47

Chapter Four.   The Revenge of the Trance Maiden:
Imaginary Friends   77

Chapter Five.   The Ghost-Writer:
Real People and *Women and Ghosts*   95

Chapter Six.   Vietnam Domestic:
The War Between The Tates   110

Chapter Seven.   The Uses of Enchantment:
Only Children   127

Chapter Eight: Paleface Into Redskin:
Foreign Affairs   142

Chapter Nine: Truth, Secrets and Lies:
The Truth About Lorin Jones   161

Chapter Ten: The Gay Imaginary:
The Last Resort   176

Bibliography   195

Index   216

Preface

Page references are to the following editions:

Poems and Plays by V. R. Lang (New York: Random House, 1975).

Love and Friendship (London: Penguin, 1977).

The Nowhere City (London: Penguin, 1977).

Imaginary Friends (London: Penguin, 1978).

Real People (London: Penguin, 1978).

The War Between the Tates (London: Penguin, 1977).

Only Children (London: Heinemann, 1979).

Foreign Affairs (London: Abacus, 1986).

The Truth About Lorin Jones (London: Michael Joseph, 1988).

Women and Ghosts (London: Heinemann, 1994).

The Last Resort (London: Vintage, 1999).

2

Acknowledgements

In writing what follows I have incurred many debts, too many indeed to name individually here. The responsibility for any errors is of course entirely mine. I am grateful especially to all the students in my Contemporary American Fiction Seminar at the University of Newcastle upon Tyne, particularly Jon Bennett, Claire Chambers and Sally Hall, whose discussion of *The Nowhere City* was invaluable (if largely unprintable). Among other individuals who helped with queries or made useful suggestions or contributions I take this opportunity of thanking Jenny Allen, Emily Arch, Bruce Babington, Tony Badger, David Barker, Celeste-Marie Bernier, Malcolm Bradbury, Rowena Bryson, Gloria Cronin, Alison Gallagher, Richard Godden, Cindy Hamilton, Simon Jarvis, Yvonne Jerrold, Margaret Jones, James Knowles, Claire Lamont, Hermann Moisl, Chris Perriam, Elaine Safer, John Saunders, David Seed, Glynis Williams and Mike Woolf. For the opportunity to try out preliminary pilot versions of material which is developed in the book I should also like to thank the editors of *Bulletin of Bibliography; Plotting Change: Contemporary Women's Fiction* (Edward Arnold, 1990); *University Fiction* (Rodopi: 1990); *Postwar Literatures in English; Neo-Realism in Contemporary American Fiction* (Rodopi and Restant, 1992); *Forked Tongues? Comparing Twentieth-Century British and American Literature* (Longman, 1994); and *The Insular Dream: Obsession and Resistance* (Free University Press, 1995). I am also grateful for invitations to lecture on Alison Lurie to the University of Keele American Studies Research Seminar (1990), the Belgian-Luxembourg Association for American Studies at the University of Gent (1991), the Arthur Miller Centre for American Studies (University of East Anglia, 1992), the British Association for American Studies Conferences in York (1988) and in Belfast (1992), the American Literature Association Annual Conference, San Diego (1992); and the European Association for American Studies Conference in Luxembourg (1994). I am also grateful to the School of English, the Staff Travel Fund, and the Small Research Grants Fund of the University of Newcastle upon Tyne, and the British Academy for Overseas Conference Grants and Small Research Grants, as contributions to the cost of travel for research purposes. A special debt is owed to the staff of the Robinson Library, the University of Newcastle upon Tyne, especially the Inter Library Loans department, for absolutely invaluable assistance in tracking down material, and for efforts well beyond the call of duty. I know of no European critic of American Literature who can call upon a service to rival theirs. I am also grateful to the staff of the manuscript collection at Cornell University Library, the Harvard Theatre Collection and the Houghton Library, at Harvard. Although it is unusual to thank one's subject (and implies no agreement or disagreement on her part with what follows) I am also deeply grateful to Alison Lurie for granting interviews, and for generous hospitality in Key West. Above all, my thanks go once again with feeling to Alice and Cash Newman, and Chris Revie for their continuing encouragement and support, and to James Revie for welcome fun and distraction.

The author and publisher wish to thank the following for permission to quote: A. P. Watt Ltd. on behalf of Alison Lurie. Every effort has been made to try to trace copyright holders of material reproduced in this book. Any rights not acknowledged here will be acknowledged in subsequent printings if notice is given to the publisher.

Chapter One
Biographical Introduction

When Alison Lurie was first a student at Radcliffe, only one class in creative writing was available, taught by Robert Hillyer, a handsome minor poet whose manner struck Lurie as courtly, but curiously vague. (She did not suspect that he had a drinking problem.) For several weeks Hillyer collected the students' efforts, but never returned them, preferring to read aloud from his favourite books, slowly but with maximum emotion.

> Finally one day he entered the room, pulled from his briefcase what looked like all the work he had ever received from us, heaped it onto the desk and sat down. We waited expectantly. "Yer – all – such – nice – young – ladies. Only you can't write, y'know. Wasting – yer – time." Then he put his head down among our papers and passed out.[1]

Hillyer was signally wrong about one, at least, of his students. Alison Lurie went on to produce nine novels, a volume of short stories, a biographical memoir, works for children, a study of the language of clothes, and two collections of fairy tales. She won widespread popularity for *The War Between the Tates,* and became the recipient of an American Academy of Arts and Letters Award (1979) and a Pulitzer Prize (1985).

When John Leonard described Alison Lurie's prose as faultless as an English lawn – "One could play polo on such prose"[2] – he merely confirmed the prevalent view of Alison Lurie as an Anglophile, even in some ways a very English, type of American writer. Often compared to Jane Austen, Lurie tends to be seen as a paleface among all-American redskins, a writer of comedies of manners more in the mould of Henry James and Edith Wharton than of Twain or Melville. Lurie herself has conceded the influence of the nineteenth-century British novel, but as a product of gender. Given the relative lack of prominence of American women writers during her youth, she turned to British literary foremothers.

---

[1] Alison Lurie, "Their Harvard." In *My Harvard, My Yale.* Ed. Diana Dubois (New York: Random House, 1982): 41.

[2] John Leonard, "Review of *The War Between the Tates,*" *New Republic*, 171, 10-17 August 1974, 24-5.

> For a young American woman who wanted to write in the 1950s, there were very few role models. Hemingway and Faulkner offered me nothing. I wasn't going to write about bullfights or incestuous Southern families. I turned naturally to writers such as Virginia Woolf and Doris Lessing, having grown up on the English Victorian Novel.[3]

None the less it is not for nothing that Gore Vidal dubbed her "the Queen Herod of modern fiction", for Lurie's irony can be savage, her satiric thrusts all the more deadly for the deadpan manner of their delivery. As Derwent May commented, Lurie's readers often have no idea "what expression there is on her face as she contemplates the field of slaughter."[4] In the contests of her novels, the result of a resounding collision of values is rarely other than Pyrrhic victory; more often the action ends in a standoff among exhausted characters, whose foibles have been ruthlessly exposed.

Throughout her work, and in spite of her "European" reputation, Lurie has none the less focussed on that oldest of American traditions, Utopianism. In each of her novels a Utopian community – a college founded on an innovative Humanities course, a group of Beats, a millennialist sect, a colony of artists, a gay enclave, a group of progressives, feminists or (in several reprises) Liberal academics – provides the means to explore the boundaries between pragmatism and idealism, and to tackle issues of social conformity, engagement or detachment within a carefully circumscribed arena. The university campus is thus only one variant on the miniaturised or microcosmic space within which each plot is set. Influenced perhaps by her sociologist father and her own involvement in the Poets' Theatre, Lurie is particularly adept at delineating the effects of social role-play (or role-play *tout court*) upon characters whose sense of self is permeable at the boundaries and constantly shifting. When Erica Tate laments the fact that identity appears to be at the mercy of circumstances, she voices one of Lurie's central concerns.

Perhaps inevitably, given the focus upon the social construction of the self in American literature, Lurie also follows Twain and James in an emphasis upon the child as innocent eye, revealing the hypocrisies of circumambient adults. In her case, an informed knowledge of children's literature adds a consciously

---

[3] Jay Parini, "The Novelist at Sixty," *Horizon* March 1986: 22.
[4] Derwent May, "Review of *The War Between the Tates,*" *Listener,* 20 June 1974, 808.

intertextual dimension to her adult fiction. Women's writing is always particularly sensitive to the ways in which female acculturation and socialisation are promoted by such "texts" as folklore, myth, fairy tales, movies and advertisements. Lurie's retelling of classic fairy tales in her 1980 volume, *Clever Gretchen and Other Forgotten Folktales*, deliberately selects tales from the available body of folklore in order to reconstitute a tradition and to promote images of women as brave, clever, resourceful, able to defeat giants, answer riddles, and outwit the devil, rather than as waiting passively for their prince to come. Two other volumes for children, *Fabulous Beasts* and *The Heavenly Zoo*, are designed to facilitate imaginative liberation, in the one case in a Borgesian collection of legendary animals and their tales (e.g. "The Vegetable Lamb", "The Basilisk"), in the other by recounting the stories of the stars, whether Greek, Biblical, Indonesian, or Native American. As well as editing a series of reprints of traditional children's literature, (*Classics of Children's Literature 1621 –1932*) Lurie has also published a variety of essays, now collected as *Don't Tell The Grownups*, in which she emphasises the way in which children's literature can be subversive of the social norm, an aid to imaginative and thus to political freedom. For Lurie there is no distinction of seriousness between children's and adult literature – each category deserves equal attention.

Similarly her 1981 volume *The Language of Clothes*, a serious examination of the history and interpretation of costume, begins from the premise that one set of signs is translatable into another, that clothing may be envisaged as a sign system, and that human beings communicate in the language of dress. In each of her novels Lurie foregrounds a similar interaction – in specific terms, between novel and folklore, sociology, political science, or biography, or more generally between art and life. Despite a concern for craft which satisfies the most demanding formalist aesthetic criteria, Lurie never loses sight of the sense in which art and life interpenetrate, in which paradigmatic plots abound, not just in literary culture, but also in general culture. In consequence her readers gain a sense of real life as being structured according to patterns familiar from literary culture, just as literary culture may be structured according to patterns familiar from real life. As Susan Stewart expresses it in her intertextual study of folklore and literature: "our neighbourhoods are full of Madame Bovarys, Cinderellas, Ebenezer Scrooges, Constantine Levins and wise fools, as much as fictions are full of people from our neighbourhoods."[5] In this sense Lurie is distinct among contemporary American novelists in her ability to conjoin self-conscious forms with thematic meat. By employing intertextual devices, she calls into question received literary and cultural definitions, interrogating the relation of fantasy to reality, and displaying an intense fascination with levels of truth. In interview Lurie argued that

> I think any way that we project ourselves into the world is a kind of sign. Like all signs, it can be genuine or false or something in between ... When you write, put on a costume, or furnish a room, you are working in a system of signs that have a meaning just as a word has a meaning. It is an indefinite system because no signs will mean the same thing to any two people. But this is nevertheless the system we have to work in. [6]

It is worth remembering that when we say "novelist of manners" we are in fact often talking about fiction which pays close attention to the reading of social signs. Lurie's novels, like those of Wharton or James, are in some respects semiotic comedies, comedies of the sign.

In typically mischievous fashion, Lurie also offers a bonus for regular readers in the use of "carryover" characters (rather in the style of Barbara Pym or Anthony Powell) who reappear from one novel to another, often at a tangent to the main action. Principal actors in one novel (e.g. Erica Tate in *The War Between the Tates*) may be mere asides in others (Erica in *Only Children*, Emmy in *The War Between the Tates*, Paul Cattleman in *Foreign Affairs*) or have walk-on parts (almost everybody in *The Truth About Lorin Jones*). It is a technique which has two principal effects. Firstly, as the reader "recognises" a character, the impression is created (rather as in popular or series fiction) of a stable fictional world. At the same time the recognition of a character as belonging in another novel highlights fictionality. More generally therefore the technique interrogates the notion of a framed reality, reminding the reader that, in Tom Stoppard's phrase, every exit from the stage is an entrance somewhere else, that beyond the frame of art, life has its own horizons.

Alison Lurie's early experiences offer several clues to the prevalence of the Utopian scenario in her work and the characteristic

---

[5] Susan Stewart, *Nonsense: Aspects of Intertextuality in Folklore and Literature* (Baltimore, Johns Hopkins, 1979), p.26.
[6] Martha Satz, "A Kind of Detachment: An Interview with Alison Lurie." *Southwest Review*, 71 (1986): 198.

opposition between idealistic commitment and ironic detachment.
Born on 3 September 1926, in Chicago, and brought up in New York
and White Plains, Westchester county, Lurie was the daughter of
Liberals with left-wing leanings. (She remembers Norman Thomas,
repeatedly a socialist presidential candidate, visiting the house). Her
father Harry, Latvian-born, was a professor of sociology and became
the founder and executive director of the Council of Jewish
Federations and Welfare Funds, a social work agency. Sociological
issues feature prominently in several of Lurie's novels, particularly in
connection with the workings of small groups – fraternities in *Love
and Friendship*, cults in *Imaginary Friends* – and social workers are
major characters in *Imaginary Friends* and *Only Children*. Although
Lurie's mother, Bernice Stewart, did not work outside the home, she
was no conventional housewife. She had had to support herself from
an early age following her father's death, had worked her way through
college, and was then a journalist for the Detroit Free Press, editing
the book and magazine section for some 15 years.[7] Married in her
early thirties, she was in her 35th year when her daughter was born.
Lurie herself has ascribed her satiric viewpoint partly to background:

> My father was a sociologist, my mother had been a
> journalist, and I think both of those professions are
> ones in which you can't help but take a step back
> from things. A sociologist is trained to do that and a
> journalist has to do that or else he or she would be
> sitting in the city room weeping all day long.[8]

The influence of idealistic and progressive parents clearly countered
any easy detachment from social issues.

    A second important influence was the manner of Lurie's birth
– by the high-forceps delivery method, which left her damaged in one
ear. As Lurie herself puts it:

> I was a skinny, plain, odd-looking little girl, deaf in
> one badly damaged ear from a birth injury, and with a
> resulting atrophy of the facial muscles that pulled my
> mouth sideways whenever I opened it to speak and
> turned my smile into a sort of sneer.[9]

---

[7] For this, and for other biographical information I am deeply grateful to the author
herself who allowed me to conduct two interviews with her, in London, 7 June 1988,
and in Key West, 19 February 1991.

[8] Martha Satz, 195.

[9] "No One Asked Me To Write A Novel," *New York Times Book Review*, 87, 23 (6
June 1982), 13.

By the age of eight or nine Lurie was fully aware of these disadvantages and concluded that no one would ever want to marry her, she would never have children and would remain an ugly old maid. She was proved wrong on all counts. (She has been twice married, first to Jonathan Bishop, from whom she separated in 1975 following his religious conversion, and then to Edward Hower, a fellow novelist.   She has three sons and three grandchildren). Nonetheless as a child she noticed that adults praised her various creations, from fudge brownies to rag rugs and poems, as "perfectly lovely", but "No one ever told me that I was perfectly lovely, though, as they did other little girls. Very well then, perfection of the work." She turned to writing as both enormously enjoyable and as a magically transformative experience, a "kind of witch's spell": "With a pencil and paper I could revise the world."[10] Lurie was the elder of two sisters. In "Witches and Fairies" she recalls the kind of fairy-tales in which there are two sisters, the older ill tempered, spiteful and plain, the younger gentle, kind and pretty.

> I didn't have to read what her name was, I knew already: it was Jennifer Lurie. My baby sister, who everybody said was as good as she was beautiful, would grow up to marry the prince, while I would be lucky if I didn't end up being rolled downhill in a barrel full of nails.[11]

The barrel of nails is the fate of the malevolent goosegirl in the story dramatised by plain Mary-Anne and beautiful Lolly in *Only Children*. Lolly goes on to a tragic fate in *The Truth About Lorin Jones*, while Mary-Anne achieves success, marriage and children.   Unlike Jane Austen's world, adult sisters are relatively rare in Lurie's novels – with the exception of the antagonistic Myra and Dorrie in *The Last Resort*, and the sisters in "Rabbit", one of whom is responsible for the other's death.   Emmy, Verena, Catherine, Lorin, Mary-Anne, and Vinnie, are only children or have brothers, Erica Tate has a younger sister, described as perfectly horrible.   No doubt a Freudian would have a field day with this material. The more prosaic explanation may simply be that which explains the high number of orphans in Victorian novels – the need to eliminate characters who would be redundant to the plot. In Lurie's fiction, nevertheless, ugly ducklings may become

---

[10] "No One", 13.

[11] "Witches and Fairies: Fitzgerald to Updike." *New York Review of Books* XVII, 9 (2 December 1971): 6.

swans but swans have more of a tendency to turn back into ugly ducklings.

Significantly, like Mary-Anne and Lolly's, Lurie's childhood also included attendance at a day school, Windward, founded by progressive socialists. Lurie was part of this Utopian project from the ages of seven to twelve. She had attended a public (i.e. state) school for a year but the experience had not been a success. Lurie had learned to read at the age of four and was thoroughly bored in the sate system, which at that time in America focussed on the "three R's". At Windward she had the run of the school library, there were excursions to local factories, pets and an ant-farm, the type of activities which are now fairly commonplace but were then very unusual. After Windward, Lurie went back to the state system for two years and then to Cherry Lawn, a coeducational school in Connecticut (Mike Nichols was a fellow boarder). Almost by accident she then enrolled at Radcliffe, planning to major in English. Once there, she swiftly discovered that if she chose instead to enter the recently created field of History and Literature, she could take Harvard courses, use the Widener library and have a Harvard professor instead of a Radcliffe graduate student as a tutor. The advantages were both intellectual and erotic. Radcliffe was then all-female, in the restrictive sense of the term. Men were allowed to visit only at specified times and in the public rooms on the ground floor. Upstairs the approach of any male (e.g. a plumber) was announced with warning shrieks of "Look out! Man coming." Two thirds of Radcliffe women were virgins. Harvard did allow women in the undergraduates' rooms but only before six in the evening and providing that the door remained ajar. Lurie found these rules baffling. ("Didn't the Dean of Students know that sex could take place before supper?")[12] Later she realised that they may have been introduced to enforce class principles, since they effectively prevented Harvard men from sleeping with any women with daytime jobs. Radcliffe students remained resourceful; three quarters of them were eventually to marry Harvard men. One room with a window opening onto a terrace was much in demand among the more adventurous women:

> One of its occupants during my time later worked for a brief period as a high-priced call girl, while another became an English duchess.[13]

---

[12] "Their Harvard": 43.
[13] "Their Harvard": 44.

Lurie clearly enjoyed her years at Radcliffe, and felt lucky to be there, as opposed to her male contemporaries who were fighting in the war.

> World War II was a central fact of adult life – it began on my thirteenth birthday, and when it ended I wrote in my journal: "It's not being war is hard to imagine. There's a kind of childish haziness around it, so that being grown-up means there being war".[14]

Petrol, meat, butter and sugar were rationed and even in the affluent surroundings of Radcliffe the menu featured such appetising delights as Shrimp Wiggle and Carrot Surprise. The men whom the Radcliffe women met as freshmen had a tendency to vanish at the official draft age of eighteen and a half, Harvard Yard was full of Navy officers in training, and everyone knew, or knew of, someone who had been killed in action.

Though they were not protesting about it, the Radcliffe women knew that they were distinctly second class citizens in the Cambridge academic community, lodged at a chilly distance from the main campus, and invisible to their instructors who addressed mixed classes as "Gentlemen". There were no women on the faculty, all Lurie's textbooks were written by men, and women could not usually use the Harvard libraries. Since society girls usually went to Wellesley or Smith, it was assumed that Radcliffe women were bluestockings; cartoons in the Harvard *Crimson* regularly portrayed them as "dogs", ugly grinds. When Lurie's friends invited B. J. Whiting, a popular Chaucerian scholar, as guest of honour at a dinner, he looked at the design of grotesque exotic birds on his plate and remarked, "At Harvard we have pictures of the buildings on our china. Here, I see, you have portraits of your alumnae."[15] Rather than resenting this, the women laughed appreciatively. Lurie's first tutor, David Owen, dismissed all her questions with the remark, "The trouble with you is you're a worrier like my wife." She counted herself exceptionally fortunate later to find, in Joseph Summers, a magnificent tutor. Lurie went to the lectures of F. O. Matthiessen, Harry Levin, I. A. Richards and Henry Aiken, and in her final year joined Albert Guerard's fiction seminar. (The group included future novelists Alice Adams, Stephen Becker, Robert Crichton, and John Hawkes). The writing of the present was not itself covered in Harvard courses. "The Contemporary Period" ended in 1922 with Aldous

---

[14] "Their Harvard": 36.
[15] "Their Harvard": 42.

Huxley. Levin's course on Proust, Joyce and Mann was considered daringly modern.

Harry Levin's influence, however, was strong in another sense. If anything, it was drama rather than the novel which marked Lurie's years in Cambridge. Levin's courses on Elizabethan and Jacobean drama were enormously popular, and covered English drama from its origins in church ritual and mummers' plays to the closing of the theatres. Lurie wrote her undergraduate dissertation on the relation between the sexes in Jacobean comedy, focussing on Middleton and Heywood. Entitled "Love and Money" it considered the relation between capitalism and romance in the Jacobean period. (The History and Literature field had been created in part as the product of a feeling that literature had become too specialised and refined, and that one way to connect back to the world was through history). The dramaturgical interest of Lurie's fiction has a long pedigree. More importantly, perhaps, Lurie became involved at Harvard in the Poets' Theatre, founded in 1950, as a loose affiliation of writers determined to revive poetic drama. A fluid and eclectic group, the Poets' Theatre set out to generate work by poets who would also act, administrate, direct and sell tickets, while retaining control of their own writing, and promoting the emergence of a new American verse theatre.[16] Already a published poet and the winner of a poetry contest, Lurie was a founder member, having become involved through Edward Gorey, whom she had met at Mandrake, a small arty bookstore run by the wives of two Cambridge graduate students. The group was very much a writers' theatre, and included Gregory Corso, Hugh Amory, James Merrill, John Ashbery, Donald Hall, Frank O'Hara, Richard Wilbur, Lyon Phelps, John Ciardi, Kenneth Koch, Richard Eberhart and V. R. (Bunny) Lang, among others. Dylan Thomas gave his first American reading of *Under Milk Wood* for the Poets' Theatre in the spring of 1953; Beckett gave them permission to do the first American production of *All That Fall*. Plays by Lorca, Middleton, Yeats, MacLeish, René Char, Paul Goodman and Louis Simpson were among those produced. Edward Gorey did many of the set designs and artwork, and his late-Victorian taste dominated the visual aspects of some productions. (Frowning cherubs recur on the posters).

---

[16] The history of the Poets' Theatre remains to be written. Lurie gives her account in her biography of V. R. Lang. See also Nora Sayre, "The Poets' Theatre: A Memoir of the Fifties." *Grand Street* 3, 3 (1984), 92-105; and Frank O'Hara, *Selected Plays* (New York: Full Court Press, 1978), the appendix to which provides photographs of productions and set designs.

The Poets' Theatre was in many ways a highly idealistic and Utopian project, on the part of a group who were deeply serious about the importance of art. Lyon Phelps composed a manifesto "The Objectives of the Poets' Theatre" in which he emphasised the need to foster a theatre which foregrounded language rather than visual effects. In addition:

> the training of an audience is inseparable from the training of ourselves as poet-playwrights.[17]

At the first production (1951, O'Hara's *Try! Try!*) the audience laughed – and were roundly rebuked at the intermission by Thornton Wilder, who lectured them angrily on the importance of verse drama. Nora Sayre, an early member, saw the group as responding to an acute hunger for European culture. There were strong echoes of surrealism and several members wrote plays about Orpheus (known to the group as "Orpheus things"). Noh plays, which needed little or no scenery and few actors, and were therefore cheap to produce, were also popular. In Lurie's account[18] the idea of reviving poetic drama was a response to the feeling just after the war that poetry had become too separated from real life and the common reader, that it should come out of the study and library, to reach a wider audience. Many of those involved in the early days had followed Harry Levin's courses, and had also read widely in Classical drama, particularly Sophocles. Although verse drama may therefore sound somewhat arcane, the Poets' Theatre was in fact looking out from the ivory tower to a wider world. "Orpheus things" were more intertextual or parodic than reverently classical. In V. R. Lang's *Fire Exit*, Eurydice was in a burlesque theatre, and Orpheus was the mainstay of the Mozartiana L. P. Record Company. *Try! Try!* may have been a Noh play, but it involved a returning veteran confronting his wife as he arrives back from the war – a highly topical theme. The European influence yielded, however, as the movement tipped towards a more essentially American theatre. The Beats were on the horizon – indeed several members of the group are now thought of primarily in connection with the Beat movement.

Like any theatre group, the Poets' Theatre was fairly tempestuous, the first of Lurie's Utopias to reveal its flaws. As Lurie remarks,

---

[17] Box VII, Poets' Theatre Collection, Harvard Theatre Collection. Dated 28 November 1950, p.5.
[18] Key West Interview, 19 February 1991.

> The emotional temperature of the Poets' Theatre in
> the early days was high, for most of the younger
> writers and their friends were in love with Bunny and
> with each other.   There were secrets, confidences,
> collaborations, poems and dramas *à clef* passed from
> hand to hand, public quarrels and reconciliations, and
> the best scenes were not always played on stage.[19]

Flurries of telegrams of resignation citing "artistic differences" tended
to arrive just before dress rehearsals, forcing defeat on the opposition.
Money was scarce, and at first the group were essentially strolling
players. At their first physical theatre, a small loft, there was so little
backstage space that in warm weather the actors waited for their
entrances in an alley outside the theatre, dodging garbage thrown out
by a neighbouring restaurant.   The auditorium held 49 on folding
chairs. When a production sold out two more people could perch on a
sink – through since it dripped it was a rather dampening experience.
During one financial emergency invitations were sent out for a
fundraising evening, at $2 to attend, $5 to stay away, and $6 to bring
somebody who had not been invited. The group – effectively led by
Bunny Lang – could be merciless at demolishing the pretentious. In
the spring of 1952 they produced a one-act play, *The Center*, by Cid
Corman, a Boston avant-garde poet.   The play was tragic and
symbolic.   Characters   included   "The   Old   Man",   "Second
Philosopher", "A Child".   Lang, infuriated by Corman's lack of
attendance at the casting meeting or rehearsals, dressed the actors in
union suits (long underwear) dyed salmon pink, and replaced the
chosen Stravinsky symphony with the Elephant Polka.   The
performance went extremely well – but as a comedy. Corman arose
shouting with anger at the close, as the curtain went down to
thunderous laughter and applause.

   Corman was sharing the bill with Alison Lurie. Lurie was
involved in the Poets' Theatre from 1950 to 1955, in the years when it
was a bohemian and radical group. (Later the increasing need for
money was to propel it into a more respectable academic and social
milieu).   There were a number of gay men in the group and a
distinctly countercultural aura.   When a fire inspector, about to
threaten closure on safety grounds, asked V. R. Lang, "Do you have
AC or DC?" she replied "Oh we have *everything*" and he promptly

---

[19] Alison Lurie, *Poems and Plays* by V. R. Lang (New York: Random House, and
London: Heinemann, 1975): 14.

fled.[20] At this point only the most bohemian of Cambridge residents attended the productions. Lurie wrote two plays for it, kept minutes of its board meetings, and did the costumes and make-up for a large number of its productions. Although clearly very involved, she took a clear-sighted view of some of its participants. As she notes,

> Among the original members as well as those that joined later not one was single-mindedly anxious to "revive poetic drama". [Bunny's] motives were less worldly than most, for she did not principally hope to rise in society, to go on the professional stage, to get her poetry published, to become locally famous, or to meet possible lovers. Each of these ends was attained by some member of the theatre.[21]

This situation, in which young people confront choices between artistic or worldly goals, is treated ironically in Lurie's *Smith: A Masque*, performed on 21st and 23rd May 1952, as part of an evening of plays which also featured *The Center* and Richard Eberhart's *The Visionary Farms*. The production took place in the courtyard of the Fogg Museum, a location with excellent acoustics but no changing rooms. The actors dressed in the arched galleries above, terrifying the curators lest they damage some priceless painting or statue. Lurie appears on the playbill both as the author and (as Alison Bishop) as the costume designer. *Smith* was reviewed by Michael Maccoby in the *Harvard Crimson*.

> The final piece, as a sharp contrast to the symbolism of the first and the morality of the second, is both superficial and amusing. This fantasy *Smith: A Masque*, by Alison Lurie, describes the dilemma of a young graduate who must choose a life's work. The graduate, played by Tom Kennedy, must select among Juno and wealth, Venus and artistic fame, or Minerva and scholarship. Smith, an obstinate fellow, will have none of them and the goddesses immediately despatch him to points unmentionable.[22]

Maccoby found the performance thoroughly enjoyable, suggesting to him that the Poets' Theatre did not need to wrap themselves in "misty clouds of symbolism and obscure verbiage" to please their audience.

---

[20] A pity in some respects as a fire later destroyed most of the records of the group. The surviving papers in the Harvard Theatre Collection are partly singed.

[21] *Poems and Plays* by V. R. Lang: 19.

[22] Michael Maccoby, "The Poets' Theatre", *Harvard Crimson*, 23 May 1952.

A photograph (22 May 1952) in the *Crimson* subtitled "Pleasure or Knowledge" shows Kennedy trying to choose between the rival claims of Venus (Allyn Moss) and Minerva (V. R. Lang). Essentially a vaudeville sketch version of the Judgement of Paris, in rhymed verse, the play included songs for which Lurie wrote the words to well-known tunes (e.g. "Marbles and Chalk" an old blues song which was a favourite of Lang's). Smith, a young man clad in standard Harvard ingenu costume of chinos and seersucker jacket, opens the action by declaring his intention to avoid the fate of his audience and side-step the shackles of social conformity:

> None of you live where you would like to live
> Or do your real desire. You hesitate,
> Middle-aged, greedy, guilty, second-rate.
> You all got caught. I'm not going to get caught.
> I'm not going to do anything I ought.
> I'm going to live. (p.1).[23]

Juno's temptations include the attractions of a Cadillac, a perfect tan and West Palm Beach which are roundly condemned by Venus as exemplifying bad taste:

> Art after all demands integrity
> Don't think that means you won't have fun with me.
> (p.4).

The picture she paints of the artist's career runs from a rented attic to the editorship of a review:

> Which ten years later may devote to you
> An issue. Half a century from now
> Bons mots you made during domestic scenes
> Will be retold in little magazines,
> And, smiling graciously, you will allow
> The Authorized Edition to appear. (p.5).

In response Minerva (in horn-rimmed glasses and an owl-topped academic cap) paints a dreary picture of Smith as a worn-out hack at forty-five, offering instead the delights of a scholastic career culminating in publication in *PMLA*. Smith remains untempted, proclaims his independence – and is carried off to Hell. "Enter Jones" – and the play begins again. Without wishing to overemphasise a work intended for laughs, the play shows a developed taste for satire and, in the three fates which the goddesses script for Smith, an interest in issues of social acculturation.

---

[23] The manuscript is located in the Harvard Theatre collection. It lacks page 9. Page references follow quotations in parentheses.

Smith was not Lurie's first experience of writing for the theatre. On 20th and 21st February 1952 the group presented "An Entertainment Somewhat in the Victorian Manner" which included tableaux vivants, lanternslides, musical interludes, poetry readings and short plays together with "Full Orchestra And Irish Harps", according to the advertisements. Admission was free, since the performance took place in Christ Church Parish House, and no charge could be made for admission to a church. The Parish House was filled to capacity, with a big crowd. Lurie's contribution was *Sir George and The Dragon: A Marionette Play.*[24] There were four characters, George, Mrs. Why, Sir Hugh, and the Dragon, each played by two actors, once speaking, one miming. In interview Lurie described the play as a mock Christmas mummers' pageant, transferred to Cambridge with the characters given Cambridge identities. In the play Lurie exploits the disjunction between heroic, male pretensions and the bathetic realisation, in the character of George who opens the action lamenting that

> This quasi-military dress
> Is not authentic, I confess.
> I bought my helmet at the Coop –
> They told me it was meant for soup. (p.1).

From this reference (to the Harvard Co-operative Society in Harvard Square, which sold books, clothes and household items) the play translates the action into contemporary America, where the local community value their dragon as a useful heat source and a handy means of disposing of tiresome citizens. (He eats poets when necessary). Dressed by Brooks Brothers, George is the ultimate preppie, as is his friend Sir Hugh, a product of both Harvard and Groton (New England's most prestigious prep school), played by Hugh Amery who had been to both. Even the dragon has a Christmas box from S. S. Pierce, Boston's equivalent of Fortnum and Mason, and cordially invites his opponent to join him for a civilised drink before the duel. George, however, refuses obstinately. His role is ready-scripted by literary tradition and he will not deviate one whit from it.

> Dragon: You want all the conventions
>   Observed?
> George: Everything Malory mentions.
>   The cry, the challenge, and the taunt. (p.5).

---

[24] I am grateful to Aison Lurie for supplying me with her copy of the play, annotated with local references. Page references follow quotations in parentheses.

With the archaic cry of "Avaunt! Avaunt!", battle is joined, and the dragon struck down, to the horror of the other characters who fail to appreciate the joys of traditional genre and rebuke the hero in no uncertain terms. George is defensive:

> An artist can expect no praise
> From those whose lives he strives to raise.
> No member of the bourgeoisie
> Ever appreciated me. (p.5).

But when Sir Hugh refuses to knight him, on the grounds that he has not committed any good deeds, merely "a mean dragonicide" (p.6) George changes his tune. Artificial respiration restores the dragon to life, and to the accompaniment of supernatural voices off, drums, trumpets and lightning, the hero gains his title, to general rejoicing. No man is a hero to his dragon, however. The latter has the last words.

> But who's congratulating me?
> I go through this farce endlessly
> And nobody ever knights me. (p.7).

Primarily an entertainment, the play none the less demonstrates a firm grasp of the conventions of the mummers' play, intertextually revamped, and a readiness to puncture aristocratic and artistic pretensions. George's slavish belief in the necessity of observing conventions – social or artistic – looks ahead to other characters in Lurie's fiction who find themselves ready-scripted into a damaged – or damaging – social identity. George is a figure of fun, but he follows a macho agenda:

> I ought to do some noble deed.
> I ought to kill something. (p.1).

Lurie's role was not only that of the dramatist. Costumes for the entire evening were in charge of "Mrs Jonathan Bishop". The costs ($18.57) included the rental of a helmet for Sir Hugh, a dragon's head, a Chinese hat and pigtail, and a colander. Arguably Lurie's experience backstage at the theatre may have been even more significant than her two experiences as dramatic author. She did the costumes and make up for a great number of the productions (e.g. John Ashbery's *Everyman*, Richard Eberhart's *The Apparition*, O'Hara's *Try! Try!*, and Lyon Phelps' *Three Words in No Time*). In interview Lurie commented that the experience of knowing how the theatre works is bound to have had an effect on her work:

> You see what it's like behind the scenes and what the
> contrast is between the Poets' Theatre's (not very

immense) glamour of what you see on stage and all the confusion and makeshift that goes on behind.[25]

The legacy of the Poets' Theatre was a double one, firstly in the influence of drama (and of working in a small group with Utopian aims) on the content of Lurie's fiction, but secondly, and more prosaically, on the fact that her fiction was ever published at all. Lurie's writing career was not all plain sailing; there was a gap of some 10 years between her first short stories and the publication of *Love and Friendship*. Lurie's first major work, *Leonard and Others*, a novella written when she was just out of college, focussed upon a young instructor at a boarding school who falls in love with a student. It is striking that in this first work of fiction Lurie situated events within an institution – viewed from a decidedly dystopian perspective. In interview, Lurie commented on the sense at a boarding school of an "upbeat mystique, you know, we're all working together, we're having a wonderful time, we're cheering for the school team, and we're singing in the school choir. Everything is wonderful".[26] Leonard Zimmern featured as a rather sour character, who saw the underside of the myth. Although the novella was never published, he was to survive as a character in almost all of Lurie's later novels. A second, full-length novel, *The Guided Tour* concerned four young Americans in Europe, Jamesian innocents abroad. Chloe Newcomb, the Jamesian heroine, bored by the guided tour which she is taking with her best friend and the latter's parents, meets two expatriates living on family money. As a result she comes to see the underside of Europe. If the guided tour offers a European proto-Disneyland, with scenery and exotic food as major components, the expatriates provide access to a Europe of poverty, desperation and crime. Set in 1950-51 the novel includes a particularly sinister expatriate living by his wits. It is never entirely clear if he has CIA connections, or is merely involved in black market activities, smuggling cars to Spain. As events unfold towards disaster, one couple remain in Europe, one return to America. Lurie had herself visited Europe in 1950, spending time in Britain and in Paris, Salzburg, Vienna and Munich. (Not merely tourist attractions; Munich had of course been badly bombed). The four chapters of the novel are each set in a different European city and the emphasis is very much upon the disjunction between tourist stage-sets and the historical wretchedness behind the scenes. Astutely

---

[25] Key West Interview, 19th February 1991.
[26] Key West Interview, 19th February 1991.

foreshadowing later critics' comments on Lurie's coolness, V. R. Lang described it as written in a style of "stark impassivity."[27]

Lurie's published fiction also anticipated some of the concerns of her later work. In "A Story of Women", published when she was just twenty years old, Daisy, a rather literary girl who has just read *The Great Gatsby*, dreams of going to Europe while submitting under protest to the attentions of her mother and emphatically domestic sister, who are fitting her for a party frock. The dress is made of white silk, closely resembling the mother's wedding dress. The opposition between the sisters' views and life-choices is skilfully dramatised, in an understated fashion, and the central dilemma (art or marriage) presented via indirection. "Hansel and Gretel", published five years later, is a darker tale, reversing the central situation of the fairy tale, to feature old people, rather than children, at the mercy of authoritative others. Mr. Mahans (Hansel) and Rettie (Gretel) are residents in an old people's home, who walk out of its repressive precincts and into the realms of forest fantasy. The folktale elements are again understated. Rettie is the active figure; Mr. Mahans is passively led. He dreams that he will be eaten, presumably by the sinisterly named Dr. Hex. The twist on the tale is that this witch figure is **inside** the supposedly safe and protective institution; the witch's house in the forest is actually a welcome destination, a refuge in the flight from oppressive authorities in league with the family. The tale looks ahead to the escape of Vinnie Miner (*Foreign Affairs*) from the imprisoning conventions of age and sex, again with a mediating fairy tale structure, and to the folklore motifs of *Only Children* and *Women and Ghosts*.

By 1951 Lurie was the author of two substantial works of fiction, but had published only two short stories and a small group of poems. It would be 1962 before *Love and Friendship* saw the light of day. Lurie has given her own account of the years of rejection slips in "No One Asked Me To Write A Novel"[28]

> Twice in my life I deliberately tried to break the habit of writing. The first time I was 26; I hadn't had a manuscript accepted for five years, and my first novel had been turned down by six publishers. (p.13).

By now married with a two-month old baby, Lurie accepted her husband's breakfast suggestion that she cut her losses and give up:

---

[27] Letter from V. R. Lang to Alison Lurie, 3 November 1954, Houghton Library.

[28] "No One Asked Me To Write A Novel," *New York Times Book Review*, 87, 23 (6 June 1982), 13, 46-8.

> After all, Alison, nobody is asking you to write a
> novel. (p.13).

Abstention lasted less than a May morning in the park.

> Now that I wasn't a writer the world looked flat and
> vacant, emptied of possibility and meaning; the spring
> day had become a kind of glossy, banal, calendar
> photography: View of the Charles River. "This is
> stupid", I said aloud. I stood up and pushed the baby
> home and changed him and nursed him and put him
> down for a nap – and went back to the typewriter.
> (p.46).

Two years later, now with two rejected novels and two children in
diapers, Lurie gave up again, for over a year. Beset by well-meaning
friends and relatives suggesting that she give more time and attention
to her family and stop doing something which appeared merely to
make her unhappy, she concluded that

> Evidently, what we had been taught was true: a
> woman had to choose between a family and a career;
> she couldn't have both like a man. By marrying, I
> had lost my powers. I had published two children, but
> my two novels had been born dead. (p.47).

She threw herself into togetherness, family picnics, the baking of
cookies and casseroles, and the other pursuits considered appropriate
for a 1950s wife.

> I told myself that my life was rich and full.
> Everybody else seemed to think so. Only I knew that,
> right at the center, it was false and empty … I passed
> in public as a normal woman, wife and mother; but
> inside I was still peculiar, skewed, maybe even
> wicked or crazy. (p.47).

For some thirteen months this state of affairs persisted. Then in 1956
V. R. Lang died suddenly of cancer. "Disturbed, even frightened" by
the suddenness and senselessness of this loss, and by the way in which
memories were already fading Lurie decided to put down on paper
everything that she knew of her, as fast as possible before it could be
forgotten. She wrote entirely without thought of publication, or
indeed of any other reader at all.

> First, I noticed that I felt better than I had in months
> or years. Next I realized that I wasn't writing only
> about Bunny, but also about the Poets' Theatre, about
> academia and the arts, about love and power. What I
> wrote wasn't the whole truth – I didn't know that –

but it was part of the truth, my truth. I could still cast
spells, reshape events. (p.47).

Above all Lurie realised that the point of Bunny Lang's life was that
she had done what she wanted "not what was expected of her". (p.47).
Lurie determined to write on, even if she were never to be published,
since what **she** wanted to do was to write. Two years later friends
who had read the memoir of V. R. Lang arranged for it to be privately
printed. Two years after that the brother of another friend passed his
copy to an editor at Macmillan, who asked if there was a novel – and
accepted *Love and Friendship*, written almost without hope of
publication, entirely for Lurie's own pleasure. The experience is one
to which Lurie returns in *The Truth About Lorin Jones*, in which Polly
Alter, a painter whose career has stalled, is kick-started back into
creative activity by the experience of writing a biographical memoir of
another artist, Lorin Jones. At the close of her story Polly also realises
that she cannot ell the "whole truth" about Lorin, but that she can be
true to her own knowledge of events. Interestingly Polly makes this
decision after a trip to Key West where she also meets her future
husband. Bunny Lang spent time in Key West with the man who was
to become her husband, Bradley Phillips. Faced with as many
versions of Lorin Jones as she has sources – alternately describing her
as shy, schizoid, spiteful, unscrupulous or generous – Polly opts for a
metabiography in which all her findings are pluralistically presented.
In her introduction to Lang's collected poems and plays, Lurie
comments that

> when someone dies, each of the survivors is left with
> a slightly different image. With Bunny, who had so
> many moods and roles, these images were perhaps
> more different than usual.[29]

Her memoir also discusses the way in which Bunny could slip
smoothly into different parts – as society hostess, chorus girl, Irish
charwoman, member of the Canadian WAC, carer for an elderly
father, idealistically committed to poetic drama, yet capable of
dreadful revenges. She adored disguise and when she turned up on
Lurie's doorstep dressed in drab, middleaged clothes, in her role as
commission saleswoman for a "Your Child's Lifetime" photograph
plan, she was almost unrecognisable. Rosemary Radley in *Foreign
Affairs* – alternatively playing the roles of English lady and Cockney
charwoman – owes something to Bunny Lang. Lang, however, was
not just an actress, but also a director. "She spontaneously invented

---

[29] *Poems and Plays* by V. R. Lang: xvi.

an interesting character for whoever she met."[30]   Since most of the
young people involved in the Poets' Theatre were impressionable, and
none too sure who they were,

> They were excited to be told, and often behaved
> afterwards in line with Bunny's definition.   Thus it
> might be said that today the character of everyone
> who knew Bunny is partly her creation.[31]

Lurie's own heroines are often exposed to similar scripting, for good
or ill, both by individuals and society.   Katherine Cattleman adopts the
role of stereotypical California girl, and becomes unrecognisable to
her husband.   Vinnie Miner finds that Chuck Mumpson's repeated
description of her as a good woman actually makes her do a good
deed.   Bunny Lang's acting abilities also highlight the extent to which
role-play can move the actor from frame to picture, eliding the
distinctions between life and art.   In her final illness, she gave a poetry
reading, haggard in black velvet, sobbing out a long elegiac poem
until most of her audience were weeping,

> but when the lights went up I could have sworn the
> dark circles under her eyes had been improved with
> greasepaint.   Really dying, she still played at dying, as
> if she would make death just one more costume.[32]

Lang's last play, *Et In Arcadia Ego*, a modern anarchist pastoral, took
its central characters to a paradisal island, where utopia promptly went
sour.   Its metaphors centre upon the image of the Ice Age and the
extinction of the dinosaurs.   Despite this emphasis, Lang was unaware
that the title phrase originally meant "death, too is in Arcadia" and
when informed, promptly changed it to *I Too Have Lived in Arcadia*
to dispel the suggestion.   Lurie's latest novel, *The Last Resort*, makes
a similar play with the notion of death-in-paradise, as a doomed hero
in Key West attempts at several reprises to stage his death, only to be
repeatedly thwarted, and eventually reprieved.   Death is there only for
others.   Originally entitled *Endangered Species*, the novel focuses on
the hero's career as a naturalist and his efforts to save the manatee
from extinction.   (Other species have already gone the way of the
dinosaurs, despite his efforts).   He is also writing a biography –
though an ecological example of the genre, featuring a famous copper
beech.   As the novel demonstrates, Lurie's debt to V. R. Lang was not
short-lived.   Reading her memoir is an intensely moving experience.

---

[30] *Poems and Plays* by V. R. Lang: 27.
[31] *Poems and Plays* by V. R. Lang: 28.
[32] *Poems and Plays* by V. R. Lang: 52.

Perhaps because it is such an honest portrait the human being comes alive off the page, undimmed by reverence or sentimentality, and irritating, amusing or enchanting the reader by turns. Above all the book refuses to impose any easy paradigmatic structure on a very various life.

The facts of Lurie's own subsequent career are largely a matter of public record. It is no accident that *Love and Friendship* is set in Convers, a fictional new England campus which bears a strong resemblance to Amherst, where Lurie's husband taught from 1954-57, that *The Nowhere City* moves its location to Lost Angeles, where he taught from 1957-1961, or that the fictional university in upstate New York of *Imaginary Friends* and the Corinth of *The War between the Tates* have been identified with Cornell, where he took up a teaching post in 1961. Along the way Lurie had worked as an editorial assistant for Oxford University Press, in the Boston Public library, and even as a ghost writer, writing up scientific data for articles by meteorologists, psychologists and city planners among others (Bonetti) while bringing up three children. Lurie herself began teaching courses in creative writing and children's literature at Cornell in 1969, and is now Frederick J. Whiton Professor of American Literature. (Children's literature was an astute and to some extent a pragmatic choice, since no other professor had laid a territorial claim to that field at Cornell.) She teaches part-time, allowing her to spend time writing, in her second home in Key West and in the London flat which she bought with fellow novelist Diane Johnson. Lurie regularly exchanges manuscripts with Johnson, for comments. Philip Roth also read a number of her earlier novels and offered constructive criticism. She remains true to her Liberal upbringing. (She allowed herself to be arrested during a sit-in at Cornell in protest against Cornell's investment policy in South Africa.)[33] Perhaps because of her progressive background and the strong role models offered by her mother and female teachers, Lurie does not seem to have felt victimised by men and has demonstrated a welcome ability to get round or over the obstacles before her. (Though one might note that it took her 10 years and four novels to get the lowest of teaching posts at Cornell). In interview Lurie made light of the problems faced in juggling work and family at a time when day care was generally unavailable.[34] She adopted a strategy of "play-pen pals" – other

---

[33] Molly Hite, "Belles Lettres Interview," *Belles Lettres* 2 (July-August 1987): 9.

[34] Dale Edmonds, "The World Seemed So Empty To Me If I Wasn't Writing." *Negative Capability* 6, 4 (1986): 152.

women who wanted time to paint or write – with whom childcare was shared. She also counted herself fortunate not to face the pressure to "get on" in a conventional career. Unlike other writers of her acquaintance she did not have to write to support herself financially. As a result of this rational and pragmatic attitude, Lurie rarely features among the role models for contemporary feminists. She none the less sees herself as working in a female line and identifies herself as a feminist. To Dorothy Mermin she commented that "I think it's a mistake to believe that there's one female line which is intensely personal, subjective, intuitive, emotional. That's not the only female line. There's also a line in Fanny Burney and Jane Austen that is just as true as the other."[35] Rather than preaching to the choir, Lurie's feminism is intelligently strategic in method. In the same interview she comments that

> Suppose you want to write a feminist novel today, and you don't want to convince only the converted. You want to convince people who are not seriously feminists, and you'd even like some men to read it. Well, if you write *The Women's Room* you're not going to get very many nonconverted readers.[36]

Comedy poses particular problems for women writers, often triggering accusations of lightness or triviality. Lurie however argues that "that's just as good a way to get at things, to laugh at them, as to shout a them."[37] Where polemical feminist writers tend to be dismissed as overserious ("women have no sense of humour") women who are comic novelists habitually face accusations of lack of ballast. The cult of the victim (Sylvia Plath as icon) is almost as damaging as the myth of Superwoman. It would be easy (indeed it is akin to what Polly Alter considers à propos of Lorin Jones) to construct a biographical sketch of Alison Lurie which emphasised immigrant background, birth injury, sibling rivalry, academic misogyny, the tragic death of a close friend, domestic drudgery and a tune played on the second fiddle to husband and children. The paradigm is almost as familiar to the twentieth century reader as the "trials and tribulations" formula was to the nineteenth. It would be equally easy to emphasise Lurie's relatively comfortable background, private schooling, Ivy League education, class advantages, European connections and three

---

[35] Janet Todd (ed.), *Women Writers Talking* (New York: Holmes and Meier, 1983): 83.
[36] Janet Todd: 92.
[37] Janet Todd: 91

residences.   Life is, fortunately, rather more complicated than
biography allows for.

As is fiction. An authentic fictional voice, Alison Lurie has
attracted relatively little academic attention, perhaps because her
portrayals of campus life are too close to home, perhaps because her
sophisticated directness and intelligent wit are highly resistant to easy
categorisation. In this respect readers have proved wiser than literary
critics. Lurie's novels are eagerly awaited, in very different quarters,
and widely reviewed. (After America and Britain, she is particularly
popular in France). As one reviewer remarked, "The novels of Alison
Lurie are almost enough to make one believe in the dubious notion
that reading fiction is fun."[38] Essentially realistic, her richly textured
fictions are deceptively readable, their dramatic tone and scenic
construction lending themselves successfully to other media. (Both
Imaginary Friends and *The War Between the Tates* have been adapted
for television). Although sexual intrigue is generally the mainspring
of her plots, Lurie's talent for satire, her concern with the interplay of
fantasy and reality, her moral seriousness, and her interest in feminist
issues make her a distinctive presence on the contemporary literary
scene. Critical accounts of her work, however, remind one of the
early response to John Updike, as someone who had nothing much to
say but said it rather well. Though tending to highlight Lurie's prose
style and sharp wit, critics rarely suggest an intellectual agenda to the
works, and almost never a specifically American agenda. It is
assumed either that Lurie writes comedies about the three M's –
marriage, the middle classes and morality – or that she is a campus
novelist working with a narrow palette and a restricted range of
character types. Is she really "American" in her fiction? Or merely an
East Coast paleface with her eyes looking firmly towards Europe? In
what follows, I offer a different Lurie, profoundly engaged with
intellectual and social questions, and firmly within an American
tradition. *This* Lurie, I will argue, starts her career in *Love and
Friendship* with an extended interrogation of the masculinist basis of
American Transcendentalism, and of the homosocial basis of
American culture, using a gay novelist and a wicked parody of male
fraternity rituals to queer assumptions of heterosexual "normality", a
theme to which her latest novel, *The Last Resort* returns, satirising the
sociobiological assumptions which are the ground of homophobia.
The Nowhere City, a Hollywood novel, engages with the Adorno-
Benjamin debate of the 1930s, on the significance of popular culture.

---

[38] Elizabeth Dalton, "Review of *Real People,*" *Commentary* 48, 2 (August 1969): 60.

Imaginary Friends turns its attention to a different version of Utopianism, the religious cult, basing its analysis on American small group sociology. Vietnam through the domestic lens is the topic of *The War Between the Tates* which takes George Kennan's politics as its organising metaphor. *Only Children* moves back in time to the American Depression, using fairy tale and folklore motifs to underline the adult idiocies resulting from romantic paradigms and wish-fulfilment fantasies. *Foreign Affairs*, set in Europe, and haunted by Henry James, offers an emblematic rewriting of the "International Theme", which comprehensively scotches most of the American protagonist's illusions about genteel traditions. Throughout, Lurie has an uncanny ability to serve critical, even radical, aesthetic purposes within a popular form. Even those volumes which appear most aesthetic in their focus – *Real People, The Truth About Lorin Jones*, and *Women and Ghosts* with their employment of the genres of diary, biography and ghost story to question the relationship between art and life – interrogate the psychological and the economic bases of art, in order to mount a full-scale attack on the assumptions of genteel good taste, and the literature that compromises with it. As the next chapter will demonstrate, it is no accident that this is a writer who saw her first novel publicly burned in America.

Chapter Two
Hell Week with Emerson and Thoreau: *Love and Friendship*

> The very simplicity and nakedness of man's life in the
> primitive ages imply this advantage at least, that they
> left him still but a sojourner in nature. (Thoreau,
> *Walden*).

Love and Friendship introduces two of Lurie's characteristic
themes – patriarchy and its discontents, and the opposition of nature
and culture, in a novel which stakes its claims to a territory which is
peculiarly American. It is something of a truism that American
cultural myth validates the retreat into isolation, with the consequent
rejection of the restricting forces of civilisation, the latter often
female-identified (Aunt Sally, Dame Van Winkle). Whether Huck is
lighting out for the territory, Natty Bumppo for the prairie, or Thoreau
for Walden Pond, the myth is overwhelmingly that of the male as
solitary sojourner in nature, entering the wilderness to gain access to
truth. Isolation is a key emphasis – whether the male is actually alone,
as in the Emersonian or Thoreauvian versions, or in the major variant,
in which he has as his companion a "buddy", who, generally by virtue
of race, is deemed uncultured, outside of, or marginal to the symbolic
order, almost himself a part of nature. Huck and Jim, Natty Bumppo
and Chingachgook, McMurphy and Chief Bromden: it is a story
which we all know so well that it hardly bears rehearsal.[1] Feminist
critics have argued, in response, that American literature offers
particular difficulties for women. Judith Fetterley contends that the
female reader is continually asked to identify with men and against
herself.[2] The title of Nina Baym's influential essay speaks for itself:
"Melodramas of Beset Manhood: How Theories of American Fiction
Exclude Women Authors."[3] Carolyn Heilbrun describes *Deliverance*
as "the latest in a series of fictional escapes into the 'territory' where
women do not go, where civilisation cannot reach, where men hunt

---

[1] Classically stated in Leslie Fiedler, *Love and Death in the American Novel* (New
York: Criterion Books, 1960).
[2] Judith Fetterley, *The Resisting Reader: A Feminist Approach to American Fiction*
(Bloomington: Indiana University Press, 1978).
[3] Nina Baym, "Melodramas of Beset Manhood: How Theories of American Fiction
Exclude Women Authors", *American Quarterly* 33 (Summer 1981): 123-39.

one another like animals and hunt animals for sport."[4]   In *Love and Friendship* Emmy Turner follows in the footsteps of Emerson and Thoreau as solitary sojourner in nature; variations are struck on the "buddy" motif; and the myth of the New Eden – that divinely appointed second chance represented by America – comes in for re-examination. The relationship of women to the myth is complicated. As outsiders in patriarchal culture, women have also been held in relative isolation from each other and from any sense of social consensus.[5]   In a culture which validates isolation as a means to truth, women are therefore doubly disadvantaged: they are, in a sense isolated from isolation, understood as a transcendent virtue. They are positioned as the old story of culture from which the new story must distinguish itself, to form a new cultural myth.   In the European cultural paradigm woman is nature, not culture. But when nature becomes culture, she is briskly redefined, repositioned and consigned to repetition. Huck Finn, after all, lights out not once, but twice. Aunt Sally is an old story as well as a female story. As he says "I been there before."[6]

In the figure of the solitary sojourner in nature, the reader is of course confronting what has been variously described as a masternarrative, grand narrative or metanarrative, towards which postmodernity has displayed considerable incredulity – whether voiced through Foucault's localism, new historicism's anecdote, or any other opposition to totalising claims. Jean-François Lyotard's is the clearest exposition available. For Lyotard "the grand narratives of legitimation" (historical or religious), which have claimed access to the true nature of things, are open to question and to temporary replacement by "petits récits" (little stories) with more modest, local ambitions.[7]   The question of legitimation remains, of course, insistent. If we accept that the grand narratives have collapsed, we are in a position where the social subject dissolves in a dissemination of language games. Lyotard evinces the proliferation of new languages available to us – machine languages, matrices of game theory, new systems of musical notation, the language of the genetic code. Since nobody is fluent in all these languages, the possibility of a universal

---

[4] Carolyn Heilbrun, "The Masculine Wilderness of the American Novel," *Saturday Review*, 29 January 1972, p.41.

[5] Joanne S. Frye, *Living Stories, Telling Lives: Women and the Novel in Contemporary Experience* (Ann Arbor: University of Michigan Press, 1986), p.26.

[6] Mark Twain, *The Adventures of Huckleberry Finn* (London: Penguin, 1966), p.369.

[7] Jean-François Lyotard, *The Postmodern Condition*, trans. Geoff Bennington and Brian Massumi (Minneapolis: University of Minnesota Press, 1984) p.51.

metalanguage recedes – grounds for pessimism in some quarters. On the other hand, the delegitimation of the masternarrative results in a re-affirmation of narrative itself, as a central instance of the human mind, and a mode of thinking fully as legitimate as that of abstract knowledge. In this argument then, narrative is no longer in retreat in the face of abstract denotative, logical or cognitive procedures. If, as Lyotard affirms, "Narrative is the quintessential form of customary knowledge",[8] the work of the novelist becomes of central cultural importance.

In support of his vision of the centrality of narrative Lyotard makes three important points. Firstly, he notes that popular stories recount positive or negative apprenticeships: the successes or failures of the hero bestow legitimacy upon social institutions or role models. Secondly, narrative form lends itself to a great variety of language games, allowing all sorts of other statements to slip in. And lastly the transmission itself of narratives, involving sender, addressee and hero, communicates what one must say in order to be heard (sender), what one must listen to in order to speak (addressee) and what role one must play in order to be the object of narrative (hero). In short, a narrative tradition is intimately involved with a community's relation to itself and its environment; the set of rules that constitute the social bond is transmitted through narrative. Postmodernity therefore becomes a condition in which no single instance of narrative can exert a claim to dominate narration by standing beyond it. There is no single or originary speaker, we are all, to some extent, addressees of immemorial previous narratives. Where grand narratives link little narratives, either around a referent (classicism) or an original sender (modernism) the serial disposition of little narratives (one after another) means that no one narrative can become the masternarrative, organizing the field of language elements. To quote Bill Readings

> Crudely, each little narrative does not aim to tell **the** story, to put an end to narrative; rather a little narrative evokes new stories by the manner in which, in its turn, it has displaced preceding narratives in telling a story.[9]

Art is not, therefore in the service of cultural transformation; it is cultural transformation.

---

[8] Lyotard, p.19.

[9] Bill Readings, *Introducing Lyotard: Art and Politics* (London: Routledge, 1991) p.69.

Feminist critics have also, quite independently, highlighted the centrality of narrative in relation to cultural change. Carol Christ, for example, draws an explicit parallel between telling stories and living lives.

> In a very real sense there is no experience without stories. Stories give shape to experience, experience gives rise to stories ... for those who have had the freedom to tell their own stories ... but this has not usually been the case for women. Indeed there is a very real sense in which the seemingly paradoxical statement, 'Women have not experienced their own experience' is true.[10]

Instead, women may live out inauthentic stories provided by a culture which they did not create – conventional stories of love, courtship and marriage, for example. Woman is often neither sender, addressee or hero of narrative. The creation of new literary traditions may therefore offer a prime means to cultural change. As Joanne Frye puts it,

> because the novel as form resists fixity and responds to its social context through interaction rather than simple ideological miming, its literary resources are peculiarly responsive to women's needs for alternative resolutions.[11]

As an active participant in the processes of change the woman reader may claim personal agency, setting aside cultural determinisms, to make sense of experience in different ways. Frye again:

> as novelistic narrative is an agent of interpretation, it becomes as well a possible agent of reinterpretation, not only giving form but also altering accepted forms.[12]

How far however, is it possible for the masternarrative to be completely challenged? As Frederic Jameson's concept of the political unconscious indicates, the possibility remains of the return of the grand narrative. Robert Kiely puts it in a nutshell:

> Story patterns of social coercion and victimization, of education and political responsibility cannot be

---

[10] Carol P. Christ, *Diving Deep and Surfacing: Women Writers on Spiritual Quest* (Boston: Beacon Press, 1980) pp.4-5.

[11] Joanne S. Frye, *Living Stories, Telling Lives: Women and the Novel in Contemporary Experience* (Ann Arbor: University of Michigan Press, 1986) p.6.

[12] Frye, p.21.

purged any more than language can be. Dislocated, dishevelled, deprived of respectability these patterns remain in the mind of the reader.[13]

Moreover, if the masternarrative could be completely challenged, would that be a desirable state of affairs? How is the writer to avoid the reinscription of the notion of dominance in the replacement narrative? The problem presents itself in acute form for the American woman writer – who may wish to make it new, *without* invoking the Adamic myth, to develop autonomy *without* "self-reliance", to be *in* nature without being *of* nature, and to cultivate relationality outside the buddy relationship.

In *Love and Friendship*, Emmy Turner, transplanted to the isolated New England campus of Convers College, envisages herself communing with nature in the steps of Emerson and Thoreau. Emmy's family, though not physically New Englanders, have the tradition of being spiritually so. They believe that in their four years at Convers the sons of the family "breathed in the air of a higher spiritual state" (p.11).[14] Hitherto excluded from this all-male enclave, Emmy (a female Emerson) finds the very silence and chill of Convers inviting.

> It suggested revelations in deserts and forests, Thoreau and Descartes. (p.18)

Even amidst the rigours of the New England winter Emmy's enthusiasm continues unabated:

> after all, the heroes and philosophers of New England, all the founders of the Convers tradition had lived through winters like this ... Here one could still practice self-reliance; ... one could listen through the long, cold, black evenings for the inner voice. (p.65).

What Emmy listens to, initially, is her husband Holman preparing his classes. Convers specialises in a compulsory freshman course entitled "Hum C", which explicitly encodes its public values. A lightly fictionalised version of the famous innovative Amherst course, English 1-2,[15] Hum C is loosely based on logical positivist

---

[13] Robert Kiely, *Reverse Tradition: Postmodern Fictions and the Nineteenth Century Novel* (Cambridge, Mass.: Harvard University Press, 1993) p.34.

[14] Alison Lurie, *Love and Friendship* (New York: Macmillan, 1962 and London: Penguin, 1977). All page references are to the Penguin edition.

[15] See Theodore Baird, "The Freshman English Course", *Amherst Alumni News* 5 (1952), 194-6; James H. Broderick, "A Study of the Freshman Composition Course at Amherst: Action, Order, and Language," *Harvard Educational Review* XXVIII, 1

principles, in which the teacher goes on asking questions and the student answering until the latter learns to use words accurately. The object is to wipe the mental slate clean, so that each student can create his own moral universe anew, thinking for himself. Lurie gives a typical example:

> ASSIGNMENT II
>
> Here is a photograph, an airview of Convers College.
>
> (a) Let us assume you are now somewhere in the middle of the area contained in the photograph and you recognise this as a photograph of the spot you are now on. What do you do to recognize this?
>
> (b) Define in the context of (a) 'the spot you are now on'.
>
> (c) What difference do you see between this spot and the one in the map in Assignment No. 10? (p.24).

The aim of the exercise is to prompt the student to recognize his ability to make orders of various complex kinds. As a language game, Hum C implies that all final questions concerning truth are outmoded. It breaks up preconceptions and makes the individual abandon older beliefs. In its historical model, for example, the professor pointed to a window in the classroom and asked the students what they saw. (Response: a window). He then opened the window and stepped out onto the lawn, and (followed by his entire class) re-entered the room by the door. Asked for a definition of the door the class agreed that it was an opening for entering and leaving a room. Pointing to the still-open window, the professor again asked the class what they saw. The new definitions were more careful. In addition the course had an operationalist basis. One assignment set out to establish that the length of an object (a line in a visual illusion) was merely the sum of the operations performed in its measurement. To extrapolate: a word means what it means to the individual. He is the operator of its meanings. Significantly the historical course had empowering aims. Originally designed for non-literary students, who lacked confidence in their writerly abilities and had little access to canonical texts, the underlying assumption of the course was that the student does know something, and that he can be encouraged to communicate his knowledge drawing on his own experience. Students were likely to be asked to write about football, maths, or machines. They were

---

(1958), 44-57; Gail Kennedy, *Education At Amherst: The New Program* (New York: Harper and Brothers, 1955).

encouraged to see their own knowledge as legitimate – rather than as needing to be legitimated by a master narrative. The course was empowering only in one respect, however. Amherst, like the fictional Convers, was all-male.

Although debarred from her husband's lectures, Emmy Turner sets to work to take the course by proxy, eager to participate in a language game, which, as she is swift to recognise, has distinctly American assumptions, potentially providing a point of access to the masternarrative.   The point is made explicitly in a conversation between Holman and Emmy.

> "They keep asking questions simply to clear away all
> the rubbish that everyone takes for granted and what's
> left is what you really believe; what you really see, I
> mean, the way *you* see it and nobody else.   Like
> Emerson."
> "Emerson?" Holman raised his head.
> "Yes, like Self-Reliance ...   Convers now probably
> looks a lot like Concord used to ... when they were all
> thinking about the same things as in Hum C." (p.66).

Holman is less than appreciative, however, of his wife's newfound interest in Transcendentalism, though he keeps his thoughts to himself.

> She would always want to see every idea from an
> emotional point of view ... He did not mind – women
> should be that way. (p.67).

Ironically bearing out his thoughts, Emmy contemplates him in sour silence.

> I am more isolated than anybody ever was in
> Concord, she thought ... they had friends to talk to. I
> bet Emerson talked to his wife. (p.67).

Appropriately, perhaps, the result of the ensuing conversation is that she does see Holman afresh; she sees him as decidedly unattractive and falls out of love with him.

Far from Convers producing a higher spiritual state, Emmy finds that the converse is true as she ends up communing with nature in the arms of an appropriately named lover, Will Thomas. Just as Hum C's refusal of metaphysics delivers its students to sense experience, so Emmy's idealism collapses into sensuality. As she reflects, "When I listen to my inner voices they only say things like: 'I think I will call up Will,' or 'Let's give Emmy the largest piece of pie.'" (p.201). In the quest for places in which to make love, ranging from the duck marsh to a tool shed and a disused railway station,

Emmy does get to know the area reproduced in the maps and aerial photographs discussed in Hum C, in some detail. Moreover she gets to know it quite literally on the ground. Most of the love affair is carried on in the great outdoors, often in emblematic locations. At one point Emmy and Will are observed by Allen Ingram, a visiting novelist who is astonished at the sight of a couple making love out in the snow. In spite of the weather, he notes, the woman is naked to the waist; and quite brown, a fact which he ascribes to local history:

> I imagine there must still be a good deal of Indian blood hereabouts. Beyond them ... were the fields which were lush with corn and squash and tobacco ... last fall. (p.180).

In point of fact Emmy is tanned from a recent holiday in Bermuda. The comment returns Will and Emmy to a scene imbued with origins, in references to indigenous peoples and crops. Making love in the great outdoors however, exposes Emmy first to poison ivy and then to the full savagery which civilized society turns upon instinctual pleasures. Emmy's return to ethical origins takes place in a narrow and precisely calibrated society in which the social self triumphs over the impulse to nonconformity.[16]

As this false Eden reveals its true colours so Hum C comes in for reappraisal. When Holman is alerted to Emmy's adultery he finds his suspicions revolving through his mind as if part of an assignment. The mid-term exam, which he has just finished correcting, all now seems to refer to him.

> This is an Optical Illusion. What do you do to see these lines not only as lines but as an Optical Illusion? What other kinds of Illusions have you come across in your experience? (p.261).

In addition, when Holman follows the method of Hum C, relentlessly cross-questioning Emmy, the results are neither personally nor ethically satisfying. By these means Holman transforms the prints of the cleaning lady's galoshes in the snow into evidence of adultery with three different people – none of them actually Will Thomas. Having by this stage already abandoned Will, Emmy speaks nothing but the truth when she denies Holman's accusations. The precise linguistic truth, in this case, wipes the slate clean in a less than moral sense. Lurie's novel, therefore exposes the male language game, with its pretensions to privileged truth, and idealistic moral content, to

---

[16] See Amanda Lohrey, "The Liberated Heroine: New Varieties of Defeat," *Meanjin* 38 (1979), 294-304.

experience – and finds it decidedly wanting. Hum C is, in Emmy's description, nothing but a "stupid word game" (p.26).

Not all language games remain, however, as local and unlegitimated as Hum C. Slowly the possibility emerges that there is a second story underlying the masternarrative of Transcendental idealism – a story organised upon corporate, economic and distinctly male principles. Rather like *Who's Afraid of Virginia Woolf?* the novel emphasises the mythic substructures and archaic practices of the academic community, and by extension of society at large. In its cyclical movement from Autumn to the following summer, in the presence of Will as mock fertility god (impregnating the Dean's wife) and in satiric references to rites of passage and initiation, animism and magic, the novel sets in motion a parodic transformation of Walden into Wasteland. One interpolated language game is particularly significant. At a dinner party, Julian Fenn reveals just how little Convers actually acts on its stated aims. When teaching *Walden* Julian takes it seriously enough to spend a weekend living rough in the woods with his students. The result is censure by the Dean who maintains that it is not the role of a teacher to suggest actions to the students but to deal exclusively in ideas. Hum C remains a language game, not a narrative implicated in cultural change. Holman agrees that Convers is false to its stated ideals: "right here in town they're running pagan rituals ... at the fraternities." (p.42). In the story of his own fraternity initiation which he goes on to tell, animal worship looms large. The pledges are sent out to buy a terrier, which is christened James Dawg and confined in squalor with the pledges for the whole of Hell Week. At the end of the week the animal is supposedly slaughtered, and the festivities conclude with the great Dog-Eating Ceremony as the pledges, blindfolded, are passed parts of the unfortunate animal's insides to eat. (It is in fact raw calf's liver.) The initiation rite includes two elements of especial narrative interest. It is preceded by a ceremony of inquisition in which (rather as in Hum C) the pledges are interrogated about their sexual practices. Telling the right story is crucial:

> If you had no heterosexual stories to tell ... it was best to make some up, or else you would be questioned on still more embarrassing matters. (p.43).

As anthropological study indicates,[17] fraternities are both overtly homophobic and implicitly homoerotic – rather like classic American literature. Fraternity initiations cleanse young men of the despised "feminine" or "effeminate" self, bonded to mothers, humiliating them and exposing them to various forms of mock death in order to wipe out the past, break pre-existent bonds and rebond to the brotherhood. (At one point in the novel Holman worries about the choice between supporting his mother financially, or paying his fraternity dues. p.123.) Given that sexual expression is communicated and learned through discourse, the discourse associated with fraternity practices operates as a strategy of knowledge which sanctions the deployment of male power in acts of sexual aggression. Peggy Reeves Sanday has investigated the incidence of fraternity gang rape, for example, in which the woman (often unconscious through alcohol) is a surrogate victim in a drama in which the main agents are males interacting with each other. In group activity of this nature homoerotic desire is "simultaneously indulged, degraded, and extruded from the group."[18] What the ritual says is that women "ask for it". (Participants are often shocked by the charge of rape.) By defining women as "wanting it" the men simultaneously convince themselves of their heterosexual prowess and bond to each other by coparticipation in· a forbidden act. Holman expounds further on his fraternity activities, describing "Pig Night".

> Everybody brought in the easiest lays they could find, see ... God, what a collection ... Pigs. But turn out the lights and you couldn't see them ... Girls like that will do anything. They enjoy it actually. (p.290).

As Holman's stories indicate, the "right story" is a narrative that excludes or degrades women, while paradoxically functioning as a guarantor of heterosexual "normality". Importantly Holman's account of his fraternity ritual is based on fact (an individual fraternity[19]) and describes practices which are still current.[20] As rites of initiation and

---

[17] See Peggy Reeves Sanday, *Fraternity Gang Rape: Sex, Brotherhood and Privilege on Campus* (New York: New York University Press, 1990) for a definitive discussion and comprehensive bibliography.

[18] Sanday, p.12.

[19] An account of fraternity initiation ritual by a contemporary writer. Alison Lurie, Personal Interview, Key West, Florida, 18 February 1991.

[20] See Sanday. Richard Ford, "Rules of the House," *Esquire* 105,6 (1986), pp.231-4 describes initiation in the 1960s. Mark C. Carnes, *Secret Ritual and Manhood in Victorian America* (New Haven: Yale University Press, 1989) describes the earlier period, discussing all types of fraternal organisations. While the American

passage, fraternity rituals share common characteristics with many of the classic American cultural myths of virgin land, new beginnings, and regeneration through violence. Fraternity initiates, then, act as addressees of an immemorial narrative, a well-established social script.

The point is made explicit in the remainder of Holman's account of the initiation ceremony. As well as themselves telling the right story, the initiates also form the audience to a story. The ceremonies culminate as the president of the fraternity reads aloud the traditional *Tale of Wooglin*, which describes the famous hunter Wooglin and his march through a great desert with his faithful companion James Dawg. In this Disneyesque parody of the buddy relationship, the starving hunter is about to collapse when Dawg rolls over on his back and looks up at him touchingly: "a voice speaks out of the sky: 'Rip Open the Dawg and Eat!'" (p.46). At this point all the fraternity brothers repeat in chorus: "Eat! Eat!" Blindfolded, lying on their backs, the pledges ingest the raw liver. As a communal male ritual the story perpetuates the real values of Convers society, and highlights the masculine exclusivity of such key American *topoi* as the errand in the wilderness, isolation in nature and the buddy relationship, here underpinned both by the approving chorus of the social group, and by the voice of God. Teleological and social sanction combine. The fraternity ritual, then, teaches how to tell the right story (what one must say in order to be heard), how to react as a member of a community (how to listen in order to speak), and (in the pledges' dramatic imitation of Dawg's position) what role one must play in order to be the object of narrative.

As opposed to the idealism of Hum C, the fraternity story legitimises a dog-eat-dog mentality. Julian comments that

> It must have been cannibalism originally. After all, that christening ceremony; the dog became the 25th pledge. You were actually eating a freshman. (p.46).

Holman demurs. "Nobody really dies. The dog was our scapegoat." (p.46). Scapegoats do not remain, however, comfortably enclosed within Holman's little narrative. Where Hum C is not legitimated by

---

masternarrative emphasises individualist isolation, the nineteenth century was actually a century of joiners. In 1883 70,000 men belonged to college fraternities. (How many of them became canonical American authors?) Fraternal groups (the Red Men, the Knights of Pythias) whose only activity often consisted of elaborate rituals, expanded membership to 5.5 million in 1896, of a total male population of 19 million. The influence of fraternity and fraternal rituals on American literature could stand more investigation by literary scholars.

the community, fraternity discursive practice extends into the frame tale of the novel, expanding from local anecdote to masternarrative. In feminist analysis fraternity rituals have been described as a "sexual subculture".[21] Arguably, however, the ritual inscribes the majority culture, the dominant narrative, within the ostensibly oppositional culture – the converse culture – of the university. Commenting on the Amherst fraternities Gail Kennedy argues that

> The fraternities represent an entrenchment of the world without inside the college community. They are the centre of a kind of social education that reinforces the conventional values of our society in an environment where those values are being analyzed.[22]

When Holman tells his anecdote, he does so in order to reaffirm his membership of an elite group. But, *by* telling it he betrays the vow of secrecy taken at his initiation; he breaks the bond which guaranteed his status, the compact which dictated what role one must play to be an object of narrative. When asked why he was prepared to undergo ritual humiliation, Holman replied that he looked forward, in the future, to watching others being victimized in their turn. Fraternity members resort to abusing others (women, new pledges) in order to renew their sense of the social power of the brotherhood. In fact, however, they have become (in Sanday's analysis) "subjected beings who submit to fraternal authority and mold their identity to fit the mythologies of masculinity."[23] To put it another way, the initiates may associate themselves with the great hunter, Wooglin, but are in fact playing the role of James Dawg.

In the plot of Lurie's novel the apparent subtext usurps the public discourse, expanding from anecdote to action as mock death becomes real injury and a succession of scapegoats fulfil the community's darker needs. Julian Fenn is disgraced and ousted, largely because his children set fire to a campus house. Will Thomas's ambiguous status is suggested by his first appearance in that house. Clad in highly expensive (but second-hand) clothes, he resembles "a burglar who shopped at Brooks Brothers." (p.72). As his clothes suggest, Will lives off the academic community, if at one remove from full elite status. He is a writer – of music – though inspiration has faltered of late. As a failed artist he occupies the legitimate role of society scapegoat. He describes himself as "one of

---

[21] Sanday, "Introduction".

[22] Kennedy, p.130.

[23] Sanday, p.175.

the staunchest upholders of society there is. I play my part. I'm the local failure, no-good artist, seducer of little girls. Why, it's chaps like me that keep society going." (p.192). Significantly Will has a language game all of his own – ultra modernist music. When he performs, he plays a series of musical jokes on his audience, entirely for his own private amusement. (To the language of music most of the inhabitants of Convers are stone deaf). On the Lumkins' piano (on which C-sharp above high C is half a tone flat) he particularly enjoys playing Chopin's C-sharp minor waltz. He plays "Trumpet Voluntary" for Holman, mocking his pompous triumphalism, and inserts a stanza of "Oh, Susanna" when performing his latest composition for Emmy – who remains reverently appreciative. As an artist, although Will satirises society, he does not challenge it. He does not allow the game to cross over into the mainstream. Indeed Will draws a very firm distinction between art and life. When Miranda takes comfort in Dean Lumkin's pleasantness (as opposed to his wife's scornful behaviour) Will comments that

> It's the same tune: don't let yourself be fooled by different performances. (p.105).

Miranda counters that as a musician he should see that performances do make a difference to meaning but Will disagrees:

> In art it does. In life, it's just decoration. "Miranda Fenn, I am going to send you to the county poorhouse!" doesn't sound any better if it's set by Verdi and sung by Callas. (p.195).

As a lover, however, there are disadvantages to Will's belief in foundational truth, in meaning as prior to language. Emmy finally rejects Will for a related reason. Will cannot promise to love her forever, only that he loves her now. (p.329). He is true to the principles of Hum C, that every man is alone and responsible for making up his own moral universe, and recognises that time may compromise or destroy his assumptions: "how the hell can I promise what I'll feel for the next ten years? You want me to lie to you?" (p.329). He will not confuse words with deeds. Emmy would prefer him to express an idealistic intention – even a fairly fictional one. His fate is appropriate. At the close Will's affair with Emmy is simply erased, delegitimated by Holman who comes to the conclusion that his wife never really had an affair – that it was mere infatuation, a flirtatious game.

Miranda Fenn, however, suggests a form of legitimation of a more damaging kind. Miranda has always been interested in magic and goes in for table-rappings and reading tea leaves. It is she who brings Will and Emmy together, jokily suggesting that she cast a spell to relieve Emmy's boredom, introducing her to Will, and later reuniting the lovers as a go-between. A surrogate rebel and artist, Miranda takes a vicarious pleasure in arranging an adulterous affair – for others. She enjoys her role as confidante to her friends and relatives who

> occasionally laid small sections of their lives at her feet. She listened, she interpreted – rearranging the bits and pieces they brought in. Advising them what to think and do, and then looking on while her words were made flesh, was her deepest pleasure. (p.278).

It is also Miranda who makes a wax effigy of Betsy Lumkin. Magical belief, of course, hinges upon the idea that words can become deeds, and have consequences in the physical world, that the game can be played for keeps. The ambiguity surrounding magic is a productive one in Lurie's plot. On the one hand, it is perfectly clear that Betsy's pregnancy owes nothing to supernatural intervention and everything to Will. Miranda's spell is just a game. But Miranda draws a dark conclusion in the welter of recriminations and self-accusations at the close.

> We all want to be guilty, because guilt is power. It's the proof that one's magic works. (p.347).

In the absence of other grand narratives, the inhabitants of this American Eden find their legitimation only in guilt.

At the end of the story the process of scapegoating culminates in physical damage. In the course of the novel Dicky Smith, a tiresomely doggy student who hounds the staff with his bundle of dog-eared manuscripts (p.252) is rechristened "Fido". In a concluding disaster, during student unrest, Holman is implicated in pushing Fido into the burning foundation pit of the new Religion building, where he is semi-incinerated. Significantly Fido's heterosexual identity is suspect. Holman describes him as a "pansy bastard" (p.323), and speculates that in expelling Smith and his two fellow ringleaders the college is glad of the opportunity to get rid of "those three queers" (p.324). Holman may not actually have pushed Fido in, but he is a willing spectator, just as in the fraternity ritual. As a result Holman almost risks becoming the scapegoat himself. When Professor McBane comments that Smith's intentions were basically good Holman, unwisely, quips,

> How can we know that? In Hum C terms we can only take account of words and actions, not intentions. (p.325).

McBane promptly turns upon him in denunciation: "In you I see the kind of Doppelganger I have created with this course." (p.325). Appropriately, Holman is saved from ruin by another operator of a language game – the novelist-within-the-novel, Allen Ingram, who refuses to confirm Fido's story that Holman pushed him. In his view, to lie convincingly is part of the writer's art. (p.334). Lurie, however, makes Holman's guilt unambiguous. He confesses to Emmy: "'I stood there and watched him burn. And I liked it … Guilty,' he said finally." (p.342). Just as it is guilt and scapegoating which hold the fraternity together, along with its macrocosmic society, so Holman's admission mends the Turners' marriage. Emmy counsels forgiveness: "if you can't forgive yourself," she says, "how will you ever forgive me?" (p.344). They reunite in shared guilt, Emmy assuring Holman that her money will pay Fido's medical bills and wipe the slate clean, Holman looking forward to a long residence in Convers. Two fraternities have asked him to become their advisor (p.326).

At the close of the novel Emmy has a moment of realisation. She need not, after all, choose between staying with Holman and marrying Will. "I belong to myself" she realises. (p.343). Emmy *has* found herself at Convers, but the self in question is not, perhaps very much worth finding. She has entered a male masternarrative – but not the one she anticipated. Remembering how her brothers had returned from Convers boasting of their sexual exploits she realises that not only did their activities apparently not cancel out the spiritual gain from attending the college, they almost seemed necessary to it. Emmy reflects that she also can now claim to have sown her wild oats at Convers. (p.338). Emmy's attempts to break into male traditions have been ironically rewarded. At the close of the novel she watches Miranda's children playing blind man's buff:

> Something was wrong with the game, though. "But they're all blindfolded!" Emmy objected. "Yes", Miranda replied, "They like it better that way." (p.350).

The tableau of the blindfolded group, an image crossing over from fraternity ritual into the main narrative, recalls Emerson's comment in "Self-Reliance":

> what a blind man's buff is this game of conformity … most men have bound their eyes with one or another handkerchief, and attached themselves to some one of these communities of opinion.[24]

---

[24] Ralph Waldo Emerson, *Essays* (London: Dent, 1971), p.35.

While Lurie's swingeing satire exposes the illusions at the centre of the masternarrative, the implications for cultural change remain open-ended. In the portrayal of Convers, *Love and Friendship* therefore suggests the difficulty implicit in any counter-discourse, the danger of reinscribing the norms of the dominant discourse within its apparent contestation, as (to quote Richard Terdiman)

> the contesters discover that the authority they sought to undermine is reinforced by the very fact of its having been chosen, as dominant discourse, for opposition.[25]

Rewritings, counter-texts run the risk of slippage from oppositional to surreptitiously collusive positions. Revising the masternarrative may see its return in subtextual form. The contemporary reader may wonder to what extent Emmy has progressed or merely degenerated morally. When the novel was published, readers in the Midwest were in no doubt: *Love and Friendship* was burned in two small towns as too shocking.[26] Clearly, 1960s America had not come as far from the nineteenth century masternarrative as might be thought.

So does Alison Lurie consign the novel itself to the status of one more word game, unable to challenge the masternarratives inscribed in culture? Not quite. Throughout the novel Emmy's actions are placed in ironic perspective by a technical device. Lurie ends each chapter with a letter from Allen Ingram, the visiting novelist, whose own novel advances in tandem with Lurie's, and finishes at its close. While the plot of Lurie's novel concerns heterosexual love, the plot of Ingram's is not described in his letters to his friend: Ingram is homosexual. As a result he is impervious to Emmy's charms and immune to the two major obsessions of all the other characters – heterosexual love and anxiety over contract-renewal, in the dog-eat-dog academic world of Convers. The play between frame and tale (to recur in *Imaginary Friends*) restores a sense of the power of narrative to revise events and meanings. Allen describes Emmy as a "serious, enthusiastic, Bryn Mawr type of deb" (p.205) and Will as a "sulky-charming young man who drank steadily" (p.51). He has no interest in Betsy's pregnancy, and news of a wedding (p.292) leaves him unmoved. Uninvolved, he functions as a chorus or commentator on the action, diminishing its importance by

---

[25] Richard Terdiman, *Discourse/Counter-discourse. The Theory and Practice of Resistance in Nineteenth Century France* (Ithaca: Cornell University Press, 1985), p.6.

[26] Janet Todd (ed.), *Women Writers Talking* (New York: Holmes and Meier, 1983), p.91.

taking a longer view – and eventually leaving Convers behind for the world without. In a sense, he reassures the reader that there is a world out there, beyond the apparent microcosm. Convers, in his view is only one small town, not a representative universe.

> The world ... is a disorderly, dirty scrap heap. Convers, on the other hand, is a botanical or zoological garden. (p.204).

The story is local, not microcosmic.

Nor does Allen himself provide a totalising alternative narrative. Emmy's story may run in parallel to Ingram's male tale, a male narrative of love and friendship, but Ingram's letters are clearly not indicative of male letters in the broader sense, as belles lettres. He, too, is an outsider to Convers and to many of the assumptions of the American masternarrative, if only because he is gay. His letters challenge notions of heterosexual "normality" in essential ways, foreshadowing the main theme of *The Last Resort*, in which he makes a passing appearance (p.195). Moreover, Ingram continually reminds the reader of the fictional status of events, and of fiction as game. Pondering how he would have treated the incident of the Fenns' fire, for example (p.89), he realises that he would have invented a larger conflagration, and wonders if he practises sufficient economy of cause and effect. The reader begins to see the fire as a fictional event rather than as "real". Letters inevitably give the reader a sharp focus on the construction of the subject in language; we assume that we should "read between the lines" to some extent; that letters offer only a partial account. Because the reader is given only Allen's letters to Francis Noyes, and none of the replies, and because the letters frequently refer to incidents known to Francis but not to us, the letters remind us that we are only getting one side of this story – Allen's – a partial truth. Given the nature of Allen's sexual orientation, our access to the true nature of his life is already somewhat obscured. This sense of an untold story is exacerbated by Allen's reference to an unspecified incident ("Don't *apologize*. It wasn't my fault that the acquarium got broken" p.179) or past history ("that episode at Newport the day of the boatrace" p.251). Difficulties of interpretation are also highlighted. Allen spends some time reassuring Francis (p.230) that his casual references to the class differences between Emmy and Holman had no implications for his own relationship with Francis. (Allen and Emmy are of a higher social class than Francis and Holman). Allen's narrative, then, reminds us that he is not trapped in the narratives of Convers, and that there are other narratives – his as-yet-unpublished novel, the other side of the story of the letters – which will follow on from the close of Emmy's story.

As a result, Emmy's story is not so much definitively "placed" or dominated by Allen Ingram, as it is extended, as the sequential, serial narrative opens out, potentially, to the next petit récit. In this respect it is noteworthy that both Emmy's story and Ingram's novel reach their central climax together. When he starts writing his "big blood-and-tears scene" (p.230), Emmy has a major row with Will and breaks off their relationship. In the attendant ruckus Holman, chasing Emmy up a back road in a fury of jealousy, crashes into Ingram's adopted dog, Beowulf, resulting in (as Ingram puts it) "a real scene" (p.272) of blood and tears. It is almost as if James Dawg has come to life and crossed over from the fraternity tale, to the love affair, and into the pages of Ingram's account. Until this point major events were relayed to the reader by an omniscient narrator. Ingram was merely an observer (p.204). But the final disaster – Fido's immolation – is not presented directly or omnisciently, but through Allen's epistolary account to Francis. Godly omniscience has yielded to a first person narrative, which has moved from novel proper to letters, almost as if the action of *Love and Friendship* were transferring itself to the control of a succeeding novelist, who is organising the field of language elements to different ends. Ingram takes up – and takes over – the story and as he does so converts the novel into a serial disposition of little narratives. Allen Ingram concludes *Love and Friendship* in tones of ringing finality:

> The novel is FINISHED, this year of economy and discipline is over. (p.351).

But the novel in question is his. The reader has less sense of finality about Emmy's fate. In Ingram's last letter he describes meeting Emmy at the kennels where he is leaving Beowulf, until the dog's rightful owners can pick him up. (This "Dawg" will not go out into the wider world.) Emmy assures him that he should not worry about abandoning his faithful companion. If he takes the dog with him it will only cause problems with friends and connections. If he wants another dog, she says, he can always buy one (just, as the fraternity does, just as Holman pays off Fido). And – as the reader realises immediately – just as Emmy can. Emmy abandons Will at least in part because of the problems which living with improvident, promiscuous, unrepressed Will would cause with her well-bred family and friends. Will is also James Dawg, used in the process by which Emmy reaches autonomy, finds herself in nature and recreates her relationships, but ultimately too lacking in breeding to meet Emmy's class-bound criteria. Emmy has gone through her own initiation ritual and rite of passage and has had her victims too. And there will be others. The sequential aspect of Emmy's story is not merely implied. In *Foreign Affairs*, Emmy's son Freddy, now grown-up, realises that she had a series of other lovers

> For the first time he considered his mother as a possible adulteress and recognized that her qualifications for this role were excellent. (p.43).

Earlier Emmy had not much liked Will's whimsical suggestion that if the Convers ladies found out about their affair, they would have their sewing club make Emmy a big scarlet letter A. (p.208). Later, a guilt-free Hester Prynne, she follows her own inclinations, and becomes the operator of her own meanings rather than the victim of the social script. In the end, then, *Love and Friendship* succeeds both in satirising the masternarrative and in preventing its re-inscription. No single instance of narrative – the American masternarrative, the conventional tale of adultery, Allen Ingram's story, *Love and Friendship* itself, or even *Foreign Affairs* – can claim to dominate narration by standing beyond it.

Chapter Three
Walter Benjamin Goes to Hollywood: *The Nowhere City*

With Lurie's second novel, *The Nowhere City*, the satire on
Utopian pretensions reaches out into the title itself. Quite literally "U-
topos" (Nowhere); Lurie's Los Angeles is an emblematic locale, a
modern Erewhon, a city almost equally divided between Hollywood
dreams, the armament industry, and the Beat generation. Into this
ambivalent Eden comes Paul Cattleman, commissioned to write a
history of the Nutting Research and Development Corporation, a
military-industrial complex, and his wife Katherine, who finds the
lack of historical sense and the emphasis on physical health as a prime
moral value almost as irritating in Los Angeles as in Samuel Butler's
original.[1] Like a Hollywood comedy of the sexes (*The Philadelphia
Story* perhaps) the novel enjoys a deliberately contrived and schematic
plot, in which Paul takes a mistress (Ceci, a painter), and then
Katherine a lover (Iz Einsam, a psychiatrist) whose wife, Glory Green,
a film goddess, promptly seduces Paul. When Paul palls on his lover
Ceci, Utopia reveals itself as nowhere, nothingness, a state of
emptiness and absence. Paul's history turns out to be "Nutting" in
every sense, commissioned merely for the purpose of incurring a tax
loss, and shredded immediately on completion. Katherine, on the
other hand, overcomes her initial distaste for the West Coast and
embarks upon a journey into the future. Precisely because she is
"nothing" and nobody knows her, she sheds her social inhibitions and
finds the courage to change. In Los Angeles Paul and Katherine
switch roles. Paul is "going nowhere" fast, and ultimately returns to
the East, to Convers, with all that it implies. Katherine becomes Kay,
a stereotypical Californian blonde, and remains. Although it is
suggested that it is healthy to try out new roles, ambiguities remain.
The reader is left to consider whether Katherine is merely a chameleon
without principles, adapting to any new social environment by a
process of protective colouration, or whether Paul is to be judged
wanting for his inability to change.

Reviewers have tended to see the contrivance of the plot,
which cuts between its major characters in filmic mode, as a
weakness. R. G. G. Price noted its "schematic comedy"[2] as offering

---

[1] Samuel Butler, *Erewhon and Erewhon Revisited* (London: Dent, 1951).
[2] R. G. G. Price, "New Novels," Punch, 248 (17 February 1965), p.258.

almost too many correspondences and parallels. The binary plot of
the novel, however, has a deeper resonance than critics have allowed.
Nor is the resemblance to Hollywood comedy accidental. In her
second novel Lurie deliberately – and daringly – engages with one of
the most significant aesthetic controversies of the twentieth century,
the debate between Walter Benjamin and Theodor Adorno concerning
the potential of new technology and especially artistic technologies, to
promote social emancipation, a debate which was also couched in
terms of the Utopia/Dystopia dialectic. In choosing Los Angeles as
her setting, Lurie deliberately selects what has been termed the most
mediated town in America,[3] almost unviewable except through its
various mythic or fictional filters. Any novel set in Los Angeles
becomes, almost by default, metafictional. There can be no pretence
of mimetic illusion. A deforming optic is always already in place.
Whether the reader draws upon images culled from the American
dream of Scott Fitzgerald (*The Last Tycoon*), the apocalyptic
nightmare of Nathaneal West (*Day of the Locust*), the early historical
marketing of Los Angeles as the land of fruit and sunshine via the
"mission myth", or the Noir version promoted by Chandler, James M.
Cain and James Ellroy, Los Angeles is never neutral. To quote Mike
Davis

> Los Angeles ... polarizes debate: it is the terrain and
> subject of fierce ideological struggle.[4]

Intellectuals have tended to gaze at Los Angeles as into a crystal ball
to capitalism's future. In *Dialectic of Enlightenment*, Theodore
Adorno and Max Horkheimer argued, famously, that Los Angeles was
the embodiment of American capitalism, focussing on Hollywood and
on the fashion in which it undermined the revolutionary potential of
the masses by promoting consumerism. Unblinded by rhetoric or
image they focussed upon economic history in order to underline the
fact that "the basis on which technology gains power over society is
the power of those whose economic hold over society is greatest",[5] a
role foregrounded also by Lurie in the shadowy but all-powerful
Nutting organisation, which uses its sophisticated technology (the
Undat machine) simply to shred Paul's manuscript and erase the

---

[3] Michael Sorkin, "Explaining Los Angeles," *California Counterpoint: New West
Coast Architecture 1982*. San Francisco Art Institute 1982, p.8. Cited by Mike
Davis, *City of Quartz: Excavating the Future in Los Angeles* (Vintage, 1990), p.20.
[4] Mike Davis, *City of Quartz: Excavating the Future in Los Angeles* (Vintage, 1990),
p.20. Davis offers an excellent account of the mythos of Los Angeles.
[5] Max Horkheimer and Theodore Adorno, *Dialectic of Enlightenment* (London:
Herder and Herder, 1972), p.121.

awkward truths of its economic history. For Adorno and Horkheimer the culture industry in Los Angeles is in collusion with the dominant ideology, undermining the revolutionary potential of the masses by its family-centred consumerism. The architecture of Los Angeles – the little family boxes – appeared to embody this process in its flimsiness and easily discarded quality. The organisation of space in the city therefore carried its own rhetoric, as it does in *The Nowhere City*. Lurie organises her novel into five parts (Mar Vista, Venice, Westwood, Hollywood, International Airport) each introduced by original advertisements reproduced from the *Los Angeles Mirror News* and *Los Angeles Times*, suggesting the subordination of individual characters to their social and commercial environment, and maintaining reader-awareness of the economic underpinnings of the American Dream. One side of the street in which Paul and Katherine rent a house turns out to be earmarked for the construction of a freeway; the buildings, wish-images styled for different dreams (Spanish haciendas, a French chateau, a Swiss chalet, English country cottages) are simply jacked up and moved elsewhere, marginalized to the demands of the machine. Utopia threatens to become Autopia.[6] Just as Adorno and Horkheimer saw the culture industry as negating the role of the masses as instruments of historical change, so Lurie's Los Angeles is portrayed as a place without the dimension of time. Katherine complains that there are no seasons, the months no longer mean anything, the days of the week are interchangeable (stores remain open on Sundays) and day and night have also become fluid entities: when out in a restaurant for dinner she finds others consuming breakfasts. As a consumer-paradise, Los Angeles defeats the historian, and destroys his attempts to place it in a meaningful chronology.

If this were all there were to *The Nowhere City* the reader might well enjoy it as merely another in a long, if worthy, tradition of exposés of Hollywood Babylon. Lurie, however, engages in quite specific and detailed fashion with the major challenger to Adorno, Walter Benjamin, and constructs plot, character and symbolism in order to create a series of discussion points bearing upon the debate. To understand the wit and ingenuity of Lurie's novel, it is necessary to review the debate briefly and to summarise the key points. Quite apart from the difficulties of translation, Benjamin's work, in particular the Arcades project, is fragmentary and not easily

---

[6] The term is taken from Peter Reyner Banham, *Los Angeles: The Architecture of Four Ecologies* (London, 1971).

accessible. Benjamin has however been fortunate in having two excellent commentators, Susan Buck-Morss and Richard Wolin, on whom I shall draw extensively and gratefully in what follows.[7]

Essentially the Adorno-Benjamin debate of the 1930s springs from Adorno's detailed epistolary responses to three of Benjamin's writings, especially "The Work of Art in the Age of Mechanical Reproduction". Benjamin had originally intended to focus his work on the "prehistory of the nineteenth century", to exhume rudiments of prehistory (myth, fable) beneath the apparent novelty of the array of commodities and inventions which swept the century. He planned to show that the modern regressed to notions of cyclical time dominant in prehistoric life and to notions of eternal recurrence – since the apparent "novelty" of the commodities concealed the fact that they were in actuality thoroughly interchangeable. (As an example of the reproduction of the always-the-same, under the semblance of the perpetually new, Benjamin cited the chorus girl line in a review, and the presentation of woman as a commodity, a mass article, in which individual expression is camouflaged and packaged into an identifiable type[8]). Adorno, however, saw Benjamin's argument, especially in its evocation of wish-images in the collective unconscious as harbingers of a potential new order, as having dangerously utopian elements. For Adorno the suggestion that the recourse to prehistory was not just a regression but an awakening in the collective mind of the memory of a prehistoric classless society was particularly alarming. Adorno saw Benjamin as having relinquished his earlier critical conception in favour of constructing a positive Utopian moment in the relation between modern and prehistoric. As Wolin succinctly puts it,

> For Adorno, it would be more accurate to describe both periods through the category of Hell ... than through the category of utopia.[9]

Benjamin had, in his view, become guilty of idealizing the potentially Utopian side of commodity production, romanticizing prehistory as a Golden Age, and appealing (in the flirtation with imagery of the collective unconscious) to the illusory notion of solidarity, cloaked in

---

[7] Susan Buck-Morss, *The Dialectics of Seeing. Walter Benjamin and the Arcades Project*, (Cambridge, Mass.: MIT, 1989); Richard Wolin, *Walter Benjamin. An Aesthetic of Redemption* (New York: Columbia University Press, 1982).

[8] Buck-Morss, p.191.

[9] Wolin, p.177.

archaic images, in a quasi-Brechtian hypostatization of such notions as "collectivity" and "proletariat".

The debate became sharper when Benjamin wrote "The Work of Art in the Age of Mechanical Reproduction", an essay considered so radical at the time that the Institute for Social Research only printed it once the term "communism" had been replaced with "the constructive forces of humanity".[10] Benjamin sketched a succession of phases in the evolution of aesthetic history. The argument goes something like this: The work of art originally had a ritual or cultic function, becoming imbued with a hallowed character as a result. Its immutable uniqueness was the hallmark of its authority, a uniqueness inseparable from its singularity in time and apace, and from its being embedded in a tradition. Such works of art possessed what Benjamin termed an aura – referring to the customary historical role played by works of art in the cultural legitimation of social functions. The aura is the "unique phenomenon of a distance, however close it may be".[11] Unapproachability is a major quality of the cult image. With the Renaissance, however, Benjamin detected a movement from the ritualistic to the secular cult of beauty. Art then begins to struggle for its autonomy which is revived by Romanticism, then threatened anew by the rampant commodification of art in the later nineteenth century. Reaction then occurs in the creed of "l'art pour l'art", which offers a kind of theology of art, restoring the aura within a framework of non-utilitarian aesthetic values. All attempts to relate the work of art to social and utilitarian concerns are now resisted. For Benjamin the most significant aspect of the production and reception of works of art in the twentieth century was the intervention of technical means into these processes – particularly as concerning photography, film, and music. By substituting a plurality of copies for a unique original, mechanically reproduced art destroyed the singularity in time and space on which the art object depends for its claim to authority and authenticity. Every work now becomes replaceable. Cult value is replaced by exhibition value, and the locus of attention shifts from the work of art itself as a privileged entity to the point of intersection between work and onlooker. (Benjamin makes the point that the cult work was previously seen by few and often only shown on ritual

---

[10] Wolin, p.183.

[11] Walter Benjamin, "The Work of Art in the Age of Mechanical Reproduction" in *Illuminations*, ed. Hannah Arendt (London: Fontana/Collins, 1973) p.224. First published as *Schriften* (Frankfurt: Suhrkamp Verlag, 1955).

occasions, citing the elk on the cave wall, the curtained Madonna, the statues in inaccessible high places in cathedrals).

Today the emphasis on exhibition value is absolute. In literary terms the death of the author and birth of the reader, reader-response aesthetics, reception theory and theories of representation and the gaze, all respond to this change of emphasis.[12] For Benjamin, this development opened up untapped potential for the political employment of art, subordinating art's status as an object of aesthetic enjoyment to its function as an instrument of communication. Film, collectively produced and readily accessible, was the prime example. In film the image is secularized, its distance abolished – the audience can see close-ups of the famous, for example. By bringing art to a mass audience, film offered a democratization of the reception of the visual image. Technology might therefore be seen as potentially progressive. If industrialization had created a crisis of perception due to the fragmentation of space and the speeding up of time, film could itself slow down time and construct new spatio-temporal orders, providing the audience with an opportunity to study modern existence reflectively and critically. (Benjamin praised Chaplin's performances, for example, for mocking the fragmentation of modern existence in his jerky sequences of small motions). The photograph can bring out aspects of the original which are not available to the naked eye. Film can construct a time-free Utopian space, tailored to our requirements.

Benjamin's emphasis on perception in relation to society is particularly important. In his argument the film has enriched our field of perception with methods which can be illustrated by those of Freudian theory. Just as slips of the tongue went unnoticed before *The Psychopathology of Everyday Life*, now film has allowed close-ups, slow motion, re-runs, and enlargements to expand space and time. Thus

> The camera introduces us to unconscious optics as does psychoanalysis to unconscious impulses.[13]

Benjamin did have some reservations. In film the actor loses his "aura"; the image becomes separable, transportable (a process which Benjamin compares to the sense of estrangement one feels before one's own image in a mirror). In compensation

---

[12] Ellen J. Esrock, *The Reader's Eye: Visual Imaging as Reader Response* (Baltimore: Johns Hopkins University Press, 1994) makes suggestive points in this connection.
[13] "Work of Art", p.239.

> The film responds to the shrivelling of the aura with an artificial build-up of the "personality" outside the studio. The cult of the movie star ... preserves not the unique aura of the person but the "spell of the personality", the phoney spell of a commodity.[14]

(It is an argument to which Lurie pays particular attention, in the creation of the starlet, Glory, and her psychiatrist husband, whose research concerns perception and social delinquency, unconscious optics by another name).   For all his reservations, Benjamin nonetheless highlighted positive aspects of technology.   Although industrialism had been appropriated for its own purposes by capitalism, he saw possibilities remaining of reactivating its original promise, to deliver a humane society of material abundance, and welcomed the potential for democracy and liberation in film.

Not so Adorno.   In ascribing revolutionary possibilities to film, Benjamin was, in Adorno's view, simply wrong, particularly as concerned the cult of stars.   He saw the rapid images of film as rendering the spectator more passive and its illusionist qualities as a powerful means of seduction and manipulation.   For Adorno mechanically-reproduced art lends itself to the ideological co-operation of the masses within the existing social framework.   It does not tend towards political emancipation.   In his 1938 essay, "On the Fetish Character of Music and the Regression of Listening",[15] he emphasised commodification (art moving from use-value to exchange value, from the challenging pleasures of listening to the formulaic and undemanding jingles and hit-tunes of mass entertainment); the regression to cult in the idolisation of the star; and the creation of the fan, who buys the art-object not for its intrinsic aesthetic merit but because of its commercial popularity (songs bought or films marketed purely on the name of the artist, functioning like a brandname). Instead he waved the flag for radical avant-garde artists such as Schoenberg who reject the unitary aura in favour of a fragmentary or dissonant aesthetic.   To sum up, Benjamin stands accused of collapsing art into society in functional terms, sacrificing aesthetic autonomy in favour of reproducible and therefore accessible art. Adorno preserves the radicality of art at the expense of universality. If Benjamin forfeited the measure of distance art needs vis à vis

---

[14] "Work of Art", p.233.

[15] Theodor W. Adorno, "On the fetish character in music and the regression of listening", in Theodor W. Adorno, *The culture industry: Selected essays on mass culture*, ed. J. M. Bernstein (London: Routledge, 1991), pp.26-52.

society, to ensure its critical function, Adorno maintained it. But in order to preserve itself by distance from the majority world avant-garde art renders itself necessarily more and more esoteric, to escape the reifying network of commodity production and thereby maintain its powers of negotiation and refusal.[16] Avant-garde art is critical – but, alas, it is also distant. (The revolutionary potential of Schoenberg remains singularly unrealised).

Esoteric, however, is not a term applicable to *The Nowhere City*, with its apparently conventional plot, its accessibility in terms of generic associations (romance, utopia, comedy of the sexes, Hollywood novel) and its exploitation of a variety of motifs from light entertainment (a chase sequence, scenes reminiscent of horror movie and western, soap opera and science fiction). Yet, without specifically invoking such concepts as "aura", "commodification" or "reification" Lurie engages profoundly and specifically with the debate, creating a novel which succeeds in uniting the popular with the critical. Both popular art (the film industry) and the avant garde (the Beats) are thematised in the pages of the novel – and each plays a role in Lurie's critique of the existing social order. Lurie is clearly not interested in preaching to the converted. Most readers do not curl up comfortably with Theodor Adorno or Walter Benjamin – but a great number do curl up with Alison Lurie and her dramatisation of their arguments. Just as in her work for the Poets' Theatre, *The Nowhere City* demonstrates Lurie's ability to serve critical, even radical, aesthetic purposes within a popular form. In its opposition of Paul and Katherine, Beats and movie industry, heaven and hell, *The Nowhere City* initiates a process of critical debate and self-reflection on the part of readers who would be instantly deterred from continuing by any overt engagement with the Benjamin/Adorno debate. Lurie adopts neither Adorno nor Benjamin's reasoning wholesale – the point is to engage the reader in the debate between them. Far from programming readers towards one particular way of thinking therefore, *The Nowhere City* presents both sets of arguments in fictional form.

These are large claims. If we turn to the novel, however, they are claims which reward careful investigation. Lurie sets out to test Benjamin and Adorno in the context of a feminist analysis, constructing a plot which centres upon Paul's relationship with three women, respectively envisaged as an art object (Katherine), an artist (Ceci, a Beat painter) and an artiste (Glory). On a simple level his trajectory appears to suggest a process of aesthetic coarsening, as he

---

[16] Wolin, p.208.

moves from Katherine (a true beauty and all his own) to Ceci (a serious Underground painter, who is promiscuously liberal with her affections) to the fraudulent charms of Hollywood décor and the arms of a starlet.   The process is clearly modelled on the historical evolution sketched by Benjamin from the cult of the beauty to the avant garde to the mechanically reproduced. Paul, himself an expert in the sixteenth century, describes Katherine in terms which emphasise the unique, the spiritual and the artistic.

> She had the grace and tint of a Botticelli – and almost
> exactly the profile of the nymph who holds out a
> flowered robe to cover Venus as she rises from the
> sea. (p.16).[17]

Significantly Katherine, sexually inexperienced and generally extremely aloof, does not reveal her beauty easily.   She is distinguished by distance, by her adherence to tradition (as represented by her parents' antique furniture, a whole collection of objets d'art) and by her considerable unwillingness to remove herself from her established place, in Cambridge, Massachusetts, to join Paul in Los Angeles. Paul admires her for these qualities:

> Hers was a real, a classic beauty, subtle, fine and
> private – not blatant and public like the Hollywood
> sort … [She] was invisible from fifteen feet. (p.311).

In the denouement of the novel, however, Katherine's invisibility proves deeply ironic. At the close, after being at a party for more than an hour, Paul is still unable to find her anywhere, despite repeated enquiries after his pale, shy, brown-haired wife. Then Kay is pointed out to him, joking with a group of men:

> a pretty girl in tight yellow pants, with a smooth
> California tan and ash-blonde hair pulled up on her
> head … an obvious Los Angeles type; he remembered
> vaguely seeing her over there earlier in the evening.
> "Oh, that's not her," Paul started to say, when the girl,
> laughing at some joke that had been made, turned her
> face full in his direction.   He realized that it was
> Katherine. (p.316).

To Paul's gaze Katherine's transformation is a catastrophe. She has become a copy of any number of Los Angeles girls, a type reproduced all over California, accessible and no longer his. From Katherine's point of view however, the process may be one of liberation – both

---

[17] Alison Lurie, *The Nowhere City* (London: Penguin, 1977). Subsequent quotations are to this edition of the novel. (First published by William Heinemann in 1965).

sexual (an emphatic loss of her suborgasmic status) and individual. The "object" has escaped from the constraints of space, time and tradition and become autonomous.

The process is not merely an individual one, however, but has political ramifications. The novel begins by setting different visual images – archaic or modern – in a critical perspective. At the beginning of the novel Katherine's object status is firmly emphasised, as Paul gazes at his reclining wife, "a pleasing arrangement of pale round pinkish shapes, the important places marked with curly brown hair." (p.9). Katherine, however, in the grip of a sinus headache, feels as if her head were being squeezed into a metal box. Involuntarily Paul then pictures Katherine in terms of this image:

> he saw her naked body topped by a tin can with a pink and white paper label – advertising canned apple-juice, perhaps, or apple-sauce. (p.10).

As an object of Paul's desire Katherine is first introduced as objet d'art, then as a commodity mediated by its advertising image. The reader is kept aware of both frameworks – Utopian and dystopian – in the slippage of imagery between the archaic and the commodified. It is also no accident that Paul supplies apples to his fantasy image. Paul's image of Los Angeles is emphatically Edenic, offering "the sense of infinite possibilities" (p.15). His mind moves immediately to archaic Utopian images suggesting the "garden of the New World" topos, associating Los Angeles with the sixteenth century:

> a city of walled gardens like the imaginary gardens in late medieval romances, full of allegorical blooms – fruit and flowers ripe at the same time. (p.15).

Here, he fantasises, still with the accent on distance and unapproachability, he might find "other paraphernalia of courtly love: the impenetrable castles ... the worship from afar of the beloved movie starlet". (p.15). When, however, he proffers both flowers and a luscious peach to Katherine, she refuses, with "the face of Persephone, he thought, offered food in Hell." (p.17). For Katherine Paul has a reason – a job, an office – to be in Los Angeles, whereas as a mere accompanying wife she is "just nothing here. Nobody knows me or wants me around" (p.19). Paul's flowers wilt beside her for lack of water. When the couple attend a party (having first been welcomed at the wrong party, such is the interchangeability of homes and décor) she proclaims loudly against the falsity of Los Angeles:

> Everything's advertisements here. Everything has a wrong name ... it's always a lie like in advertisements. (p.48).

For Katherine Los Angeles is summed up by the giant revolving doughnut advertisement – "that big empty hole going around and around up in the air ... that's what this city is! ... a great big advertisement for nothing!" (pp.48-9). Perhaps rather obviously, Paul's utopian/archaic imagery, littered with remnants of myth and fable, is contrasted with Katherine's dystopian sense of the commodification and final emptiness of mass fantasies disseminated by the advertising media.

In contrast to Paul, however, Katherine's disenchantment allows her to discover that there can be no return to the archaic. In this respect one scene is particularly significant, a visit which she pays to the "G. J. Putty" art museum, an exclusive location, not open to the general public, which contains Old Masters which "few people had ever seen." (p.66). Katherine is determined to enjoy these cult objects, fighting her way against the direction of the masses in a series of crowd and traffic jam scenes, to reach the desired seclusion.

> She held her breath ... until they entered the museum; then she looked only at the floor. She shut her eyes to the view ... waiting for the sane views, miraculously preserved for hundreds of years. (p.70).

In terms of her perceptions Katherine is fully in "cult" mode here, blanking out the world outside and preparing to revere the miraculous objects. When she opens her eyes, however, it is a shock.

> Her first impression was of behinds. Rose-pink behinds by Boucher; white behinds by Ingres; misty Impressionist behinds and full, fleshy Rubens behinds. (p.70).

Nearly all the paintings are of nudes. The room oozes sensuality from its still-lifes of ripe fruit to its sofas with the legs of beasts "as if waiting the convenience of this crowd of whores" (p.70). Where a divine presence is signalled it is in a painting of Leda, in the process of being raped by the swan. Quite clearly cult status has yielded to the exhibition – or even the exhibitionist – function. When the guard, leering, suggests a visit to the Amours of the Gods tapestries in the upstairs bedrooms Katherine flees. The paintings have been "greedily transplanted" (p.70) from their places in time and space, their aura lost and with it their uniqueness. They have become a mere collection of behinds, rather than individual works of art located in particular painterly and cultural traditions. Similarly the animals in the Putty zoo have been "forcibly torn from their natural habitat" and gaze miserably at Katherine "not realizing that she was their fellow" (p.71). These animals lack "the hysterical stared-at gaze of animals in public zoos" (p.71) – they are privately owned – but, just like Katherine, they are wretched objects of the gaze. As Mary Anne Doane has argued,

> The fetishistic representation of the nude female body, fully in view, insures a masculinisation of the spectatorial position.[18]

The sexual politics of looking is emphasised. When Katherine's companion, Suzy, describes Leda euphemistically to her little daughter as "petting" the swan, casting Katherine "a look of adult conspiracy" (p.70), Katherine refuses to cast it back. She dissociates herself from the dominant social optics in which women collude with the male-oriented gaze.

But another attraction is offered at the Putty mansion, the buffalo which, if something of an American icon, are at least indigenous. When Suzy's stationwagon gets stuck in the mud in an orchard of fruit trees, and is charged by the buffalo the scene transmogrifies from the imagery of European art to an emblematic American encounter between technological and natural forms. The machine, in this case, is quite literally stuck in the garden. For Katherine Eden has turned apocalyptic. She notes the buffalo's "black bulging eyes", "satanic horns" and bare, dirty hindquarters. But Katherine's encounter with the cult of beauty has begun to teach her how to resist. She promptly takes command. "You can't go back so you'll have to go forward" (p.75), she instructs Suzy, telling her to smash ahead, over he resistance of a young tree. The stationwagon cannot be put into reverse; there is no way back to some unspoiled state of nature. Imagistically Lurie dramatises here the dominance and destructive nature of the technological. There is some damage (Katherine's dress is split up the side to her thigh) but they nevertheless make their escape. The archaic images are left behind. The episode is clearly proleptic.[19] Katherine's later liberation involves a violent sexual encounter with a similarly hirsute and animalistic Dr. Einsam, as a result of which she too moves on.

If Katherine has begun to take the first steps in the process of assuming responsibility for her own actions, Paul's progress is

---

[18] Mary Ann Doane, "Film and the Masquerade: Theorising the Female Spectator," *Screen* 23 (1982), p.85.

[19] Horst Kruse notes that the scene dramatizes her incipient emancipation from a Puritanical background and foreshadows her future growth. More generally he comments that "the juxtaposition of the world of the museum visitor and that represented in the exhibit is particularly suited to induce epiphanic recognitions of self and the discovery of one's true identity." (p.414). See Horst Kruse, "Museums and Manners: The Novels of Alison Lurie," *Anglia*, 111, 3-4 (1993), 410-38.

decidedly retrograde. When Paul pictured Los Angeles as Utopia, regressing to archaic images of walled gardens, he also had a Utopian social agenda. His fantasy is accompanied by an illusory image of a classless society, in which labels and categories no longer exist. Paul envisages Los Angeles as a place where people no longer classify him – unlike New York or Cambridge. When a waitress (Ceci) brings him a book to read, he rejoices that he is being treated as an individual "not as a mechanical task" (p.29). When the book turns out to be Beckett's latest play, Paul finds Ceci pleasantly unclassifiable. Is she a waitress? a beatnik? an artist? On the face of it Ceci seems to offer some evidence for Adorno's thesis – as a working class woman, a member of the masses, both reading and producing avant-garde art. Her husband has painted her ceiling with a jungle of exotic trees, plus surrealist images of winged lizards, a woman with a bird's head, and a dog with a toaster for a body, with trees descending into the pipes and moulding. Nothing archaic about these images! Inventive and imaginative, as inseparable from its place as a fresco, entirely unique, and transforming the machine by its presence (e.g. the toaster and pipes) the painting has no exhibition value at all. Indeed Ceci refuses point blank to show or sell her own paintings (p.86); hers is a creed of *l'art pour l'art*. As a member of the Beat community her life apparently figures as a direct reproach to the consumer society, rejecting materialism, competition, the work ethic and sexual repression, in favour of love, art, friendship and honesty.[20] Paul finds their affair not only "a unique experience" (p.79) sexually but, in its apparent simplicity, entirely outside his usual conceptual map. ("Nearly all she said or did was like a collection of road signs in a strange language." p.83). Like a pioneer in a new world, Paul is in unmapped territory among unreadable images. Unlike Katherine, Ceci is not in the least aloof or distant. Far from playing hard to get, she simply takes off her clothes and gives herself to him. Post-climax she lies completely exposed. Paul's gaze lingers on her, finding it an odd experience to watch a woman who conceals nothing.

> Most of the girls he had known preferred to do it in the dark, or at least in the dusk. And they always pulled their skirt down or the sheet up afterwards; however boldly they might have shown themselves earlier. (p.80).

---

[20] For an illuminating account of the Beats in Los Angeles see John Arthur Maynard, *Venice West: The Beat Generation in Southern California* (New Brunswick: Rutgers University Press, 1991).

In contrast, Ceci is quite uninterested in covering Venus; she habitually wears no underwear and displays her charms quite unaffectedly. Ironically, however, though Paul thinks he is the gazer, he is himself an exposed object to Ceci. In the café he realises that Ceci has known who he is all the time; he is wearing his Nutting security badge, emblazoned with "Secret Paul Cattleman" and his photograph. Paul is always "classified", in both senses of the term, as labelled and as secretive or concealed. The wearing of the badge makes him feel "that one is continually among strangers or fools, like an exhibit in a museum" (p.24). Now that he has exhibition value, Paul also finds his identity traduced and threatened. In front of the camera Paul had tried to appear serious (suppressing his usual grin). As a result, the mechanically-produced image belies his real self. The photograph has a solemn expression "like that of a depressed twin brother, whose portrait he had chosen to wear over his heart" (p.25). Fragmentation and splitting are produced by the reproduction of the image. Avant garde Ceci escapes the gaze by indifference to it; Paul is trapped in the headlights by the forces of capital.

It is however the photograph which turns out to be Paul's salvation in an encounter with the local police. Lurie focuses in several episodes upon the moral problems of disengagement from society. When Paul goes shopping with Ceci in the Joy Superdupermarket, a "maelstrom of consumption" (p.53), with its ranks of brilliant cans and boxes and its "forbidden fruit, out of season" (p.55) Ceci cheerfully shoplifts a packet of wild rice. She has no social conscience at all. When Ceci describes her fellow Beats as the "cats" (counter-cultural slang meaning) it is against a background of pet food embossed with "full-colour portraits of eager, affectionate dogs and sensuously cute kittens" (p.54). Ceci's own "kitten face" and "cat's half-smile" (p.57) as she rubs against Paul suggest that her image flows between the two poles – the countercultural and the sex-kitten – and that Paul approaches her much as he approaches the forbidden fruit. His perception of Ceci is conditioned by his own less than innocent intentions. Ceci's own delinquency also raises questions. She is, after all, purloining a luxury item, a commodity which can have no status as a necessity of life. Accounts of other thefts by the Beats (a tweed jacket, an inflatable pool-monster, a set of expensive Japanese china) suggest a parasitical relation to society and a lingering desire for its products. Although the Beats transform their cars into works of art – hotrods covered in symbolic designs of flames and monsters – they are prepared to swindle Paul by cannibalizing the vehicle which he has selected (p.127). The moral point is explicitly debated at a storefront café in Venice. For the Beats, Paul is the delinquent. Nutting is "making death" (p.128) as opposed to their own refusal to "hustle for death or deception" (p.130). Paul's defence – the contracts are not military, they are manufacturing television parts – falls on deaf ears. For the Beats, following in Adorno's footsteps, television is "a carnivorous, brainwashing monster" (p.128). Paul's subsequent defence – that nothing is created at Nutting – is even more damning of the majority culture:

> the purpose of this whole economy is to expend as much time, money, and material as possible without creating anything useful. Otherwise, see, the productive capacity of the country would get out of hand. (p.130).

When not creating death in weaponry, Nutting holds back the production of useful objects, a case-book example of industrialism subordinate to capitalism. Paul, however, argues that "You can't opt out of your society" (p.130), on which the Beats rely for economic sustenance, law and order and military protection. At this point the protectors of law and order take on physical existence in the guise of the Los Angeles police force on a drugs bust. To Paul's horror he finds himself caught in a television scenario. As in "detective movies" (p.132) a search is made by a policeman who "spoke out of the side of his mouth to his partner" (p.133). When Paul says, "Listen, officer. You're making a mistake" (p.133) he realises that he has just uttered "a stock line from TV drama" (p.133). In the cell, scenes from TV plays run through his head. He is saved, however, by Nutting, specifically his security clearance badge, ample proof that he has already been thoroughly investigated and is "clean". On the station counter this photograph (as opposed to Paul's beatnik costume) represents his real self:

> Secret Paul Cattleman staring solemnly at the ceiling of the police station, in his real clothes. (p.137).

Safety lies in the mechanically-reproduced and transportable image (the photograph is passed from hand to hand as the police confer), not only for Paul (who is immediately released) but for the Beats themselves. Because Paul was arrested (for possession of antacid tablets) the other Beats, who *were* in possession of illicit substances, were not searched. And as they have just been raided they promptly settle down to some serious smoking, safe in the knowledge that the police are unlikely to return for some time. If the episode apparently equates Nutting with TV, arms, mechanical reproduction and the oppression of the masses, it also establishes a critique of the avant garde group. Paul's experience suggests that he is a cog in the Nutting machine, and by implication that the Utopian autonomy of the Beats is also subordinate to the majority culture. The focus on delinquency also deserves further comment. In the 1950s and 1960s delinquency became a major theme for sociological and psychological study. Earlier seen as an individual personality disorder, by the end of the 1950s deviance was understood as socially determined, just as in more organized social protest movements. Thus Cloward and Ohlin argued that the delinquent was not a deviant but a conformist to the norms of a deviant subculture, in order to gain the fruits of success by aberrant means, for example.[21] Paul's notion of a sexual underground clearly marks him as a deviant only within the majority culture. Paul may think that he is embracing the avant garde but his concept of the Underground is of a series of furtive adulteries which will never threaten the social façade of his marriage (p.239).

From this point on, Paul's flirtation with the counter-culture cools rapidly. Forced out of Ceci's apartment by the presence of other guests, he finds himself perpetually in quest of a private space in which to make love. (Lurie makes it very obvious that there are no spaces outside society, that willy-nilly Paul and Ceci are part of the social set-up.) Driven back upon his own home for an assignation, he is considerably disconcerted when Ceci demonstrates her unwillingness to adopt his standards, cheerfully loitering, stark naked, at the uncurtained kitchen window which forms a "natural picture frame" (p.164). Ceci is contrasted implicitly with Katherine, represented here by one of her pictures, a facsimile of a medieval manuscript in which everything is boxed in – a wall round a garden, a wall round a castle, a border of thorns, another border and a frame. Ceci is perceptive: "that girl is really in a bad way." (p.164). Unsurprisingly, Ceci is able to read the organisation of aesthetic space more intelligently than her lover.

One scene indicates how thoroughly conditioned by his environment Paul actually is. Infuriated by the scrapping of his history, "the expensive public manufacture of nothing" (p.184), Paul prevails upon Ceci to venture into the great outdoors. He is eager to return to his erotic prehistory "to get back to that state of innocent delinquency" (p.186) which marked his youthful amours in the woods and fields of New England. In Los Angeles, however, nature is not much in evidence, the ground hard and stony, the vegetation sparse

---

[21] See Richard Cloward and Lloyd Ohlin, *Delinquency and Opportunity* (New York: Free Press, 1960).

and very little available in the way of cover. After a prolonged search for a suitable trysting place Ceci rebels:

"Where're we going to?"

Paul stopped. "Nowhere." (p.189).

His words are truer than he thinks. Despite the lack of cover, Paul induces Ceci to make love out in the open, in full view of any passers-by. Previously so enchanted with Ceci's unselfconscious display he now registers uncomfortably that he has got "from Walden into 'The Waste Land', from private pastoral to public lust" (p.191). Their exhibitionism also has unfortunate consequences. In the rather uncomfortable knee-skinning process, Paul loses his wedding ring and inadvertently reveals his secret – that he still sleeps with Katherine. Ceci's response is immediate. She hits him with her handbag, describes him (pungently) as a two-timer, and condemns him in ringing tones: "You're just nowhere." (p.194). When Paul attempts to embrace her she steps back so that he clasps empty space (p.195) and hurtles down a bank. Paul and Ceci's relationship has gone nowhere; he is left with nothing in a denuded landscape, a living dystopian exhibit. Originally a worshipper of the unique cult object, Paul converted to avant garde art and a more accessible beauty only within the dominant framework of the mechanically reproduced image and its sponsors in the majority culture. It is entirely logical that his next step should be towards Hollywood.

Katherine, however, has also had a brush with delinquency in the shape of Dr. Einsam for whom she works as a research assistant on his major project, "A Preliminary Study of Some Relationships Between Perception and Delinquency". Einsam's consulting rooms suggest an image of purgatorial torment for Katherine, who cannot help picturing to herself his distressed patients. Ostensibly there is nothing Utopian about Iz; he appears to have embraced the commodity culture wholeheartedly. His office is dominated by a machine, the Fraudulent Response Perceptor, or cheating-machine, which reveals that almost anyone will cheat if they believe that they can get away with it (including the experimenters, who use strategic misrepresentations to influence their subjects, hustling, if not for death, at least for deception.) The technological is firmly linked with the fraudulent, and with the exploitation of desire. Einsam jokingly proposes using Katherine as a reinforcement device. "Maybe we could plug in Mrs. Cattleman somehow; say we have her sit next to the subject during the experiment, in a tight sweater, to encourage him… Or maybe we should just give a bottle of gin to the ones who make the highest score." (p.144). Katherine is almost as infuriated by the equation of her body with a bottle of gin as she is by the implication of a fundamental lack of moral responsibility in individuals, easily influenced by the sight of Katherine-as-object. Machines also dominate the research team's leisure moments. They are perennially occupied in intensive discussion of the advantages and/or the drawbacks of various mechanical devices, from computers, tape-recorders, calculators and cars to electric blenders, and washing machines. Einsam has even done a study of the effects, on the attitudes and perceptions of the possessor, of the purchase of a deluxe, Norge washer-dryer. Yet as a self-styled anarchist, Iz is committed to creating disorganisation, ignoring rules, and setting his own agendas. For Iz the absence of seasons, or even ordinary routines, makes Los Angeles a place of freedom and possibility, in which anything is possible. "If there is no schedule, then you are free to work out your own schedule" (p.173) he comments. Under his tutelage Katherine, for example, gives up make-up which she has never liked, ceasing to cater for an implied gaze. His sympathetic questioning (ambiguously professional; the reader is unsure if he genuinely sympathises or is merely deploying a psychiatrist's commodified emotional manner) releases her buried emotions in floods of tears and cures her sinusitis on the spot.

Importantly, it is by exploiting the gaze that Iz offers Katherine the key to controlling her misery. In his diagnosis she and Paul have had a silent agreement that she will not notice his adulteries. She has colluded with him in what she will and will not "see" in their relationship. In Iz's analysis, Paul is now leaving clues of an increasingly overt nature for her to pick up, presumably to give him a reason to end his relationship, or to provoke declarations of love. "Try a little experiment", he counsels. "Don't say anything to him this time. If this clue isn't picked up, I bet there'll be others." (p.180). Katherine now converts Paul into the object of her gaze – forcing him by her indifference to exhibit his delinquency in ever more overt displays. What she terms "Paul-watching" (p.199) turns out to be productive, a game which she rather enjoys. She remembers with some amusement, for example, Paul's bafflement when she did not react to his display of his dirty clothes and bruises after the fight with Ceci. Katherine recalls Paul's behaviour while typing pairs of nonsense syllables for the project.[22] The context suggests that Paul

---

[22] Allan Paivio's experiments in the 1960s, concerning imagery research in the field of verbal learning, involved investigations of how people remembered pairs of unrelated words. Nonsense pairs are a case in point. See Esrock, p.197.

has now become a subject in the "perception and delinquency" project, even a laboratory animal. As Iz comments, "He's trying to tell you something. I had a German Shepherd like that once." (p.199).

In a parallel and reversal to Paul's experience with Ceci, Katherine now encounters her own problems in negotiating between public and private space. As a result of new building construction, the project has to move offices. When Katherine sees the new plans for the allocation of space she realises that they have been "allotted nothing", they have "no place to go" (p.199). On the conscious level her action – she races straight to Iz's apartment to tell him that they are going nowhere – is reasonable enough. Given, however, that Iz has previously warned her that he admits to his apartment only women with whom he intends to sleep, it has unconscious motivations which are fairly obvious. Katherine wants their relationship to move forward, rather than going nowhere. She cannot acknowledge her motives; she can only enter his private space with a "public space" alibi. Iz, on the other hand, uses his preceding individual definition of his space as purely erotic to bully her into bed. He defines his own Utopian space, independent of the surrounding social geography, and sets up his own rules, but as a result the degree of Katherine's autonomy is open to question. Although she is liberated-by-orgasm (something of a topos in novels of the 1960s) the degree to which this is a positive individual emotional event, or a merely automatic yielding to desire, is a question posed in all its complexity. In brief, is Katherine asserting her own desires? Or is she undergoing manipulation (pleasurable, but ultimately passive) much as the masses submit to the beguilements of the culture industry? These issues are also foregrounded within the erotic scenes themselves. No vicarious romantic illusion is offered to the reader. If the first encounter is disappointing for Katherine, the second (functionally as unsuccessful but considerably more relaxed) takes place in front of the eye of the television screen. "Look! We're on television," Iz observes, drawing Katherine's attention to their bodies, dimly reflected on the screen, "Like scenes from the faded print of a French art film, anonymous shadowed faces: *L'homme barbu et la femme*." (p.222). If the anonymity and stereotypical nature of this image repels, worse is to follow. Where this encounter suggests a contamination of individual desire by the mechanically-reproduced, Katherine's subsequent experience foregrounds technology in more intimate terms:

> a well of desire opened inside her, as if a huge
> washing machine had been turned on, with steaming

water and suds, foaming, splashing, thrashing, faster and faster. (p.223).

The comparison of woman and machine suggests that Katherine's interest for Iz may not be entirely distinct from his previous study of the Norge washer-dryer.[23]

Does technology deliver on its promises of abundance and liberation? Or has Katherine merely been exploited? The question is further complicated by the presentation of the erotic scenes, in memory. The reader is positioned at one critical remove from the event, as the scenes of erotic liaison are not presented directly, but in flashback when Katherine is on a shopping trip. Consumerism therefore frames the erotic event, and unconscious optics dominate the presentation; the scenes are filtered through a succession of different lenses. Katherine recalls three separate sexual occasions, with each memory punctuated by reference to the sunglasses which she is purchasing – the tints of their lenses (rather like a filter in a film) successively changing the shop around her to green, mauve or brown. To Katherine these changes are welcome, suggesting that she prefers illusion to actuality. "It was pretty; better than the reality." (p.222). The memories flash through her mind "like a movie run through a projector at high speed" (p.221). She is buying sunglasses at least in part as a cover for her own guilty confusion. As a guilty adulteress she is sensitive to the gaze of others and protects herself from exposure. Wearing glasses, she can see but not be seen. As Mary Ann Doane notes, the woman who wears glasses constitutes one of the most intense visual clichés of the cinema, an image heavily marked for motifs concerned with repressed sexuality, knowledge, vision and desire. Without glasses a woman is *shown*, as spectacle. Wearing glasses may signal the woman's appropriation of the gaze, as active looking rather than as deficiency of vision (particularly in the example of sunglasses which imply no ocular weakness):

> in usurping the gaze she poses a threat to an entire system of representation. It is as if the woman had forcefully moved to the other side of the specular.[24]

In addition, in the scene, the cutting between erotic reverie and retail therapy is both suggestively cinematic and implies the lack of personal

---

[23] The conjunction of orgasmic woman with domestic appliance (e.g. spin dryers and washing machines) is a topos common to soft porn scenarios. I am grateful to my Contemporary American Fiction class of 1995-6 for the illuminating discussion of this scene.

[24] Mary Ann Doane, "Film and the Masquerade: Theorising the Female Spectator," *Screen* 23 (1982), 83.

emotion in Katherine's relationship to Iz, rather as in a contemporary formulaic "sex and shopping" plot. Unlike the popular formula-writer, however, Lurie does not cater to the reader's more dubious wish-images. The reader is distanced from the event, and forced to recognise the different frames (ideological and optical) through which it can be viewed. Recalling herself from memory to the present Katherine changes her glasses ("The store flashed out in a coarse confusion of real colours for a moment" p.223) before swiftly donning a harlequin pair with brown lenses. In the store mirror her face is now reflected as if deeply suntanned, with "great dark slanted eyes" (p.223). The suggestions of altered ethnicity – skin tone and eye shape – anticipate Iz's comment that she sleeps with him, because he is foreign and not of her class (p.233), as if he were a holiday romance which did not count. Iz is Katherine's illusion of classless fulfilled desires, as Ceci is Paul's. In the mirror a succession of strange faces follow each other, creating an image of Katherine's identity as fluid, performative rather than essential. She is trying on identities – and the ability to do so is usually associated with the dominant rather than the dominated. Indeed, it is at this point that Katherine crosses over into Utopian mode. "Nobody was watching her; she was in Los Angeles, she reminded herself again, where nobody saw or cared what she did. And at this thought ... came a little burst of giddy euphoria." (p.221). In little the scene offers the reader several different versions of Katherine's experience – as liberation into free sensuality, appropriated on her own terms, or as transmuting sensuality into the coarse, the mechanical and ultimately the commodified, subordinate to the machine and the roles which it projects. As if responding to Nietzsche's call for "many eyes" Lurie provides a multiplication of distinct perspectives, to produce a complex portrayal of the phenomenon under inspection.

The consumer emphasis remains relentless. Back on the sidewalk, Katherine notes the women shopping, wearing costumes "out of a chorus line or a comic book" (p.224), interchangeable in their tight Capri pants and tops. Across the street an ad portraying a lifesize woman climbing into a giant coffee cup proclaims "Indulge yourself". In the dress shop beneath, Katherine now purchases her own Capri set. Not only is the shop designed as if for a stageset by Gordon Craig, with assistants who look like dancers or actresses, but to Katherine's horror she encounters a customer who looks familiar:

> a sophisticated-looking girl in her twenties, a very Hollywood type, in dark glasses and yellow slacks, shiny pale brown hair... Suddenly Katherine knew

who she was. She raised her hand, half-waving and half warding off; her reflection did the same. (p.226).
The stranger is Katherine, a copy in a mirror of a copy in "real" space. There are of course no prizes for the reader who guesses the identity of the two figures before Katherine does. (As compared with the ending of the novel, the reader has been better educated in critical observation than the unfortunate Paul.) The question raised here is a vital one. Does Katherine passively become a copy, yielding to the dictates of advertisement, the culture industry, the commodification of the individual? Or does she begin to have an inkling that the staging of her femininity – a form of active role play rather than inauthentic conformity – may be her best strategy of resistance?

Appearances at first suggest a negative outcome. At their next rendezvous in his office, Iz switches rapidly between the roles of lover and boss. He is very much in control, erotically and industrially. Postcoitally naked he replaces his glasses to dictate a series of letters to a similarly naked Katherine, before donning his undershorts to become "the comic butt of a silent film comedy, one of those respectable bearded gentlemen whose clothes are always being stolen by Chaplin and Keaton" (p.234). Like Katherine he switches from role to role; like Katherine he is presented through a scrim of movie imagery. He also proposes to continue the experiment on Paul, suggesting that Katherine test her newly-discovered orgasmic abilities on her husband. Predictably the ensuing encounter is a fiasco. When his wife propositions him in forthright fashion Paul feels "as if he were in a Frankenstein movie" (p.242) and wonders if Ceci had "got out of his head and into Katherine, so that she was deliberately imitating, or rather was possessed by, Ceci." (p.245). Who is now the copy self, who the original? Paul rejects Katherine's advances, assuming that she has been studying a sex-manual: "I don't want you to learn any techniques" (p.247). For Paul the new, the technically innovative, the copy self is a disaster.

Up to this point it may well seem that Lurie inclines to Adorno's side of the argument. Paul and Katherine do not appear to have found any form of salvation in Los Angeles. But the novel provides a complicatory factor – and something of a counter argument – in Glory Green. The initial impression of Glory is not prepossessing. The reader is introduced to her, in the middle of a marital row occasioned by her desire to seek out her fans. Clad in "the conventional costume of a kooky starlet on vacation" (p.32) and heavily made up, Glory has a voice which has been so intensively trained for the purposes of expressing and eliciting desire that "she

could not even telephone for a plumber without sounding sexy."
(p.32). For Iz, Glory is a case-book example of the psychopathology
of everyday life. She has forgotten in various places, handbags,
suitcases, packages, contracts, a pregnant police dog and a pink Edsel
car, *inter alia*. This time it is her bathing suit – providing a good
excuse to visit Palm Springs to buy a new one and offer the fans an
opportunity for homage. Though Glory attempts to sweet-talk Iz
(modulating her tone into "a vibrating whisper of the kind that comes
out of theatre amplifiers during close-ups" p.35) he is unswayed.
Glory appears to be entirely dependent on fan-worship for her
emotional and auratic sustenance. Deserted by Iz, Glory is next
encountered contemplating a ten foot mechanical pink Christmas tree,
under which she has just been photographed, together with prop
presents (supposedly from fans) for press and publicity purposes. The
tree has all the attributes of a machine – its lights flash on and off
while the musical base plays *Silent Night* over and over again. The
scene is almost akin to a tableau dramatising the role of the work of
art in the age of mechanical reproduction, conjoining the starlet, the
fan, the photograph and the musical jingle. The presents include two
dogs offered to Glory by a redundant Indian princeling. "The way
Glory understood it, he went and let his country have an election, and
they didn't pick up his option." (p.91). The last phrase suggests that
politics is understood only in terms of movie contracts, starring roles,
and popularity with the audience. Glory herself can only construe her
experience of abandonment in terms of a film-role, Miss Havisham in
Great Expectations. The silver angel's hair on the tree recalls to her

> the scene in that old English movie – what was its
> name? – where the crazy old lady burns up in her
> room. Because long ago her boyfriend stood her up
> on her wedding day, and she flipped... It was with
> Jean Simmons. (p.90).

Film may have made the classics accessible to Glory, but it does not
appear to have done very much more. The novel is subordinate here
to the film image, its title forgotten, its individuality subsumed in the
generic formula of "spooky" (p.90) horror film, and star vehicle.
When an intruder is sighted in the garden (in fact, Ceci's ex-husband,
Walter Wong) the chapter modulates into a chase sequence, as Glory
rushes from room to room, snapping on the lights and locking doors
and windows ahead of the putative prowler, "exposed as if on a stage"
(p.95) with the Asian intruder appearing "like a villain out of the
grade B spy thrillers of her childhood" and the Christmas tree

providing the soundtrack . Earlier Glory had felt ugly and rejected, despite the fans' adoration:

> Like a goddess betrayed by a god, it made absolutely no difference to her that temples still stood all over the land in which her image was worshipped nightly by multitudes, that praises and petitions arrived daily from the faithful. (p.94).

It is rather a different matter, however, when the intruder gazes at her "without admiration or desire, rather with an expression of inscrutable disgust" (p.95). The practical reason for Walter's look of repulsion is not hard to find. With five types of skin cream on her face and body, and toilet tissue wrapped around her pink bouffant hairdo, Glory resembles "one of those Egyptian gods who wear the heads of beasts" (p.94). The cult image is definitively equated with the horror movie: "she looked like something out of a Dracula film" (p.97). In this encounter between representatives of avant-garde and popular art forms, as each stares at the other, framed in the glass doors, both appear equally enmeshed in a world dominated by the phoney film image.

Lurie's intricate plotting, however, makes the point that Glory's relation with her fans is distinctly more ambivalent than it might appear. At the premiere of *Dancing Cowboy* Glory is scheduled to rush up "spontaneously" and kiss Rory Gunn, her co-star, in order to demonstrate her sincere admiration for him as an actor. (The event has been cleared by the studio and both agents, and the media alerted.) Both stars stage the event in good filmic fashion, manipulating space and time, he walking slowly to give the world a good look at his profile, she waiting for "a good clear space to open up between her and the photographers" (p.213). Unfortunately at this point a real fan emerges from the crowd, races Glory to the target and pushes her out of the way. Glory promptly punches the teenager on the jaw, to a chorus of photographers' flashbulbs. The logic of the event is inescapable. Glory, the starlet, encourages fans, until she is persuaded to copy the role of fan herself vis à vis Rory. (Her agent attempts to mollify the injured teenager by telling her that "Glory is a fan of Rory Gunn's same as you are." p.214). It is her fate therefore to be copied. She may think that the action can be slowed and the space manipulated to suit her purposes, but the fan speeds up and outdistances her. The fan is not quite as passive and helpless as social commentators might think. In a sense, here, the audience intervenes and takes over the scene. In broader terms Glory is perpetually vulnerable to copies. On the set of her current picture Glory scrutinizes a group of new starlets for possible rivals. The girls are marketable commodities, "branded" as the classy brunette, the sultry brunette, the redhead and so forth. The picture, a science-fiction musical comedy, set on the planet Nemo (nobody) offers Glory a lead part, though played with antennae and green hands. It appears to make a comedy out of Utopia, deforming the actress to the needs of the formula. (Glory's films lean towards the generic, tending to undercut arguments for the critical function of film.) The culture industry is also presented as just that, an industry. Of all the characters in the novel it is Glory who is seen working hardest, here rehearsing sweatily all day, with an evening ahead of "commercial socializing" (p.216), a dinner date with Rory Gunn. When the latter event is reported (as planned) in the papers, it convinces Iz that he has been replaced in her affections. Glory is at real risk of seeing her emotional needs discounted by the movie industry; her agent has already discouraged her relationship, on the grounds that marriage to a psychiatrist would damage her image with her fans.

It is however in the figure of the fan that Lurie's plot turns the tables on Paul, establishes Katherine's autonomy, and reunites Iz and Glory. If Katherine and Paul appear to have been overtaken in various ways by their surrounding environment, Glory, who is right inside the culture industry, is shown as developing the ability to defend herself. In order to blank out the image of Glory as disliking fans, she is convinced to hire a private secretary to answer her fan letters – and Iz supplies Katherine. The plot foregrounds and ironises the nature of mechanical reproduction, by subjecting the major characters to a series of role-swaps, imposing copy-selves as the three plot lines (Paul, Katherine, Glory) come together in a series of climactic events. In the first sequence Katherine visits Glory to assume the role of secretary and finds herself becoming Glory: *she* is to sign letters and photos as "Glory Green". Katherine is also confronted with the distance between media role and actual person. In preparation for her visit Katherine had gone to see Glory in a screen musical, which projects an image of a brave, new world "in which everyone was handsome and physically vital, ageless and brand-new" (p.249). The novelty is accompanied by the "always-the-same" of Adorno's analysis, "a group of chorus girls with identical costumes". The audience, confronted with Glory's face in close-up, five feet high, are similarly homogenised, "lit by the reflections of Technicolor, all wore the same expression of passive enchantment" (p.249). Katherine is revolted, wondering how anyone can expose themselves to such public view. This image of Glory, however, does not survive closer acquaintance. Though her patio is adorned by a beauty sunbathing on a diving board, the pool is cracked and empty and Glory without her make-up merely "an ordinary pretty girl" (p.233). When she doles out publicity photographs of herself as "a stupid chorus girl" (p.254) displaying her cleavage, there is no resemblance to the original in beachrobe and curlers. Glory is quite well able to separate an essential self from the performative copy. When Katherine is repelled by a fan letter which asks for a photo for auto-erotic use, Glory's turn of phrase makes it clear that she is perfectly well aware of the purpose for which the "poor jerk" intends it. Her friend Ramona comments that

> its kind of disgusting to think of that creep sitting in his room somewhere playing with your photo, and pulling himself off, 'cause he can't find himself a girl. (p.256).

Glory's response – "there's a lot of people can't feel physical about what they've got at home" (p.256) with its implicit reference to Paul and Katherine - also distinguishes between fantasy and actuality. As a result Katherine recognises that she does not love Iz (though he has fulfilled several fantasy needs) and that Glory does. She sees Glory listening to a radio broadcast by Iz and realises that

> Glory was Iz's fan. She treasured these half-audible, irrelevant phrases ... as a fan might the scribbled autograph of her chosen star. (p.288).

As a result Katherine takes a moral decision, informs Iz that Rory Gunn is gay and therefore not a threat, gives up her own fantasy-foreign male, and reunites the lovers. Arguably her entry into the film world has induced a critical and reflective process to good moral ends.

Paul, however, remains in a state of mystification. Introduced to Glory by Katherine, he is initially delighted at the chance to bed a starlet, entranced by Glory's breathy voice and ample charms. The reader, however, is under no illusions concerning Glory's sincerity. Glory is staging her scene with Paul as a mere copy of Katherine's with Iz, a mechanical "tit for tat", paying Paul back in his own coin, a fact which she dramatises, ironically, in the language of clothes. Her new swimming costume is full of "coin-sized holes, ranging in size from ten to fifty cents" (p.269), through which "samples" (p.278) of her flesh protrude. The sexual encounter highlights exchange values in several senses. Paul and Glory meet at a movie executive's home, a lush location with enormous pool, the embodiment of the passive enchantment which has funded it. After a year of struggling with the ocean, Paul finds his ideal in the "tamed fresh water, in which all movement was one's own" (p.271). There is no resistance or opposition. Happily "he played with the passive water." (p.271). Glory is ostensibly just as accommodating. When the couple confront a flood in the house, they are knocked off their feet by a tidal wave of water with predictable erotic results. In Paul's view, "Physical desire had simply been turned on and flooded them like the house." (p.282). Superficially the novel encourages the stereotypical image (both novelistic and filmic) of water as floods of passion, in Paul's illicit affair in Venice, and Katherine's orgasmic washer-dryer, for example. But in fact, as suggested in Ceci's cracked bathtub, Glory's empty pool and the dried out canals of Venice, in Los Angeles "water equalled money" (p.267). As the bathing costume suggests, with its dreadfully evocative imagery of money and orifices, Lurie is capable of providing a crude subtext which reminds the reader that economics dominates the action. When Paul's attention lingers on the holes through which she is bulging, Glory, supposedly referring to the pool, asks "You want to go in?" (p.269). Glory is clearly playing the part of director. *She* watches *him*, from the pool edge; she has got rid of the others, strategically, and when she removes his clothes he is converted into the part of movie actor.

> Paul felt as if he had got into a dream, or more likely one of those surrealist movies that imitate dreams... In the flooded room, like an actor in a surrealist – no, a pornographic – film, he dug his toes into the satin bedspread and drove into her again and again. (p.279).

In contrast Glory's nakedness is "not vulnerable", more "a kind of armour" (p.275). When she compliments Paul on his performance, he feels as if he has received a film award. (p.280), though in fact he has no idea what role he is really playing in her plot. Paul is thoroughly incidental to Glory's main economic and erotic interests. Kept waiting later for hours on her filmset, he is exposed to hundreds of repetitions of one set of "fragmented lyrics" and feels that he will never forget "these trivial hedonist lines" (p.293), a comment on music much in the mode of Adorno. Paul believes that he sees clearly, unlike the inhabitants of the dream industry. When Glory explains that he was merely a means of "paying back" their spouses he refuses to believe her. For him Katherine could only by Iz's fan, not his lover – "kind of a hero-worship" p.296 – and he dismisses Glory's revelations: "It was really she who was deceived, living in a dream world" (p.297). Glory, however, knew that Katherine was sleeping with Iz, simply "From watching her" (p.296). Glory has learned to read unconscious optics, and to direct her own private movie scenario for revenge. Ironically, the truth of events is disclosed on a film set, to the background of "a jangle of trivial dream music" (p.297), by a woman who conjoins star and fan, but who is able to use the roles critically to her own ends. Paul, the academic historian and archetypal Easterner remains in a state of complete illusion.

The final scene in the sequence presents Glory and Iz's reunion. Water and machine are again juxtaposed – the star-crossed lovers finally declare undying love in a car-wash. The two are brought together both by Katherine and by the need to deal with the enraged teenage fan. With the connivance of the teenager's mother Iz has arranged a fake screentest for her, after which she will be enrolled in acting classes which are actually a form of group therapy. (Katherine's role-play has been similarly therapeutic.) The suggestion that a degree of autonomy may be fostered by role play is reinforced in the scene in the carwash. Quite explicitly Lurie designs the scene to model Adorno's description of the relation between fans, star and illusion. The scene involves both the projection and the reception of the gaze. Laura Mulvey has, famously, argued that the Hollywood spectacular uses the camera as a voyeuristic eye, permitting the male spectator to identify with the camera's gaze and possess or control the object of the gaze which is the woman, displayed exhibitionistically as spectacle.[25] Hermetically sealed behind glass (inside the car) Glory is none the less on display to her audience, eight or ten men, whose reaction to her is clearly figured as erotic. Stripped to the waist, because of the heat, damp and half-naked, they stare avidly, sweeping the car with "mockingly sensual gestures ... as if it were her own body" (p.300). The car lurches forward through the car wash, repeatedly squirted with foaming liquid, in a series of jerks. The previous description of Glory's solitary fan's activities makes the symbolism unavoidable. Inside the machine, however, there is an unconventional human being. Glory does not cater to the fans at all; she glares right back, her gaze transformed into a scowl. The problem in her marriage – her dependent relation to her fans and watchers – is definitively overcome now. Glory ignores them, and they disappear, as water blurs the faces outside the car, drowning their voices (p.301). When Iz declares his love, Glory bursts into tears: "her face was in ruins, the perfect mask streaked and wet, with clotted powder, dripping mascara and tears. 'Oh, go fuck yourthelf,' she said and burst into sobs." (p.301). Glory's sincerity is not in doubt here (she only lisps when in the grip of strong feeling). Unlike Katherine who

---

[25] Laura Mulvey, "Visual Pleasure and Narrative Cinema", *Screen* 16 (1975), 6-18.

moves towards roleplay, adopting a succession of masks and becoming hyperaware of the point of intersection between onlooker and object of gaze, Glory appears to have dissolved the mask and found herself. It is rather as if, for one moment, the boundary between inside and outside had been washed away, the water flowing inside the car (tears) and outside, the "film" with its jerky movements and deceptive optics finally subordinated to the reality. Immersion in the film world has led to the revelation of emotional truth. Of all the characters, only Glory is definitely open to emotion. And only Glory can achieve critical distance from the machine and its sponsors. The scene is played in public, but the water renders it private, obscuring the lovers from view. There is the suggestion of vicarious gratification (both by and in "jerks") but also of real emotional connection – inside the machine. Glory has been envisaged in many ways as a machine, designed to evoke a particular response from the predominantly male audience, but at the close she washes off the mask and becomes fully human.

Lurie does not exaggerate the positive overtones (at the close Iz and Glory restage their reunion exhibitionistically in public from their bed) but of the three women it is none the less Glory the starlet who is the least in the grip of illusion, the least deceived, and the most in touch with her emotions. As Iz comments, she is the proof that "a stable personality need not be a conventional one" (p.32). Katherine, more conventional, has also gained some critical distance on events. She is presented, near the close, alone in a crowd of sightseers, a mass displayed as such, "anonymous", with the common expression of "people anxiously searching for something: for success, for adventure, for love. Or ... at least searching for some excitement, for a scene, a spectacle, a hero to watch. Above all, they were looking for stars" (p.286). Katherine, however, is marked out as self-aware. She realizes that Iz was "too much the guide of the tour" (p.288) and determines henceforth to see things for herself; she has stopped being a passive onlooker on the lives of others. In a bookstore on Hollywood Boulevard she rejects a biography: "Once you've tried reality, imaginary lives seem flat." (p.290). Before her, the view widens – Los Angeles appears as an immense white city sparkling in the sunlight. In contrast Paul, a man who can never change, leaves for the East and as his plane takes off the city begins to blur. As the haze thickens, he can no longer see buildings or roads, then suddenly everything is gone. "Los Angeles had disappeared into a bowl of smog." (p.318). For Katherine Los Angeles is now a vista opening up before her; for Paul it is nowhere.

For the reader, however, the possibility of Utopia has not entirely receded. Despite the thorough demystification of the star and the culture industry, it is the historical critic, Paul, who is defeated, and the Utopian, anti-order Iz who comes out smiling. Most importantly, Glory (and to a lesser extent Katherine) may be said to have anticipated the insights of later theorists who have examined the ways in which female spectators (and by extension, women in general) assume and subvert their role as spectacle, identifying themselves in playful, ironic, defensive or aggressive postures with the object seen. Both Glory and Katherine exploit womanliness as a mask, a masquerade of femininity which holds itself at a distance even as it displays itself.[26] Honest Ceci reveals herself and is deceived and hurt. Katherine finds a mask of conformity and ceases to be the object of the gaze, imagistically filtering reality for herself. Glory is adept at manipulating the mask, but maintains a fully human dimension, untamed by the conventions within which she operates. Where the avant garde artists are connected with a variety of forms of social delinquency, film, the medium often assumed to encourage the loss of critical responsibility, teaches Katherine to assume moral responsibility for her actions. Lurie's plot adopts textual strategies which mime the processes under investigation – the copy selves and copy plots – to critical effect. Though Lurie clearly suggests that there is no "free" space outside the social system, she detects possibilities for critical opposition from within the culture industry itself. Iz, who investigates perception, is finally more able to maintain a degree of freedom than Paul, who harks back to the archaic past. Utopia or dystopia, dream or nightmare, realized or destroyed illusion, Los Angeles has been all these to the characters, leaving the reader to judge the aesthetic and social issues independently.

---

[26] Mary Ann Doane, "Film and the Masquerade: Theorising the Female Spectator," *Screen* 23 (1982), 74-87.

Chapter Four
The Revenge of the Trance Maiden: *Imaginary Friends*

If *The Nowhere City* focuses on the question of "reading" the visual image – film, art object, photograph, architecture – Lurie's next novel, *Imaginary Friends*, continues the thematisation of the operations of reading in another utopian locale, but with rather more sinister conclusions. Similarly dialectical, Lurie's third novel contrasts two forms of truth-seeking – the objective and rational (as exemplified in a pair of investigative sociologists) and the mystical and committed (in the form of their subjects, a group of religious cultists). Once again role play comes into particular focus – and with it a development of Lurie's fundamentally intertextual method.

The notion of intertextuality has been several times referred to in this study without full-scale investigation. As intertextuality is an extremely capacious term,[1] some working definitions seem to be in order. Most readers will be familiar with the term, as coined by Julia Kristeva, as founded upon the proposition that "every text builds itself as a mosaic of quotations, every text is absorption and transformation of another text."[2] At its narrowest, this has been taken to limit the applicability of the term to parody, mere allusion, source criticism, and casual generic resemblances. More commonly, however, the intertext of a given story may be defined as the set of plots, characters, images and conventions which it calls to mind for a given reader. In other words, it is not merely another text to which a work alludes, but to a totality, creating a general sense of a work of art which interacts with an entire tradition. The relationship obtaining between two (or more) texts is therefore between the texts as structured wholes. One

---

[1] For two clear theoretical accounts see Laurent Jenny, "The strategy of form", in Tzvetan Todorov, ed., *French Literary Theory Today* (Cambridge University Press, 1982), pp.34-64; and Jeanine Parisier Plottel and Hanna Charney, ed., "Intertextuality: New Perspectives in Criticism," *New York Literary Forum*, 2 (1978). For demonstrations of ways of working with intertextuality see John Hannay, *The Intertextuality of Fate* (Columbia: University of Missouri Press, 1986); Susan Stewart, *Nonsense: Aspects of Intertextuality in Folklore and Literature* (Baltimore: Johns Hopkins, 1979) and Judie Newman, *The Ballistic Bard: Postcolonial Fictions* (London: Edward Arnold, 1995).

[2] *New York Literary Forum*, 2 (1978), p.xiv, a translation of "Tout texte se construit comme mosaïque de citations, tout texte est absorption et transformation d'un autre texte." Julia Kristeva, *Semiotike, recherches pour une semanalyse* (Paris: Seuil, 1969) p.146.

can of course go one step further (following Kristeva's lead) and define a "text" as a system of signs, whether in literary works, spoken languages, non-verbal sign systems, or symbolic systems.[3]   Thus, Kristeva proceeds to define intertextuality as the transposition of one or several systems of signs into another. In its furthest expansion, therefore, intertextuality may incorporate all sorts of social phenomena. We may wish to consider that paradigmatic plots abound, not just in literary culture, but also in general culture. The term "intertextuality" can describe this sense of life as repeating a previously heard story, of life predestined by the notions that shape our consciousness. In this way "real life" may be structured according to patterns familiar from literary culture – just as literary culture may be structured according to patterns familiar from "real life". It follows that the sources underlying human actions may come from other domains of reality, as much as from everyday life situations – from proverbs, folklore, fiction, music, television commercials.

Intertextuality, then, offers an interactive model of art. Human experience may generate literature – but such experience has already been filtered through forms of artistic organisation. Lurie's semiotic expertise has also never been in doubt. It is worth recalling that her 1981 volume *The Language of Clothes*, a serious examination of the history and interpretation of costume, begins from the premise that one set of signs is translatable into another, that clothing may be envisaged as a sign system, and that human beings communicate in the language of dress. Importantly Lurie emphasises here the notion of interaction between sets of signs (clothing and social context) in terms of situational participation and involvement:

> According to Erving Goffman, the concept of "proper dress" is totally dependent on situation. To wear the costume considered "proper" for a situation acts as a sign of involvement in it, and the person whose clothes do not conform to these standards is likely to be more or less subtly excluded from participation. When other signs of deep involvement are present, rules about proper dress may be waived.[4]

Erving Goffman is not being invoked casually at this point.   The internal evidence of *Imaginary Friends* reveals a fairly close

---

[3] Julia Kristeva, *La revolution du langage poetique* (Paris: Seuil, 1974).
[4] Alison Lurie, *The Language of Clothes* (New York: Random House, 1981) p.13.
The point is made by Erving Goffman in *Encounters* (Indianapolis: Bobbs-Merrill, 1961) pp.145-6.

acquaintanceship on Lurie's part with his ideas. In this connection two of Goffman's notions are of special significance, firstly that of the relation of self to role, and secondly that of "frame analysis".[5] In the first, Goffman's most distinctive line of thought has been to adopt a dramaturgical approach to social interaction, emphasising particularly the discrepancies between the self-image which the actor presents to others in interactive process ("the presentation self") and his underlying private attitudes. Goffman's studies of such diverse groups as salesmen, hotel workers, surgical teams, games players, mental patients, argue for pervasive role playing in social situations, suggesting that the individual is always acting within a fiction, a text, which is socially evolved. In this model, the autonomous bourgeois individual subject becomes more of a "holding company" for a set of not relevantly connected selves. Some roles can be independently validated (Goffman cites that of law student), others cannot. (Goffman cites the claim to be a true believer, or a friend – two important points of contact with *Imaginary Friends*.[6]) The reality of such claims will depend upon the establishment by group members of a shared conception of the horizon or frame of a situation, of shared symbolic systems. Thus, in Goffman's view, reality is sponsored by the team. In addition, coming on to our second point, Goffman's sociological employment of frame analysis as a metaphor for the organisation of experience has been applied to theory of literature.[7] Intertextuality is the recognition of a frame, a context that allows the reader (of literature) or the actor (in a social situation) to orient himself, to distinguish "text" from "context", and to make sense of what would otherwise appear senseless. Just as a book offers a comprehensible *new* experience only because the reader has a framework of familiar points of contact between the self and the book, so in Goffman's analysis, everyday life depends upon the adumbration of a pattern or model, a conscious degree of role playing within the frame of situation, within the social text. Deciding what degree of involvement is required, mutually sustaining a definition of a situation

---

[5] Erving Goffman is referred to by name in *Imaginary Friends*, (London: Penguin, 1967) p.275. Major works include *The Presentation of Self in Everyday Life* (1956), *Encounters* (1961), *Asylums* (1961), *Behavior in Public Places* (1963), and *Frame Analysis* (1974). Although the latter post-dates *Imaginary Friends* the concept of frame is initially elaborated in *Encounters* (London: Penguin, 1961, p.20, p.25, p.26).

[6] "Claims to be a friend, a true believer, or a music-lover can be confirmed or disconfirmed only more or less." *The Presentation of Self in Everyday Life* (London: Penguin, 1967), p.53.

[7] *New York Literary Forum*, 2 (1978), p.xix.

– these are processes socially organised through rules of relevance and irrelevance, inclusion and exclusion, rules concerning "what counts" as the reality of the situation. Thus, almost identical actions may be transformed or transcribed by participants from one frame to another, via a systematic alteration which radically reconstitutes for participants "what is going on". An obvious example offered by Goffman is the distinction between fighting, and playing at fighting, in animal or human behaviour.

Imaginary Friends, then, draws upon Goffman's theories in order both to proceed intertextually *and* to thematise intertextuality. At first, the novel appears to be intertextual in a fairly traditional literary sense. Lurie's decision to name her "trance maiden" Verena, after the inspired orator of *The Bostonians*, argues for a fairly active intertextual intention, just as the cult group, the Seekers, which Verena leads, shares its name with a similar religious group in Edith Wharton's *Hudson River Bracketed*. Nor are these merely casual allusions. Both Marius Bewley[8] and Howard Kerr[9] have identified a structured intertext, a common pattern, surrounding the figure of the trance maiden in nineteenth century American literature. Representative novels – Hawthorne's *The Blithedale Romance* (1852), Howells's *The Undiscovered Country* (1880) and Henry James's *The Bostonians* (1886) – focus upon such elements as the connection of an entranced female with some kind of Utopian social enterprise, her exploitation by a ruthless mesmerist, her romance with a sceptical male, and her eventual rescue from mediumistic servitude, through the love of a good man. This is a topos with a fairly obvious normative patriarchal content, generally involving a woman who is as passive as Sleeping Beauty in her trance, the silencing of the female, the excision of her Utopian or progressive connections, and her resocialisation within the safe categories of home and matrimony. Priscilla, the Veiled Lady of *The Blithedale Romance*, may stand as emblematic of the patriarchal view of woman – totally under male control, veiled to deny her physicality, an idol obscurely in contact with spiritual mysteries, and yet exposed to prurient commercial exploitation. Priscilla's rescue by Hollingsworth marks the end of the Utopian experiment at Blithedale, and is connected with the extinction of feminist Zenobia. Similarly, in Howells's *The Undiscovered Country*, spiritualist Dr. Boynton uses his daughter Egeria as his spellbound

---

[8] Marius Bewley, *The Complex Fate* (London: Chatto and Windus, 1952).
[9] Howard Kerr, *Mediums and Spirit Rappers and Roaring Radicals: Spiritualism in American Literature 1850-1900* (Urbana: University of Illinois Press, 1972).

medium, until she is liberated from his clutches by Ford, a sceptical amateur scientist. (Shakers supply the Utopian community in the novel.) Howells also implies a precise correlation between Egeria's mediumistic gifts and the repression of her sexuality. At one point, mere geographical proximity to Ford (who is simply visiting the same location) is enough to inhibit her to the extent that her powers fail her completely.

As Kerr points out, the extreme example of the passivity of the trance maiden occurs in Henry James's "Professor Fargo" (1874) an anti-spiritualist satire, in which she is actually deaf and dumb. More subtly, in *The Bostonians*, James characterises his heroine's passivity in terms of the acculturated female desire to placate and conciliate. Basil Ransom, the sceptical rough wooer of the novel, understands Verena Tarrant's gift as a speaker as simply a willingness to please, which leads her to utter the sentiments of others without compromising her own innocence. (Because they are sexually suppressed, trance maidens are always apparently innocent although they may spring from a corrupt or "low" milieu.) For Basil, the nature of these sentiments is consequent upon the person to whom Verena stands closest, at any point, in a relation of dependency. She thus passes easily from the control of her father (ex-member of the "Cayuga" Utopian experiment, now a mesmeric healer) to that of feminist Olive Chancellor, and thence after prolonged sexual and ideological warfare into the arms of Ransom. Like Howells, James also suggests that Verena's inspired self springs from a buried or displaced capacity for passion, and he indicates a sexual basis for her gifts – as well as for Olive's behaviour.

The reader who turns from James to *Imaginary Friends* will discover that all the elements of the intertext of the trance maiden are firmly in place. Verena Roberts resides appropriately on West Hawthorne Street, in the imaginary small town of Sophis, which is located in an area of Upper New York State which was a locus for religious fringe groups in the nineteenth century. It is close to the spot where Joseph Smith met the Angel Moroni, and where the Oneida community flourished. As the narrator comments, Verena "was right in the local tradition, only about a hundred years too late." (p.30).[10] Although Verena's spirit messages, received via automatic writing, emanate from extraterrestrial beings, notably Ro of the planet Varna, this is not much more than a variant on established tradition, the result

---

[10] Alison Lurie, *Imaginary Friends* (London: Penguin, 1967). Page references which follow quotations in parentheses refer to this edition of the novel.

of the fact that "science now dominated the culture to the point where people were sitting round a table conjuring up ectoplasmic rayguns and little green men, instead of ladies in white veils." (p.14). Verena also remains firmly in the tradition of American Utopianism, her cult, at least in part, a disguised attack on the affluent society. Conspicuous consumption is roundly denounced as excessive attachment to "material clingings"; Cosmic Love is invoked, and the belief system excludes evil in favour of a vision of the universe as imbued with spirit light and benevolent power. Like her predecessors, Verena is young and virginal, resides in a distinctly lower class milieu, and initially features as passively pliant, providing her interlocutors with what they want to hear, quieting anxieties, sympathising with problems, and generally providing "uplift". One cult-member, Ken, figures as the sceptical young wooer, excluded from the Seekers when he denounces their beliefs, and subsequently kept at bay by Elsie Novar, Verena's aunt, who is using Verena, in a fashion not unlike Olive Chancellor, to promote her own emotional needs. In the denouncement the lusty Ken elopes with Verena, who abandons the Seekers in favour of matrimony.

It would be a mistake, however, to envisage **this** Verena as sinking into passivity. *Imaginary Friends* gives us the revenge of the trance maiden in no uncertain terms. As events develop Verena progresses from passively catering to her audience, towards actively attacking their cultural norms. At the close, far from being silenced, she has expanded her career to that of radical orator. A photograph in *The New York Times* shows her protesting vigorously at a political demonstration. Two "texts" (systems of signs) are actually involved here, and it is the interaction between the two which generates the ironies of the novel. When Tom McMann and Roger Zimmern, two social scientists, set up a small group interaction study of the Seekers, they use the methods favoured by Goffman: participant observation, role-playing, and non-directive techniques. The transcription of the literary intertext into the social text (and vice versa) foregrounds the whole notion of intertextuality. In addition to their literary intertext, the Seekers are also modelled on an actual group investigated by social scientists in the 1950s and documented by Leon Festinger and others in *When Prophecy Fails*.[11] Festinger and his colleagues were

---

[11] Leon Festinger, Henry W. Riecken and Stanley Schachter, *When Prophecy Fails* (Minneapolis: University of Minnesota Press, 1956). Special thanks are due to Malcolm Bradbury for comments on this source, made at the initial delivery of an early version of this chapter at the British Association for American Studies Conference in 1988. Bradbury adapted *Imaginary Friends* as a highly successful

studying the behaviour of individuals in groups which made specific prophesies, looking for evidence of increased commitment following disconfirmation of belief (on the model of such historical groups as the Anabaptists, Millerites, and the followers of Sabbatai Zevi and of Montanus.) Alerted by press reports they investigated the activities of "Marian Keech", a fifty-year-old housewife, who declared herself in contact with beings from the planet "Clarion" and prophesied the destruction of "Lake City" by flood on 21st December. (The sociologists' report omits the actual year and conceals real identities and locations beneath pseudonyms.) Mrs. Keech had initially received messages by automatic writing, and then became involved with a group called "The Seekers" operating some 200 miles away. Originally a group of college students, meeting in a Protestant church to discuss religious and ethical matters, the Seekers were swayed by their pastor's enthusiasm for flying saucers, and eventually developed an eclectic belief system of their own. Some went as far as to resign from their jobs and give away all their possessions in the anticipation of imminent world cataclysm, from which they personally expected to be saved by flying saucers. If anything, Lurie's fictional text appears decidedly *less* sensational and fantastic than the events chronicled by Festinger. In common with Lurie's group the historical Seekers frowned on meat-eating, engaged in meetings of exceptionally long duration, during which they discussed messages received from outer space, suffered from a leadership struggle between two women, and developed a clothing taboo. (Metal on the person was suddenly forbidden, leading to the frenzied removal of trouser zippers, shoe eyelets, belts and undergarments. One participant became worried about the possible necessity for immediate extraction of all their dental fillings.) When prophecy failed, Mrs. Keech explained that the group had spread so much spiritual light that God had saved the world after all. Their story attracted national publicity and was headline news for a week in the press and media, culminating in complaints to the police about their activities, threats of incarceration in mental hospitals, and flight. Like McMann and Zimmern, the historical sociologists, posing as ordinary group members and proceeding in a non-directive fashion, found it increasingly difficult to remain neutral, and often unwittingly reinforced the group's beliefs.

---

serial on British television. Lurie refers to the influence of Festinger's work on the novel in Liz Lear, "Interview with Alison Lurie", *Key West Review*, 1, 1 (1988), pp.49-50.

In addition to the intertextual doubling of referents in the case of the Seekers, Lurie also thematises the operations of reading and writing involved in the production of a text, by establishing a continuing analogy between the elaboration of a fiction, and that of the belief system of a small group. Since the establishment of the "social text" itself involves interactive techniques, Lurie thus effectively sets up a *mise en abyme* or infinite regressus, in which the novel offers both a sociology of the sociologists, and a metafictional fiction. As a result, its scope expands into a discussion of the manner in which cultural norms are established and inscribed, deviance and difference defined.

The doubling of intertexts is indicated from the beginning in Verena's residence on West Hawthorne Street, which evokes the starting point of small group study in the United States – Elton Mayo's pioneering researches at the Hawthorne Western Electric Plant in the 1930s.[12] The methods of sociological analysis – the various conceptual frames on offer – are then themselves introduced in terms of literary genres, as texts and titles. As an empirical, descriptive sociologist, Tom McMann favours the type of social diagnosis based on accumulations of case histories, known generically to the younger generation as "Nuts and Sluts". (William Foot Whyte's *Street Corner Society*, a study of street gangs in an Italian slum, is cited as a typical example of the genre.) Similarly the diagrammatic Parsonians feature as "Boxes and Arrows"; those favouring statistical analysis are involved in "The Numbers Racket". Dazzled by the prospect of collaborating as co-author with the famous McMann, Roger finds titles floating "mirage-like" before his eyes. "Anomie in a Small Town Setting" is one such; "We and It: Role Conflict in a Belief Group" is another, as Roger sets to work labelling and framing before the study has even begun. For Roger, the "real" is his career as a social scientist. The Sophis study is cut off and set apart; it does not "count" in the same way as his real life. Thus, when approaching Sophis for the first time, Roger describes the landscape of hills, barns and cows as having "all the pastoral props" (p.15). Putting up at Ovid's motel, he notes a paint-by-numbers picture, which "represented Art. Literature was represented by an old copy of

---

[12] F. J. Roethlisberger and William J. Dickson, *Management and the Worker* (Cambridge, Mass.: Harvard University Press, 1939). As director of the project, Elton Mayo launched the Western Electric Research Program in 1927, working with Roethlisberger and Dickson, and carrying out research at the Hawthorne Works in Chicago, which demonstrated the importance of social-psychological dynamics, operating in groups in the real world.

the Post." (p.16), rather as if he were stepping onto a stage set. The impression is reinforced by Roger's own role play. Following good sociological principles he conceals his professional identity beneath a cover story, the fiction that he is carrying out public opinion survey work. As McMann argues, to obtain unbiased data "You had to filter your presentation" (p.17). In short, as the later Roger wryly remarks, "with the excuse that we were seeking truth, we were proposing to lie ourselves blind to the Truth Seekers." (p.18).

On first encountering the Seekers, however, Roger finds that his methods rebound upon him. Rather than settling down to observe Verena, he finds himself the focus of observation, as Verena scrutinises his "aura" and pronounces him "a complete blank" (p.26). This unwelcome news is compounded when she obtains a spirit message from Varna for him. The message is merely a series of interlocking loops. For Roger, this experience is profoundly disquieting: "No possible statement is as uncanny as one you can't read at all." (p.29). He is cheered, however, when the term "automatic writing" occurs to him. Roger is considerably more secure with a long word between him and phenomena, preferably a word which labels and positions a text within a frame of assumptions. Verena is almost as adept, however, at framing Roger within hers, as her next message suggests. Roger, attempting to suppress a fit of laughter, finds himself silently praying to the totemic deities of his brand of sociology – Max Weber, C. Wright Mills, and Machiavelli. Verena promptly produces the message "Makes Favour. See Right Ills. O Make a Veil High", reinscribing his gods within her own textual system. The common-sense explanation is that Roger had unwittingly muttered the names under his breath, and that Verena who has never heard of Max Weber, or Machiavelli, and therefore lacks the right frame to make sense of the utterance, has simply done her best with the verbal system at her disposal. Roger, however, is quite unnerved. As his previous facility with titles indicates, Roger **does** treat the world as a text, but one which he does not expect to operate on him. He believes that he can maintain distance and objectivity, observing the Seekers without being in any way affected by them.

Thus, as a participant-observer, Roger implicitly occupies a readerly role. Indeed, the Seekers' extrapolation of a system of beliefs is overtly equated with the formation of a fiction, by Lurie's concentration on messages generated by automatic writing. Verena's first message from Varna is received when words in another hand are added to a letter which she is composing, quite beyond her conscious volition. It looks like divine intervention, and very much conforms to the popular image of what an author does.[13]   In this model, an author creates a narrative by some mystic alchemy or inspiration, and it is made public in a book which the reader passively enjoys, gaining private satisfactions. Similarly the traditional critical process focuses on the author as creator, and translates reader responses into statements about the work and its creator. The reader is thus able to operate without taking full responsibility for his or her own feelings, casting the self into a pseudo-objective role. The same is true of Roger, in his role as non-directive participant observer, aiming to offer as little input as possible to the group, while gaining professional satisfaction from it. As Miles Coverdale to Verena's Veiled Lady, Roger "frames" the Seekers as if they were a fiction, as if they "didn't count" as real people. Thus, in the absence of local kinship ties, the group provides an undemanding social life for all its members, which Roger labels an "imaginary kinship system". He participates in it, enjoying an evening at the Freeplatzers' as "almost a social occasion" (p.65). Of course, for all the other participants, it is a social occasion. Only Roger has framed it as "group interaction". Roger also assumes that the Seekers' friendship for him will end with the study (p.254). But of course, for the Seekers, there **is** no study; they are quite unaware of the frame which Roger has placed around them. Nor is their sense of kinship unreal – whereas, as a friend, Roger is almost as imaginary as Ro of Varna.

The problem of Roger's "role distance" from the social text is particularly focussed in relation to Verena. Roger originally perceives the belief system of the cult as created and authored by Verena. He describes her as "able to dream for others or to fit them into her own dreams" (p.45). In fact, however, Verena is co-authoring her text in close collaboration with the group. The Seekers' sessions focus upon the reception, interpretation and elucidation of spirit messages, with each member relating the messages back to his or her own personal framework (popular science in Rufus's case, spiritualism in Catherine's) and emphasising those aspects of the message which suit them best. In short, via reader input, a text is slowly extrapolated within a shaping culture, interacting with, and being modified by that culture.

Unfortunately Verena's openness to others allows her text to slip from her hands, passing for a time at least to Elsie, who wrests control from Verena by enforced sexual suppression. In a hysterical,

---

[13] See Hugh Crago, "Cultural Categories and the Criticism of Children's Literature", *Signal*, 30 (1980), pp.140-150.

Salemesque accusatory mode, the group stigmatise Verena as a "filthy, unclean vessel" (p.97), polluted and spiritually weakened by proximity to Ken, who is characterised as a "negative vibrational force" (p.94) surrounded by a greasy, smoky aura. Verena is forced to abase herself before them, proclaiming "I am cleaned and made pure" (p.99) only after prolonged humiliation. Roger and Tom stand passively by, capable only of non-directive comment. On one level, the scene recognises the ethical problems posed by participant observation as a sociological method. Goffman unwittingly provides a rather good example in *Behavior in Public Places* where he discusses the different classes of involvement obligations within one situation: "I have seen patients watch passively, from a few feet away, a young male psychotic rape an old defenceless mute man."[14] Disapproving glances were apparently the most which the patients in the asylum risked. Goffman, himself, also observing, appears to have risked even less. Similarly Roger Zimmern is uncomfortably reminded at this point in the novel of snapshots in *The New York Times* showing prisoners being tortured in Vietnam: "You couldn't help asking, why didn't the photographer do something? He was right there, wasn't he?" (p.104). Partly as a result of Roger's refusal to allow his objective observations to be biased by emotional involvement, Verena is now downgraded to the role of symbolic leader, while Elsie reinterprets the messages on her own terms, engineering a sharp shift in the group ethos, from its earlier Transcendental cast, towards a more Manichean, sin-oriented creed. Just as Olive Chancellor exploited Verena Tarrant's style, to transmit her own convictions, so Elsie reduces Verena to the mechanical rehearsal of another's script. Roger describes Verena as "like a painting in reproduction", "as if she were imitating herself, or reading from a script she had memorized earlier." (p.105).

The death of this particular author, however, turns out to have been very much exaggerated. Verena is able to act in a consciously intertextual fashion herself, and she gains her revenge by adopting the sociologists' own methods. Earlier, when McMann was rumbled as a professor, he had adopted the strategy of over-acting, carrying more books and papers, making ostentatious notes, muttering to himself, and mislaying objects – imitating, not so much a real academic as the popular image of the absentminded professor. Verena plays McMann at his own game, exaggerating the stereotypical role of the trance

---

[14] Erving Goffman, *Behavior in Public Places* (Glencoe, Illinois: The Free Press, 1963) p.207.

maiden into parody. In response to the repressive identification of her sexuality with sin, Verena apparently meets the group demand for purity by anorexic self-starvation. Far from internalising the prohibition against female physicality however, she externalises it, imposing her own food phobias on the group and evolving a complicated set of dietary taboos, which reduce them all to the intake of the tame rabbit. Verena also exaggerates female pliancy to the point at which her blank gaze, flat voice, and mechanical echoing of Elsie's prompts suggest to Roger, first the "waxy flexibility" (p.115) of incipient schizophrenia, then an uncomfortably close mirroring of his own non-directive techniques. Both Roger and McMann subscribe to the orthodox psychological notion (initiated by William James) that the trance maiden is possessed by an ordinarily quiescent second self, emerging only in states of dissociated consciousness. In this analysis Ro of Varna is actually Verena's subconscious. Verena's revenge is to split the two investigators into fragmented selves. McMann is eventually defined as insane himself, when he becomes convinced that he is Ro of Varna. His partner's fate is also appropriate. Roger, who had constituted Verena as his object of study, finds himself subject to Varnian academic requirements, forced to take notes at meetings, copy messages, memorise prayers and generally embark on an exhaustive course of study in which he is an involuntary D student. As a result he separates himself consciously into "Clever Zimmern" (his "real" self, the objective scientist) and "Stupid Roger" (the role he plays within the group and the person who is also erotically fixated on Verena.) Since fragmentation into alternate or suppressed selves is commonly the fate of women in patriarchal culture, where men are unitary characters, it is a peculiarly apt revenge.

One scene specifically emphasises the problems inherent in labelling behaviour as delusionary on bases of gendered norms. With Ken out of bounds, Verena makes overtures to Roger, when he consults her about the date of "The Coming", the imminent descent of Ro to earth. Erotic double entendre runs through the scene, with puns on the group's "desire for the coming" which appear to foreground the repressed sexual bases of their delusionary system. With Verena praying over him, Roger averts his eyes from her heaving breasts to take refuge in the notation of "neutral sociological details" (p.143) – knobs on a maple bureau, a mirror reflecting a non-existent waver in the window frame, a framed reproduction. Wavering between spiritual and sexual frames himself, it occurs to him to stop resisting. After all, "What Verena had always done with her gift was to guess what people wanted and then to give it to them." (p.143). Indeed, when Verena removes his shirt and jacket, on the grounds that these material clingings are preventing the Varnian vibrations from having "a chance to penetrate" (p.143), even Clever Zimmern collapses into Stupid Roger, and seizes her in his manly arms. Of course, on one level, if the reader accepts that Verena is deluded, Roger's scruples are entirely proper. He reflects that, but for the interruption of footsteps outside the door, "The Junior E [Experimenter] on the Sophis Project (National Institution of Mental Health Grant No. 789 etc.) would have raped his principal S [Subject]." (p.145). On these "objective" grounds, he should resist, as a psychiatrist is expected to resist the overtures of a disturbed patient. But who defines Verena as deluded? On less disinterested grounds, for the social study to continue, Verena must remain repressed. In Roger's theory, her dammed up sexual energy is the source of Ro of Varna. The suspicion lingers that Roger is actively repressing Verena's as well as his own emotions, an impression strengthened by subsequent events.

At the next meeting Verena announces to the group that Ro has prohibited clothing made from natural materials. Only artificial fibres created by pure science are acceptable. Having been unwilling to remove his clothes in private, Roger finds himself forced to disrobe in public. Despite Verena's assertion that "There is no shame in the True Universe" (p.160), the other Seekers also show some resistance to total nudity in the front parlour, and are permitted to borrow synthetic garments from the family wardrobe. This poses no great problem for the women, who have both Elsie's and Verena's clothing to choose from, and whose apparel, in any case, tends more towards synthetics, but it is a disaster for the males. When they reappear, Ed is wearing plastic duck waders, McMann an old nylon shirt which suggests an auto salesman in the Fifties, Bill baggy paint-streaked slacks, Roger striped pyjamas, which make him look like a comic strip convict, and Rufus swimming trunks and a floral quilt. As they descend the stairs, they are framed in a wall mirror as

> some group from the Theatre of the Absurd,
> a tall middle-aged duck hunger, a small
> convict with horn-rimmed glasses, a plump
> comedian in baggy paint-spotted pants, and a
> large used car salesman, all led by a skinny
> lunatic in Dacron socks and a flowered quilt. (p.162).

By the proclamation of new sumptuary laws from Ro, Verena at a stroke deprives the males of their chosen sartorial identity. In the language of clothes, they have been effectively struck dumb. In addition they have been forced to impersonate a dramatic character, a presentation self, quite at variance with their own internal attitudes.[15]

Up to this point Roger has been treating his involvement with the Seekers as one that "does not count" in real terms, rather as a fiction is traditionally marked off from "everyday life" on the grounds that its events are reversible, that we can "take back" their meanings by saying "it was only a story" or that we can revise their meanings by intertextual transformations and rewritings, so that (to quote Borges) "every writer creates his own precursors." Verena, however, decides not to permit this, and insists upon irreversible actions. Roger has to commit his expensive organic tweed jacket to the flames. In addition the manner in which this occurs is carefully staged by Verena so as to re-enact and revise her own preceding humiliations. **She** may be said to be acting intertextually here; the other characters are not granted the same freedom. Thus when the bonfire begins, the room fills with pungent smoke, exposing the whole group to the aura formerly ascribed to Ken – "as if some particularly strong and unpleasant astral force were present" (p.165). As the Seekers burn their garments, they proclaim "I am purified and made free" (p.166), a variant on the lesson Verena was forced to recite. Roger, on the sidelines, is still constituting himself as an observer. He notes, for example, that since Sissy Freeplatzer spent a long time knitting her woolly sweater, Verena was psychologically astute to leave her "to the last" (p.168). He still thinks that he is outside the group. But Roger's turn is yet to come – **he** is actually the last to be called upon and such is the power of group consensus that he actually does burn his cherished jacket. While the Seekers have been behaving as if invisible beings (Ro and Mo) were present at their meetings, the two sociologists have been acting as if **they** were invisible, not "really there" (p.155), just as readers do. Verena, however, now hauls them bodily into her frame. As Roger comments, it is as if "someone else, possibly Ro of Varna, was conducting a field study on American sociologists. To him, we were the white rats." (p.171). Verena thus enforces the correct degree of involvement on Roger's part, by forcing him into the "proper clothes" in Goffman's terms, those which express participation in the situation. In Sophis, Roger has to kit himself out from head to toe, in inorganic clothing. The result, he realises, observing himself re-framed in the motel mirror, is to transform him into "a small nondescriptly lower-middle class young man" (p.174) in Dacron shirt,

---

[15] The resemblance between Verena and Bunny Lang as director, forcing her protesting cast into odd costumes, is compelling.

Orlon sweater and limp slacks, a figure who now matches the motel room perfectly: "It was Stupid Roger, in his real clothes." (p.175). Verena's vengeance is thus both a class revenge and a sexual retaliation. The penalty for Roger's pretensions to superior detachment is to be forced into a position where he is entirely controlled. When next he is alone with Verena, he is deterred from *any* sexual responsiveness, inhibited by the knowledge that he is wearing "blue rayon undershorts decorated with beagles." (p.178).

It is as well to pause here to anticipate a major qualification. Although the results of Verena's actions constitute a fairly thoroughgoing revenge, Lurie fosters a productive ambiguity concerning the degree of intentionality involved. When Verena announces the new sumptuary laws, it is noteworthy that she has already donned a new, synthetic robe for the occasion. Roger catches himself thinking, "She must have *known* what was coming ... because her old robe ... was cotton velvet. But of course she knew, what was the matter with me? Was I beginning to believe, like the Seekers, that Ro was a separate entity?" (p.161). But how far does the author "know" what is coming next? Verena may be scripting the messages and pulling the plot strings without being consciously aware of her own control. (Messages may be issuing from her subconscious.) Strong hints are also dropped that McMann had advance knowledge of this announcement (he is clad in synthetic trousers) and of the announcement of "The Coming". McMann wants to test his hypothesis – that disconfirmation of the group's beliefs will not dissolve the group – and may therefore be prompting Verena with millennial suggestions, abetted by Elsie. Or, of course, all three may be in cahoots. When Roger finds out that Tom has entered the date of the millennial prophecy in the records before that prophecy was uttered, it looks like decisive evidence. Challenged, however, Tom appeals to social norms as the explanation. Given the existence of what Roger describes as "the ordinary Protestant delusionary system" (p.33), to which the Seekers broadly adhere, an announcement of the descent to earth of a god in December is strictly in accordance with tradition. Only Roger, who is Jewish, is surprised. In addition, the fictional frame also conditions events. For Roger the Varnians are purely imaginary, mental constructs, and he therefore *knows* that no little green men will put in an appearance. But the reader, especially if well versed in recent feminist science fiction, for example, has no such certainty. Inside the frame of genre, little green men are perfectly permissible. In little, therefore, the novel seems to offer a near perfect model of the various potential theories of how a text is generated. Does it originate in a single author? In that author's conscious or unconscious self? In some sort of collaboration with an Ideal Reader (the reader in his presentation self) or a Common Reader (a member of a group audience whose generic expectations must be respected)? Or is it socially produced in accordance with a well-established framework of group norms and assumptions?

These uncertainties are not merely matters of literary interest, as becomes abundantly clear in the denouement. Ambiguities as to who is in control, who is deluded, who sets the norm for the group, extend from the literary into the social text, raising the question of the ways in which cultural hegemony is established, how situational norms are defined, and deviance penalised. At the close of the novel, Verena invents a happy ending for the Seekers, announcing that the Varnians have descended to earth, that they have been incorporated into all the group members equally, and that from now on the Seekers must go forth into the world, to spread the word. When, however, Roger reads the last automatic message from Ro, previously elucidated at length by Verena, he discovers that it consists only of meaningless scrawls. Verena has deliberately engineered the dissolution of both the group and its text, in order to be free to join Ken. For the Seekers, however, the non-appearance of actual Varnians constitutes a fairly radical disconfirmation of their belief system. Tom promptly intervenes, proclaiming the felt presence of spirits within him. Reconstitution of the group is accompanied by a brisk reinterpretation of Ro's last verbal message. "I am in Man On Earth" becomes "I am in Tom McMann On Earth". Or, in Roger's sociologese, "At approximately 2.20 a.m. on December 5, Ro of Varna was accepted by the group as being incarnated in the senior project researcher." (p.231).

An exceptionally non-objective reader, Tom has had a decidedly creative input to the evolution of the group text. As a result of his overenthusiastic adoption of his new role he ends up in an insane asylum, where he is visited each week by Elsie, intent on fulfilling her desire "to make it with her god." (p.280). Unlike Verena, who has transformed her role as trance maiden on her own terms, Tom appears to have been entirely engulfed by his intertext, he is now fully on the inside of the "Nuts and Sluts" genre. It finally dawns on Roger that this has been threatening from the start. Two small groups have been involved throughout – the Seekers and the sociologists. Roger had been so intent on the activities of the former that he had failed to perceive that every development there was replicated in the group in which he saw himself as having primary membership. McMann's initial choice of subject – the effects of internal opposition within a small group – was occasioned by his own experience of opposition within a small group, his University department. Thus, the evolution of the study has been predestined by events which shaped McMann's own consciousness. Formerly a hero of sociology, McMann has lost out humiliatingly to younger men and is eager to revise and restore his status. The title of one of his essays, "The Sociologist – Seer or Statistician?", proves entirely proleptic of the generic options available to him. As the Seekers' seer he accrues once more the respect, reverence, even hero-worship once accorded to him within his professional group.

If Verena's escape depended on the use of her intertextual skills to redefine her role, moving out onto a larger stage, and leaving behind something of a dent in the cultural monolith, Tom's subsequent actions reveal the potential hazards of intertextual operations. Tom is also able to switch frames and to transpose systems. First he "takes back" the meaning of his incarceration, claiming that his madness was only an act, a role assumed originally in order to avoid criminal prosecution, and later perpetuated in order to allow him to undertake the ultimate participant observation study, of the asylum. (This paradigm is imported from Goffman, whose own study *Asylums* was carried out while posing as assistant to the asylum athletic director.) Having therefore established the fictionality of his own "Nuts and Sluts" intertext, McMann is about to move into "The Numbers Racket" in a more sinister sense. Earlier in the novel, Roger had expressed unease with the frequency of the sociologists' non-directive repetition of group opinions on the grounds that they were offering too strong a reinforcement: "If you push quantity too hard, it becomes quality." (p.61). Visiting McMann, Roger is unnerved by the ordinariness of the asylum, which is reminiscent of a small college or school, perfectly standard in every way. Roger's disquiet, the product of the lack of any obvious distinction between sane and insane, will be familiar to readers acquainted with *either* the sociological literature concerning the political definition of mental illness (Goffmann, R. D. Laing, Thomas Szasz), *or* the fictional intertext (*One Flew Over the Cuckoo's Nest, Catch 22, The Crying of Lot 49*). Roger had previously experienced a similar unease when he first visited West Hawthorne Street: "The whole place made me uneasy; it was so ordinary, so average, like the mid-point on a distribution which has no positive correlative." (p.19). In short, in her typical frame house Verena inhabited the norm, and the norm has no real existence; it is merely sponsored by the team, socially defined by the majority. It follows for Roger that "Madness can be defined as a conception of reality that is not shared by others in your environment." (p.39). But McMann's conception of reality **is** shared. He has at least half a dozen followers, and is actively planning to expand the Seekers into a mass movement, with himself as their god, drawing on his own professional knowledge of leadership techniques. Nor may he be said to be pretending to be Ro of Varna. If we take the view that identity is socially defined, then McMann **is** Ro of Varna. He has been so constituted by the small group. If thousands more were to follow him, the individual delusion would be reframed, first as a mass delusion, then as a respectable religious movement, its dietary taboos as acceptable as those of any other faith, its compulsory Dacron no more surprising than, for example, obligatory headgear in places of worship. In that case, since Tom would be spending most of his time playing the role of Ro, we would have to say, with Roger, that "Ro of Varna is insane to believe he is still Thomas McMann, a professor of sociology." (p.286). Thus, if numbers are on his side, McMann will be able to accomplish an intertextual move himself, from "Nuts and Sluts" to "The Numbers Racket", and from statistician back to seer.

Imaginary Friends thus leaves the reader to decide for him or herself what is the proper degree of involvement, whether in the social or the literary text, which readerly role to adopt and which reality team to sponsor. Roger's objectivity results in the loss of a woman whom he genuinely loved, passed up in favour of a small group interaction study. Tom's view, that the observer who remains external to events is not so much unbiased as incompetent (since the mental set of the group is what he needs to assume and understand) induces a degree of commitment which results in him actually being committed – to a mental asylum. In Verena's case, intertextuality may subvert literary and social ideologies to radical ends. But Verena's vacant place is swiftly filled by a male god who may prove equally adept at redefining his act, rewriting the past – and thus, potentially, controlling the future.

Chapter Five
The Ghost-Writer: *Real People* and *Women and Ghosts*

> Imagine a deserted estate in Northern New England
> (p.9).[1]

From its opening sentence *Real People* invites the reader into the
realms of the unreal.   The Victorian baronial mansion with its
imposing gateposts, rolling lawns, forests of hemlock and once-
famous rose garden appears to be abandoned.

> It is fifty years since the last owners lived here. The
> fountains are silent; the main entrance to the mansion
> under the heavy portico is closed, and a line of sharp
> rocks bars the drive.   The shades are drawn ... the
> drawing room furniture is shrouded in muslin.
> Behind the house the broad terrace above the lawn is
> bare except for red and green tendrils of vine
> advancing over cracked plaster and crumbling stone.
> No one walks there. (p.9).

With its shades and shrouds, its advancing vegetation and crumbling
masonry the scene is reminiscent of a latter day version of Daphne Du
Maurier's Manderley, Shirley Jackson's Hill House or any of the great
haunted houses of Victorian Gothic.   The house is not, however,
entirely empty.   There are ten "guests".   Bathos follows – for the
mysterious guests are being waited upon quite mundanely by a staff of
ten, vigorously making beds, polishing floors and doing kitchen duty.
Who are these unghostly residents?   When the narrator invites the
reader to look through the walls, the guests are all "idle or worse"
(p.10), each shut up alone in a private room or isolated cottage. From
their solitary confinement two are window-gazing, two pace restlessly,
"One writes a letter and signs it with a false name" (p.10), one is
illicitly reading somebody else's private correspondence, another is
methodically bending a pile of coat hangers out of shape, one is
picking out discords on a piano, "and one, apparently, is making love
to himself" (p.10). For the reader fresh from *Imaginary Friends*, it is
easy to assume that *Real People* takes up where it left off – in a
private asylum, a hospital or (given the images of vandalism, onanism,
forgery and voyeurism) perhaps a prison.

But the guests are artists.   In its anonymous, italicised
opening, as distinct from the diary form of the novella, Lurie

---

[1] Alison Lurie, *Real People* (London: Penguin, 1978).

deliberately involves the reader ("Imagine ... If we would look ...") in a complicitous pact to view the artists as ghosts or criminals, a race apart from "normal" society, either above its usual conditions and standards (moral or material) or below them (crime and deviancy). At one point a child, visiting Illyria with a tourist party, spots the inhabitants and asks, "Are those artists, Mom, or are they real people?" (p.50).   Lurie's own technique of weaving among her fictitious characters the names of "real" artists – Philip Roth, Louise Bogan, Robert Lowell – cultivates a similar uncertainty in the reader. Most of us do not know our modern artists well enough to be quite sure (at least on their first appearance) just who is meant to be fictitious, and who "real".

In its opening transition from Gothic to bathetic, *Real People* returns the reader to earth, but to Illyria, a Utopian artists' colony (modelled on Yaddo, which Lurie had visited on three occasions) where almost of necessity passions seethe and ideal visions are lost. A genteel writer of short stories, Janet Belle Smith, the diarist and narrator, finds herself forced to consider what constitutes reality, and just how honest she can be in transcribing it. As readers, reading her diary over her shoulder, we both collude with the voyeuristic, transgressive element of artistic activity, and enjoy a (perhaps illusory) sense of ironic superiority to her. In the process of writing her diary Janet's initial impression of Illyria as an aesthetic Eden, or Platonic world of Being (in which one becomes one's real self, "the person one would be in a decent world", p.15) gives way to the perception that hell is other people, even (or especially) fellow artists, and that this particular Shangri-La is little more than a luxurious prison. It is important to note that in writing the novel, which is so clearly set in Yaddo, Lurie was associating herself with an act of transgression. The one overarching rule of the artists' colony is that it is forbidden to write about it. "Those who do can never come back." (p.15). The ironies of the situation – the ostensible generous support for the creative act, conjoined with prohibitive censorship applied to it – are fully exploited in the novel.

The very form of the artists' colony implicitly suggests that society is prepared to subsidise its artists only if they remain invisible, sequestered and under strict prohibitions concerning the use of their material. Charlie Baxter, Marxist author of *The Red Moon*, is in Illyria fleeing his creditors following trouble with women, drink, and the Senate Investigating Committee. In real life, when the Director of Yaddo allowed a Marxist journalist a lengthy stay in 1949, two other residents, Flannery O'Connor and Robert Lowell, (both with a decided aversion to Communism), protested vigorously and the colony was investigated by the FBI.[2] In *Real People* one artist, here identified as Felix Ledger though unsubstantiated academic gossip attaches the incident to Howard Nemerov, listens patiently while the rules are explained to him – where not to walk, punctuality at meals, times when typing is permitted, how and when to clean the bathtub – and without unpacking gets straight into his car and leaves forever. The opulence of Illyria also has its own stultifying effects. Over dinner, Gerry (the author of *Wet Dreams*, a volume of poems distinguished for their frankness) misquotes one line as "five foot monkeys *arriving* on Greyhound buses" (p.18) rather than the original "fucking", in deference to the sensitivities of the ladies present. Because of the setting the artists converse at table as if they were characters in a Henry James novel (p.9). The talk has a marked theatrical tone "as if we were improvising dialogue to suit the room" (p.17). At a concert in Illyria the resident artists are banished to the upper storey, out of hearing of the music, their places usurped by an audience of socialites. In their evening clothes the guests are almost indistinguishable from those of sixty years before (p.79). When the concertgoers glance out of the brilliantly-lit music room they look straight through the artists, sitting in the shadows "as if we were ghosts" (p.82). Listening to the music on the stairs Janet feels like a housemaid in a nineteenth century novel. The concert is the kind of event (a benefit concert for an arts charity) at which many of those present are essentially worshipping the money paid for the ticket rather than appreciating the music. Nor are the artists immune from this commodification of art. Despite Gerry's hippy philosophy and Charlie's radical politics, both are happy to attend this demonstration of established privilege and power. Gerry is himself something of a performer. He lives partly off poetry readings, partly off his wife, who actually *does* work as a housemaid in exchange for free accommodation. As a poet who celebrates experience, Gerry goes on LSD trips purely out of duty, in quest of material. They are "business trips" (p.54) in every sense. Something of a slim volume itself, Lurie's tale combines a sophisticated essay on art – interrogating its economic bases and psychological sources – with a satiric portrait of American society. As the *New Yorker* reviewer was quick to grasp, Illyria becomes a paradigm for any affluent society which supports its

---

[2] See Jon Lance Bacon, *Flannery O'Connor and Cold War Culture* (Cambridge: Cambridge University Press, 1993), 57-9

artists without really valuing their work, and exploits them as markers of social status.

On a more individual level, Janet undergoes a process of self-discovery which reveals what is wrong with her work and her life. In her husband Clark, Janet has the equivalent of an eighteenth century patron, supporting her handsomely in a comfortable suburb with two children at private schools, but with restrictive effects upon her art. Like Dryden and Pope, Janet's writing shows her dependence on her patron and his social group.

> There is the same avoidance of all topics which might annoy them; the same gross or subtle glorification of their way of life; the same praise of the virtues (reliability, good taste, justice, moderation) and blindness to their faults. (p.123)

Over the years and quite unconsciously Janet has indulged in self-censorship, never writing about anything which would disturb her family and friends, until in the end she even avoids doing or seeing anything which she could not write about. For several years she has had a close, but Platonic, friendship with a painter, Kenneth Foster, assuming that the asexual nature of the relationship owed something to Kenneth's revulsion from his alcoholic, promiscuous wife, Roz, and thus his appreciation of the finer, less physical qualities of a kindred spirit, "Lovely Janet", a woman of taste, sensitivity and refinement. In the course of the novel Janet discovers that Roz's behaviour is explicable by the fact that Kenneth is gay; and that only Janet has been in the dark about this. Janet's art is a defence from commitment, responsibility, even from life itself. She has been too busy protecting her idea of herself as "Lovely Janet" to be a real person, and paradoxically only real people can write imaginatively.

Janet's progress is charted, in part, by the evolution of one of her stories, a ghost story composed and revised at intervals throughout the novel. The germ of the story is suggested by Teddy Berg who tells two ghost stories – the tale of the "distracted, dishonoured, Woman in White" (p.25) who appears in the woods, and that of the ghost of Illyria's original sponsor, Undine Moffat, who supposedly haunts his bedroom. Janet finds the idea comic – Undine was not exactly insubstantial; she weighed nearly 200 pounds at her death. The knowing reader, however, may find this ghost (and her tendency to haunt the bedroom) wholly appropriate to the ironies of Lurie's tale. Undine Moffat, the ruthless fortune hunter of Edith Wharton's *The*

Custom of the Country, loathed art, except in so far as it represented
entry into a world of money and society.[3]

Janet's original story line is brief:

> Idea for story: The plump ghost. Seen by woman
> who is dieting. Unsuccessfully? When she succeeds
> (fails?), it vanishes. Her past or future self. (p.26).

She notes approvingly that in the Eden of Illyria, artists are gods,
creating without responsibility, "for we only create ghosts – though
sometimes rather plump ghosts". (p.27). When she drafts the story,
however, "it seemed both trivial and pretentious, a thin, silly tale
elaborately overtold" (p.56). A conversation among her fellow artists
seals its doom. Janet has been trying to pour oil on the troubled
waters of the artists' colony and is mocked for her efforts.

> JANET: No, but I do think when one's been invited
> here, one is responsible after all –
> NICK: Hey! You know something? Janet has an
> imaginary friend named Wun. An Oriental. She's
> always telling us his opinions. 'Wun prefers the kind
> of art Wun was brought up on. Wun is *responsible*
> after all.' (p.73).

To Janet's horror when she rereads the story, in imagination turning
"Wun" to "I" throughout, "a tedious character appeared, sententious,
supersensitive" (p.74). By using the impersonal pronoun Janet
generalizes her opinions, announcing that they are shared, inviting the
reader to be part of a community of like-thinking people. It is a
common enough writerly strategy – even a necessary one – yet it also
gives Janet's emotions more dignity, and diminishes the personal
reference of her writing. As she suddenly realises, her best stories did
not have Wun in them but her best stories were written five years ago.

The catalyst in Janet's progress towards becoming her "real"
(i.e. unrepressed) self, and therefore a better writer, is Nick Donato, a
vulgar pop-artist with whom she has a satisfyingly physical affair.
Significantly, perhaps, she abandons her repressions and her
"ladylike" self on the night of the Fourth of July amidst coarse jokes
and Rabelaisian overtones. After making love, Nick dips his finger
into "a puddle of what looked like egg white" (p.108) and draws two
lines on Janet's body, signing his name below, just as in his drawings,
and Janet asks him jokily "if he always signed everything he'd made"
(p.108). Janet has been redefined, from artist to woman as object, a
work of art, but emphatically not in the mould of "Lovely Janet".

---

[3] Edith Wharton, *The Custom of the Country* (New York: Scribners, 1913).

> It was as if I'd turned into a different person too – or
> rather as if I'd somehow been that person all along.
> (pp.107-8).

Taken with post-coital panic Janet runs wailing into the woods in her
white dress, and realises that she has stepped into Teddy Berg's ghost
story. "Only now I was her – or her ghost." (p.110).

Back at her desk, in full retreat from the discovery of a self
which she has tried to suppress, Janet rationalizes the act as merely an
aberration. The Oriental persona reappears.

> One has to avoid making much of an incident simply
> because it doesn't match the rest of one's life – when
> one ought for that very reason to give it less weight ...
> I literally wasn't myself but an emotional vacuum into
> which was projected the kind of person Nick wanted
> me to be. The fact is, it really wasn't I who went to
> his studio, but just some anonymous, lonely, half
> hysterical woman in white, like Teddy Berg's ghost
> (p.119).

Predictably, Janet now revises her ghost story to rescript her own life
and refashion her character in a more conventional light. This time
the ingredients include a woman spending the night in a haunted
house, who imitates the cries and gestures of a ghost in a story,
possibly involving the death of her husband. "Was she my ghost, or
am I hers?" (p.119), the woman wonders. On one level the story
mirrors Janet's own experience. Life has imitated art as Janet became
the Woman in White, and art now briskly remodels it. But as Janet
realises, the new story is utterly conventional.

> There was something in the original ideas, but then I
> changed the people to types, and the precipitating
> incident from a seduction to news of a death. (p.123).

Typically the story is less likely to offend anyone in its new form – it
is firmly inside the conventions, both social and literary. Eventually
she realises that she has never written anything but ghost stories,
spiritualized versions of herself and others which leave out any vulgar
physical details. She has been living to suit her work, allowing
generic conventions to script her emotions and perceptions. Taking a
deep breath she rips up the story and starts to write about Illyria. A
bruising encounter with Kenneth sets the seal on her decision.
Kenneth describes her stories as full of self-congratulation and self-
advertisement, "a form of onanism" (p.148) dependent upon the
economic exploitation of her husband. As he speaks, her image of
him dissolves in the face of his undisguised malice:

> His Lovely Janet doesn't really exist, and never did,
> any more than my Lovely Kenneth. They were both
> just ghosts in some story we were telling each other
> and ourselves. Very charming and spiritual, like all
> ghosts, but in the end thin, transparent and boring.
> (p.153).

Up to this point the reader may well detect a punishing quality to the story, which throws an ambivalent light upon Lurie's portrait of a woman writer. The epigraph, from one of Charlotte Brontë's letters, casts Janet as representative, in a tradition of women writers who lay claim to the right to all experience, on the same terms as men.

> Come what will, I cannot, when I write, think always
> of myself and of what is elegant and charming in
> femininity; it is not on those terms, or with such ideas,
> I ever took pen in hand: and if it is only on such
> terms my writing will be tolerated, I shall pass away
> from the public, and trouble it no more.

Castigated by Kenneth, patronised by Clark, in thrall to the super-phallic Nick (much is made of his oversized attributes and tiny swimming trunks) Janet appears to learn only from men, and to remain under their tutelage. Nick, however has a female equivalent, the Eve in this particular Eden, who sows confusion among the male artists. Anna May Mundy, the visiting god-daughter of the house's director, introduces the Jungian joke at the centre of the novel. Yaddo was so named as the result of a childish mispronunciation of the word "shadow".[4] (The grounds are shaded by enormous trees. The original owners, Spencer and Katrina Trask, donated the estate only after their four children had died of diphtheria.) The landscape of Illyria gives literal form to Jung's metaphors of the shadow, the forest of the unconscious and the pool of selfhood. For Jung the process of individuation involves transcending the conscious persona by facing the "shadow" in the personal unconscious, which represents everything denied in conscious living. When the projection of the shadow is resolved, the individual then encounters a personification of the collective unconscious in figures of the anima (in men) or animus (in women).[5] Like Jung's world soul (the anima mundi) Anna May Mundy has no "real" existence, no fixed character. She merely receives the projections of the artists, all of whom interpret her according to their own desires and fears. Leonard (Jewish) sees her as

---

[4] Robert M. Coates, "Yaddo," *Author's Guild Bulletin*, June-July 1966, pp.3-5.
[5] Carl Gustav Jung, *Aion* (London: Routledge and Kegan Paul, 1959).

anti-Semitic; for Teddy (older) she is a childish innocent. For Gerry (his reputation fading) she is in love only with fame. Nick (working class) sees her as an upper class tease. Janet (disillusioned with men and feeling betrayed by Kenneth) sees her as Estelle to her godmother's Miss Havisham, wreaking revenge on men because of the dead artist who supposedly betrayed her thirty years before. Meanwhile, the real Anna May departs, rather bored, in a red sports car. The world is impervious to art. All that is left behind are the various projections of the artists, Kenneth's faint scribbled sketch, Nick's "American Girl with Coke No. 3" executed life size in metal and plastic and flashing light bulbs, Gerry's poems and Charlie's novel – all very different images of Anna May, reflected in the distorting mirrors of art. Slowly Janet recognises the parallels with her own story-telling, also a projection of herself onto others. She learns that in life, as in art, people can become distorted, mirror-images pulled out of shape by the desires of others.

Lurie's novel therefore treads a double path. On the one hand Janet's diary provides the reader with a voyeuristic access to authoritative truth – the story as it develops, without revision, jotted down each day before Janet can interpose her self-censoring artistic filters. In addition the inclusion of small playlets allows Janet's voice to be countermanded by others, and reinforces the impression of honest transcription of the "real". The first person journal allows for tentative realisations, self-doubt and vacillation; the reader can compare earlier and later evidence (retracing the career of Wun, for example) apparently gaining access to an unvarnished truth. Yet as H. Porter Abbot notes (in a study of diary fiction which includes a perceptive analysis of the structure of *Real People*) the view that a diary is a nonliterary form, in the sense that it is unpremeditated and free of artifice, will not stand up to scrutiny. In *The Counterfeiters* Gide's diarist, Edouard, describes his diary as a pocket mirror.

> The analogy is a good one because it allows us to formulate a double question: does the diarist catch herself in the mirror or does she use it to put her makeup on? (Abbott, p.47).[6]

The true self is not necessarily the hidden self, difficult of access and requiring special tools for its excavation – not is it, indeed, any single self. The diary may express spontaneous emotion in all its raw power – or it may be, in itself, a form of role play. As Abbott puts it, "it is the mystique of the diary – its illusion of sincerity – that can make it a

---

[6] H. Porter Abbott, *Diary Fiction* (Ithaca: Cornell University Press, 1984).

particularly treacherous form" (Abbott p.47). Recognising this may establish the diary's greater authenticity, offering access to a more complex form of truth.

More importantly the diary can itself play a role in the story as a live agent (Abbott, p.41). Abbott notes that just before Janet sleeps with Nick (in her view the act of a stranger-self), she had been in debate with herself in the diary concerning Kenneth's homosexuality, wondering whether he was really a stranger to her, and whether she knew herself at all.

> The seducer has an accomplice in the seduced ... her retelling of the story of her "love affair" with the painter has prepared for her sexual affair with the sculptor – prepared her and may well have led her to it (Abbott, p.41).

Janet may have projected a version of herself in the diary just as she projected various images of Anna May, to prepare for action in "real life". As she notes "We choose the literary forms that match out lives" (p.48). As a result the form of Lurie's novel constitutes its own evasive strategy, producing a highly unusual fiction, which avoids a perfect fit with novel, drama, essay or Socratic dialogue, and gives the reader room to manoeuvre in the interactive space between art and life.

The novel ends with Janet's recognition that

> You can't write with only the nice part of your character, and only about nice things ... I want to use everything, including hate and envy and lust and fear. Not only do I want to – I must. If nothing will finally survive of life except what artists report of it, we have no right to report what we know to be lies. (p.153).

But will Janet succeed? In an oddly oblique fashion the answer came some twenty five years later with Lurie's only collection of short stories, *Women and Ghosts*. The reader who turns to "Fat People" discovers that the outline of Janet's original ghost story has finally been filled in. In the short story, Ellie decides to lose weight while her husband Scott is in India, and begins to see fat people everywhere. At first she puts this down to coincidence, and to having the subject on her mind, but soon (dizzy with hunger) she realises that she is seeing fat people who are invisible to other witnesses. When she binges, they disappear. When she goes back on the diet, they reappear, only now in more sinister mode, culminating in a ghastly vision of "a huge sexless person with long stringy hair waving its arms and walking slowly towards me out of the woods." (p.139), [7] followed by hordes of angry blubbery, grey people, who besiege her apartment in a scene reminiscent of *Night of the Living Dead*. The tale ends happily as Ellie, reunited with her overweight husband, polishes off another slice of pineapple upside-down cake. "Fat People" was first published in 1991 in *Good Housekeeping*, a magazine which Janet Belle Smith's conventional neighbours – if not Janet herself – might well be expected to read. And if they did they would be reading about Janet's family and friends, without any self censorship on Janet's part.

The collection raises the intriguing possibility of an extremely clever narratorial ploy, in which Lurie becomes the ghost writer for her own writer-character. Almost all the stories in *Women and Ghosts* feature carryover characters, connected to Janet Belle Smith. In "The Pool People" Clary, Janet's daughter, is the central character. In "The Highboy", narrated by Janet, the story centres upon Buffy Stockwell, Clark's sister-in-law and features Roo (née Zimmern) and her husband Freddy Turner, son of Clark's sister Emmy. In "Counting Sheep" Charles and Miranda Fenn (Emmy's friends) put in an appearance. Roo narrates "Another Halloween". "In the Shadow" closes with the wedding of Celia Zimmern (Roo's sister) to Charles Fenn Junior, Miranda's son. In "Waiting for the Baby" Janet's son Clark is in India, attempting to arrange an international adoption, with his wife Aster (formerly Astarte, child of Josie and Steve, the Beats of *The Nowhere City*.) For the reader who recognises the connections between the characters there is an extra dimension. Rather as on Halloween, children now take on the character of ghosts (rather than the ancestors who returned as ghosts in the Ancient Roman festival of the Day of the Dead), with the repetition of names recalling the past – Celia reminding the reader of her father's long dead stepmother, Clark Stockwell and Charles Fenn referring to both the father and the son. Thematic doubling is also a feature. Karo McKay, the eponymous heroine of "The Double Poet" is split between two selves, an ethereal sibylline poetess (visiting poet in residence at Convers) and a vulgar double who sleeps with a complete stranger and begins to take over Karo's identity. *Real People* investigates whether Janet was always essentially a ghost writer, paid to dramatise somebody else's socially approved script, unable to introduce her own experiences or ideas. But the prologue to the novel, the description of the deserted mansion, is not attached to Janet – for she is one of the artists whom this disembodied frame-narrator (Lurie herself?) observes. In her diary

---

[7] Alison Lurie, *Women and Ghosts* (London: Heinemann, 1994).

Janet had come to the painful recognition that not only was her ghost story trivial and thin, but also that all her stories were ghost stories, unconvincing tales in which all physical substance was edited out in the name of good taste. *Women and Ghosts* turns the tables on the conventions. The ghosts in these stories are "fatter", altogether more substantial than the characters, in several significant respects. Lurie plays with the idea here that her identity as writer has been taken over by a character.

As a result, *Women and Ghosts* is very much the literary "double" of *Real People*; its ghosts are familiar, domestic and contemporary, haunting kitchens, pools and pieces of furniture, their role often to warn the characters (particularly the women) against potential loss of identity and substance. In "Ilse's House", for example, the ghost of a first wife (not dead but divorced and living happily ever after in Europe) returns in sisterly fashion to warn her successor against marriage to a decidedly unreconstructed male. She appears only in the kitchen (her "proper place" in her former husband's ideology) cramped into the space between the refrigerator and the wall, and only to Dinah, a statistician of a stolidly unimaginative nature who describes her first inklings of romance as "a rising curve of possibility in the relationship" (p.7). In "In the Shadow" the unblithe spirit of Celia's former boyfriend, Dwayne Mudd, pops up to interrupt his beloved in every potential clinch, with comments on the physical deficiencies of the new lover, ranging from athlete's foot, hairy ears and smelly socks to diminutive sexual organs and a taste for whores. Not so much rattling his chains as offering the sotto voce suggestion of an AIDS test, Dwayne, as his name suggests, is a very terrestrial, down to earth ghost, but his effect on Celia is to remove her from every physical contact. She becomes arguably less physical than the ghost itself.

The comic, domestic method owes something to Lurie's recent anthology of modern fairy tales, many of which also renounce the usual trappings of the supernatural in favour of domestic settings.[8] Philip K. Dick's "The King of the Elves", for example, begins in a filling station; in Naomi Mitchison's "In the Family", the hero's response to being accosted by a fairy is to get a firm grip on his monkey wrench and spirit his beloved away from danger in a rather mundane lorry. Mundanity has its own horrors, however. As Claire Messud remarked, these ghosts do not elicit a fear of the spirit world

---

[8] Alison Lurie, (ed.) *The Oxford Book of Modern Fairy Tales* (Oxford University Press, 1993).

so much as a dread of American reality.[9]   They embody the middle class woman's anxieties – the desire to be thin, married, or pregnant, the longing for a perfect identity – or at least a perfect pool. In some stories the ghosts are distinctly sisterly (Ilse, and the Indian deity who rewards the heroine with a baby). "Another Halloween" deals with sisterliness in more orthodox terms, as murderous sibling rivalry, in a story which topples over into the traditionally "spooky".   In her childhood Marguerite went out trick-or-treating with Annie, whose younger sister, Kelly, followed them. When the older girls tried to leave her behind, she ran after them and was knocked down and killed by a car. On Halloween Marguerite, now an adult, believes that she sees the ghost of Kelly in the distance, runs after her, and is herself run down and killed. Roo left Marguerite to her own devices, partly because she resented the latter's orthodox femininity; "I always felt kind of overgrown and clumsy around her; she was so daintily pretty." (p.142). With hindsight Roo's ideas change. "Now I believe women have to take responsibility for other women, even ones they don't much like" (p.152). Had she been more sisterly in the feminist sense of the term, the avenging ghost-sister might not have entrapped Marguerite. The story is conventionally "spooky" precisely because Roo wrote Marguerite off, delivering her into the bonds of the conventions, both ghostly and social. Now she is haunted by the thought that one day this "sister's" ghost will be out there "waiting for me." (p.153).

As in *Real People* one theme that haunts the stories is the commodification of art and people in the service of materialism. The victims tend either towards the stolid and unimaginative (Dinah's first solution to a ghost occupying the space between wall and refrigerator is to have the kitchen remodelled, though Ilse promptly pops up in the broom closet) or those deluded by a naïve belief in art. Celia ceases to be haunted by Dwayne when she relinquishes possession of the expensive antique watch which he had given her, on the advice that "You must hold to persons, not to things." (p.104). In "The Pool People" excessive materialism gets its comeuppance via a haunted swimming pool; in "The Highboy" from a malevolent cupboard. Buffy's mania for antiques takes over to the extent that she describes her grandchildren as temporary, as opposed to her heirlooms:

> from our point of view we own our things. But really, as far as they're concerned we're only looking after them for a while. (p.48).

---

[9] Claire Messud, "Women and Ghosts", *The Guardian*, 13 July 1994, p.8.

Janet dismisses too easily Buffy's belief that the highboy is malevolent, laughing at the idea that "we're all in danger of being injured by our possessions" (p.48). But even before the highboy falls on Buffy and kills her she had already been irrevocably damaged by her attachment to things. "Good taste" is nearly always fatal in these stories. Celia's predilection for designer garments and classy accessories is a case in point. In "Waiting For the Baby" Aster is initially scornful of the Birla Mandir temple (built in 1938), an oriental film-fantasy edifice of marble the colour and texture of banana ice cream. Even the statues of the gods are glaringly new, like Disney figures, overdressed and suggesting "vulgar commercial power" (p.110) Aster had rejected the antimaterialist tenets of her hippy parents, determined that even if her adopted child were Indian genetically it would not have the mock-Indian, hippy childhood which she suffered in America – of vague spirituality, mantras, meditation, vegetarianism and too many siblings (p.114). In an ironic twist, she now worships once more at the Indian shrine. It is only when she is overcome by her inability to exercise her own vulgar commercial power and buy herself a baby, that she flings herself down on the filthy ground in front of the goddess Lakshmi, praying vigorously.

"Counting Sheep", in which an academic involved in the Wordsworth industry in Grasmere turns into a ram, says everything about the "heritage" side of the poetry business. In all but appearance the hero was nothing but a cultural sheep anyway. He had previously rescued a sheep in an incident modelled on Wordsworth's "The Idle Shepherd-Boys" where a poet saves a lamb from a ravine; now he goes one step further and becomes one. At least as a ram, he now has a choice of ewes. As Lurie wickedly notes, "for some reason Wordsworth wasn't popular with young women scholars" (p.70), so that the Wordsworth project at Grasmere is full of frustrated males: "overrun with professors and sheep, and it was getting so you couldn't tell the professors from the sheep" (p.74). If "Counting Sheep" deals with the academic end of literary commodification, "The Double Poet" tackles the topic head on, as what Lorrie Moore once called "po' biz".[10] Written like *Real People* in diary form, the tale returns to the doubling theme, satirising the commercialisation of art, as Karo McKay, a pretentious minor poet, obsessed with her own uniqueness, finds herself stalked by a mysterious other, who buys sweaters in her name, has one-night stands with unsuitable men, and takes over her

---

[10] David Leavitt, "They're Playing Our Dirge," *New York Times Book Review*, 18 September 1994, p.12.

poetry readings. Karo has allowed her agent to negotiate some fat fees for the readings, which she loathes, and as a result is overdosing on valium. Like the residency at Convers, she took on the job for financial reasons, to provide herself with the "necessities" of life. No starving in a garret is envisaged:

> if I'm to work well I must have a warm, quiet room
> flowing with soft music; the scent and colour of fresh
> flowers; simple but perfect meals with good wine; the
> look and feel of almond silk and lace and taffeta
> against my skin (p.159).

At Convers, however, she finds that business is all. The resident writers mostly see her as a professional resource for recommendations, advice on grants, fellowships and writers' colonies, just as the queues at book signings are often headed by book dealers proffering six or eight first editions with precise instructions that she add date and place to her signature, to increase their mark-up. Karo had previously encouraged a semi-mystical view of her art, encouraging its cult status (p.161) and favouring sybilline sea-green silk on the podium. When her double inscribes "to a budding poetess" on a volume, Karo is outraged both by the trite phrase and by the sense of sacrilege (p.162) involved. It remains unclear whether an excess of tranquillisers has simply confused Karo, or whether there is a double, Not-Karo, who may have evil intentions. At the close, taken with panic when she apparently sees her place on stage usurped, Karo collapses back into her original identity as Carrie Martin, greying and middle aged, cancels all her commercial engagements – and suddenly finds that her writer's block has lifted. It remains a moot point whether the haunting double has punished her pretensions, or saved her from a fate worse than death – herself. Her own materialism posed more of a threat to her than any external stalker. Early in the story Karo had described Not-Karo as a snail spreading slime behind her, "So that once she's done the public things, I become unable to do them; it's as if they've been slimed and fouled." (p.177). But perhaps Not-Karo did her a favour. Just as writing about an artists' colony removed the writer from the unreality and the bourgeois prohibitions of the subsidised Utopia, Karo is freed from signings, readings, residencies and rehearsals. At the end she is writing again:

> she's started to hear phrases, lines, even whole
> stanzas of poetry whispering at her everywhere.
> (p.182).

This time she protects her art from exploitation, shutting the poems away in a drawer. "As long as they're safe from Not-Karo, so am I" (p.182). Freud saw the sense of the uncanny (the unheimlich) as not so much the result of an encounter with the unknown as the return to consciousness of the familiar, the homely, and domestic.[11] In *Women and Ghosts* Lurie puts the home back into the Freudian "unheimlich" with a vengeance, in a collection which leaves behind a lingering insubstantiality as to the nature of authorship – doubled intertextually between author and character.

---

[11] "The Uncanny," in James Strachey (ed.), *The Standard Edition of the Complete Psychological Works of Sigmund Freud* (London: Hogarth Press, 1955). Volume XVII.

Chapter Six
Vietnam Domestic: *The War Between the Tates*

Where preceding novels, however, have tended to deal with issues of social conformity, engagement or detachment in carefully circumscribed microcosmic locales outside the mainstream, *The War Between the Tates* (1974) brings them home to roost. Set in the period between March 1969 and May 1970, the novel chronicles the break-up of the marriage of Brian and Erica Tate, against a background of the Vietnam War, student protest, and the rise of the counter culture. Although once more set on a university campus (the imaginary Corinth) the novel refers out from a specific discussion of the social role of the university to the politics of the Cold War period, and thence back to that oldest of American traditions, Utopianism. Many readers have felt that the use of the Vietnam War as mere background to what has been dubbed a novel of adultery or of midlife crisis is indefensibly tasteless. Vietnam and its horrors are too momentous. Its events dwarf the pygmy Tates and their amorous shenanigans. As Marigold Johnson commented, it is rather as if "Jane Austen had tackled War and Peace".[1] Yet the connection between sexual and civil aggression is one which is frequently drawn. Lyndon Johnson declared that he was reluctant to leave "the woman I really loved" (the "Great Society" welfare and civil rights programme) "in order to get involved with that bitch of a war on the other side of the world".[2] In "Vietnam and Sexual Violence" Adrienne Rich argued that the bombings in Vietnam were so wholly sadistic and gratuitous that they had to be seen as acts of concrete sexual violence, an expression of the congruence of violence and sex in the masculine psyche. For Rich, the equation of manhood with the objectification of another's person and the domination of another's body lay at the core of warfare as of sexuality. "The capacity for dehumanizing another which so corrodes male sexuality is carried over from sex into war."[3] Rich complained that the slogan of the antiwar movement, "Bring the war home" (meaning disrupt "business as usual" in America, stop traffic, bring guerrilla theatre onto the streets, keep Vietnam in the forefront of public attention) had never been fully acted upon in domestic terms.

---

[1] Marigold Johnson, "To the Death," *New Review*, 1,4 (1974), p.76.

[2] Doris Kearns, *Lyndon Johnson and the American Dream* (New York: Signet, 1976).

[3] Adrienne Rich, *On Lies, Secrets and Silence* (New York: W. W. Norton, 1979), p.114-5.

It is just this project – to bring the war home – which occupies *The War Between the Tates*, in which the shaky alliance between Brian and Erica Tate mirrors the shakiness of the American consensus. The domestic battle, as they separate, provides an analogy to larger conflicts, as domestic Erica Tate (the Am-Erican State) dissociates herself from the external activities of her husband, Brian, a political scientist who specialises in the study of U.S. foreign policy. His expertise in foreign affairs extends specifically to an extra-marital affair with his student, Wendy. The ensuing civil war at home is interrupted by a temporary ceasefire, ostensibly for peace talks and reconciliation, during which Brian engages in undercover activities, while Erica stockpiles evidence of his guilt as ammunition for the future. As a result the Tates' sexual contacts become less marital than martial,

> a deadly struggle between his will to enter and her will to delay the invasion as long as possible, so that the occupation might be as short as possible. His main weapons in this battle are force and persuasion; Erica's fuss and delay ... A real victory for Erica took place on the few occasions when she was able to hold back the invading troops for so long that, fatigued and impatient, they discharged all their artillery at the frontier. (p.74).[4]

The title of the novel therefore refers out to several overlapping conflicts: the war between the sexes, between older and younger generations, and between North and South Vietnam, by analogy with the American Civil War, under its alternative title of The War Between the States.

These various conflicts are held together in the novel and "brought home" by quite specific references to George F. Kennan, architect and then opponent of the Cold War, and critic of the American student Left. Kennan is Brian Tate's hero, the public figure he admires most (p.37). A diplomat and historian, Kennan made his name as a brilliant analyst of foreign affairs. After the Second World War he was frequently at the centre of national debates on the goals and methods of American foreign policy. Three terms are of key importance in Kennan's thought (and in the novel.) He made his name with the **containment** doctrine of the 1940s, became the

---

[4] Alison Lurie, *The War Between the Tates* (London: Heinemann, 1974). Page references which follow quotations in parentheses are to the Penguin edition, London, 1977.

advocate of **disengagement** in the 1950s and spoke out in the 1960s against global interventionism (e.g. in Vietnam) and in favour of both détente and **neo-isolationism**.[5]

In *The Cloud of Danger* Kennan remarked that "Foreign Policy, like a great many other things, begins at home."[6] It is a point which is quite lost on Brian Tate who excuses his infidelity in the following terms:

> he has committed no overt act of aggression against Erica, deprived her of nothing. He had held to the Kennanite principle of separate spheres of action. Within the family, the marital sphere, he had been faithful. The idea of sleeping with Wendy in the marital bedroom ... revolted him. (p.75).

Kennan's "containment doctrine" stemmed from his view of Marxism as a pernicious and enduring threat. For Kennan the U.S.S.R. was bent on global pre-eminence, implacably hostile to the West, duplicitous and totalitarian. In 1946, in the "long telegram" (actually an 8000 word essay which made Kennan's name) he recommended that the main element of U.S. policy toward the Soviet Union should be that of "patient and firm containment" of Russian expansive tendencies, partly by the application of counterforce at a series of shifting geographical and political pressure points, partly by preventing other nations from allowing the reins of power to be seized by elements under Moscow's control. Needless to say, Kennan completely ignored American power and expansionism as a contributory factor to Soviet-American tensions. Nor did he envisage that the results of containment were to be the American coddling of satellite states and client nations, and the shoring up of dependent puppet governments, as in Vietnam. After Stalin's death, however, fearing an expansion of American militarism, Kennan espoused disengagement, advising the withdrawal of troops from Europe, for example. As a result he began to move to a neo-isolationist position, arguing that the U.S.A. should set its own house in order, regulate its own domestic affairs, before it could hope to have a political influence on others. He spoke out against American intervention in the Third World, and in favour of diplomacy as a means of solving problems.

---

[5] On George Kennan's life and writings see David Mayers, *George Kennan and the Dilemmas of U.S. Foreign Policy* (New York and Oxford: Oxford University Press, 1988); David L. Shils (ed.), *International Encyclopaedia of the Social Sciences. Biographical Supplement* (New York: The Free Press, 1979); Anders Stephansson, *Kennan and the Art of Foreign Policy* (Harvard University Press, 1989).

[6] George F. Kennan, *The Cloud of Danger* (Boston: Little, Brown), p.379.

For Kennan, the U.S.A. of the Sixties and Seventies had assumed the role of world policeman, thrusting itself in where it was not wanted, and would inevitably fall on its face.   In his analysis isolationism meant the reduction of the military establishment, a more serious attention to domestic ills, and a frank recognition that Washington had neither the duty nor the capacity to serve as mankind's guardian angel. Interestingly, he ascribed American meddling directly to the national sense of Utopian political mission.   From the nineteenth century onwards, he argued, Americans were not content to *be* something, but also had to *appear* as something lofty, noble and of universal significance. Foreign policy, therefore, tended towards the cultivation of projects Utopian in nature but barren in practical results (e.g. the negotiation of a whole series of treaties of arbitration and conciliation.)   Over-concentration on these Utopian schemes meant that Americans lost their feeling for reality, so that when war came, they saw their enemies as monsters arisen from nowhere – rather than as the reflection of deeper causes.   Kennan considered that international life would be easier if there were less readiness in America to be morally impressive and

> a greater willingness to admit that we Americans, like everyone else, are only people in whose lives the elements of weakness and virtue are too thoroughly and confusingly intermingled to justify us ... in any claim to a special moral distinction.[7]

This attack on American "exceptionalism" is very much part of the moral of Lurie's novel, in which the Tates' pretensions to superior moral status are ruthlessly destroyed, until at the close Brian and Erica are left to contemplate their own weakness:

> they will put their arms about each other and forget for a few moments that they were once exceptionally handsome, intelligent, righteous and successful young people; they will forget that they are ugly, foolish, guilty, and dying. (p.379).

If Kennan's political writings form an essential background to the defeat of the old fashioned Liberal Tates, his view of the university is equally significant in relation to the Tates' younger opponents on the campus. In 1968 a speech which Kennan gave at the dedication of a new library at Swarthmore College was printed under the title "Rebels Without A Program" in the *New York Times*. It drew

---

[7] George F. Kennan, *Realities of American Foreign Policy* (London: Oxford University Press, 1954), p.50.

an unprecedented response from students and teachers, with sackfuls of mail delivered to Kennan.[8] (The letters varied from one lady willing to support him for the Presidency, to a public challenge to a duel.) Essentially Kennan took issue with the politicisation of the American campus. For him the basis of education was "the ideal of the association of the process of learning with a certain remoteness from the contemporary scene."[9] He therefore emphasised the need for detachment, monastic seclusion, and isolation, and decried the radical student Left as over-absorbed in the affairs of the world. Kennan went on to note two dominant tendencies of student radicalism:

> On the one hand there is angry militancy, full of hatred and intolerance and often quite prepared to embrace violence as a source of change. On the other side there is gentleness, passivity, quietism – ostensibly a yearning for detachment from the affairs of the world [BUT REALLY] an attempt to escape into a world which is altogether illusory and subjective.[10]

In *The War Between the Tates* the first group is more or less equally represented by the group of angry feminists (who resort to violence when they take their sexist lecturer hostage) and the anti-war protesters. Kennan attacked these angry militants as overinspired by certainty of their own rectitude in a world of highly complex problems. He then introduced as a moral touchstone the image which becomes the sacred cow of the Tates' marriage, "The Children". Kennan argued that there are points in life where idealism must falter and be tempered by pragmatism:

> There is a point when we are even impelled to place the needs of children ahead of the dictates of a defiant idealism and to devote ourselves … to the support and rearing of these same children – precisely in order that at some future date they may have the privilege of turning upon us and despising us for the materialistic faintheartedness that made their maturity possible.[11]

In Kennan's view more harm has been done by those "who tried to storm the bastions of society in the name of Utopian beliefs" than by

---

[8] The speech and a selection of letters, plus Kennan's response, are printed in George F. Kennan, *Democracy and the Student Left* (London: Hutchinson, 1968).

[9] *Democracy and the Student Left*, p.3.

[10] *Democracy and the Student Left*, p.9.

[11] *Democracy and the Student Left*, p.9.

those who tried to create "a little order and civility and affection within their own intimate entourage."[12] It is clearly a view with which Erica Tate, devotee of domestic order and civility and worshipper of "The Children" (p.82) would concur, as opposed to Wendy who relegates the welfare of her child to second place, in favour of a Utopian commune.

As for the second group of students, the quiescent, non-involved pacifists (represented in the novel by Zed) Kennan saw them as deluded, particularly by the idea that marvellous internal resources can be released by passive submission to certain stimuli (e.g. drugs), rather than by effort and daring. (It is a view completely undermined in the novel by Erica's experience of L.S.D. which alters and enriches her career as a graphic artist.) He concluded that the students were mere rebels without a properly thought out programme for reform. As a result the period (1968) was in his view more serious and menacing than any he had previously experienced and he introduced the central metaphor of the war between the states.

> Not since the civil conflict of a century ago has this country ... been in such great danger; and the most excruciating aspect of this tragic state of affairs is that so much of this danger comes so largely from within, where we are giving it relatively little official attention, and so little of it comes, relatively speaking, from the swamps and jungles of Southeast Asia.[13]

As one might imagine, Kennan's advocacy of the university as an ivory tower, a place of apolitical detachment, drew a strong response from students. As one Harvard freshman pointed out, the possibility of being drafted and killed in Vietnam forced students to make political decisions speedily. There was no time for careful analysis, peaceful demonstration and a rational process of argument for reform:

> Though one must sacrifice a certain amount of perspective to involvement, this is a much lesser evil than being sacrificed to someone else's perspective through detachment.[14]

Others pointed out that Kennan's advice to think now and act later was in gross opposition to a government which was manifestly acting now and thinking (if at all) after considerable delay. For one student the problem in Vietnam was "due to the fact that thought has not been

---

[12] *Democracy and the Student Left*, p.9.

[13] *Democracy and the Student Left*, p.19.

[14] *Democracy and the Student Left*, p.26.

joined with action, but separated as though they belonged to the two different spheres that Kennan puts them in."[15] Several implied that Kennan and his generation should answer for the ideological bankruptcy with which America was facing crisis in Vietnam. In fairness, this was a point which Kennan himself had made, when he acknowledged responsibility for student anger, and admitted that it was his own ugly face which could be seen in the distorted mirror of the student Left. For Kennan the lack of "patriotism" in the draft-dodgers was a reaction to the exaggerated "hurrah patriotism" of U.S. schools in the preceding twenty years, the relic of the anti-Communist hysteria of the Forties and Fifties. In addition he admitted that the American political system had always been based on a division of responsibilities between, for example, the legislative and executive branches of government. The New Left had, in his view, reacted to this division of spheres by introducing the idea that everyone and anyone was responsible for everything and anything. The radical student, he concluded, was therefore a reflection, in a distorted sense, of the problems of America.

> He reflects, faithfully, but in expanded, oversized dimensions, like shadows on the wall, the bewilderments and weaknesses of parents, teachers, employees.[16]

The War Between the Tates opens with a similar image, in its epigraph from Jorge Luis Borges' tale "The Fauna of Mirrors."

> Deep in the mirror we will perceive a very faint line and the colour of this line will be like no other colour. Later on, other shapes will begin to stir. Little by little they will differ from us; little by little they will not imitate us. They will break through the barriers of glass or metal and this time they will not be defeated … Others believe that in advance of the invasion we will hear from the depths of mirrors the clatter of weapons.

In *The War Between the Tates* the securities of the Liberal Tates are increasingly questioned, distorted and rejected by their mirror selves, the children, and by extension the younger, student generation, who slowly stop following the parental example, refuse to imitate them, and evolve from mirror reflections formed in the Tates' own image, to grotesquely distorted characters, monsters in their parents' eyes, and

---

[15] *Democracy and the Student Left*, p.85.

[16] *Democracy and the Student Left*, p.216.

thence to active challenge. George Kennan's political ideas set the scene for a novel which engages in an extended investigation of such issues as passivity versus activism, Utopianism and pragmatism, issues which underline the Vietnam war, as seen in the microcosmic mirror of the Tates' foundering alliance. Images of mirrors, of distorted characters and self-images, of dehumanisation and war are therefore key motifs in a novel in which nobody at the university gets off lightly.[17]

From the beginning of the novel, Erica Tate identifies herself with America in its domestic sphere. Confronted with the dreadful behaviour of her adolescent children, and entirely indoctrinated by Brian's Kennanite views, she feels that she alone is responsible.

> A father might possibly avoid blame for the awfulness
> of his children – a mother never. After all, they were
> in her 'area of operations', to use Brian's term. An
> admirer of George Kennan's early writings, he had
> long subscribed to the doctrine of separate spheres of
> influence, both in national and domestic matters.
> (p.11).

In consequence, although Brian might advise Erica on important policy decisions, he would not ordinarily question her on the home front. As a result, the Tates' domestic life has been governed for years

> according to the principle of separation of powers:
> Erica functioning as the executive branch, and Brian
> as the legislative and judicial. (p.102).

So far these traditional separate roles within their marriage have worked for the Tates. Until recently they had lived in happy harmony with their children, geographically isolated from the campus in an attractive farmhouse on Jones Creek Road. Now developers have moved in, Jones Creek Road has become Glenview Heights, the Tates are surrounded by new ranchhouses, the creek is polluted, and the family breakfast to a background of "CHOMP CRUNCH SCRATCH", the result in almost equal proportions of Jeffrey and Matilda's noisy eating habits, and the developers' bulldozer. Clearly Erica's isolation in her separate sphere is nearing its end, just as the Spring thaw has created a mirror world of ice and snow which is

---

[17] Michael S. Helfand reads the novel as dialectical and anti-Liberal in its assumptions, valorising feminism, mysticism and communal living as the unacknowledged needs of the Tates. See Michael S. Helfand, "The Dialectic of Self and Community in Alison Lurie's *The War Between the Tates*," *Perspectives on Contemporary Literature*, 3, 2 (1977), 65-70.

dissolving. Apart from pursuing her career as an American Mom, Erica has also been writing and illustrating books for children, dealing with the adventures of an ostrich named Sanford who has taken up residence with an ordinary American suburban family. (He has his own bucket of sand for emergencies.) It is rather an apt image of her own withdrawal from the changing world about her, and of American isolationism. Erica's detachment is cruelly shattered when, waiting for her cookies to bake, she idly reads Brian's mail, and discovers that he is sleeping with Wendy. Reeling with shock, Erica notices a peculiar burning odour in the room, like explosives. It is, of course, the baking. The kitchen fills with smoke and the hot smell of scorched cookies. "The war has begun." (p.32).

The larger causes behind this spring offensive are locatable in Erica's past. On her divorce, Erica's impoverished mother had immediately embraced all things foreign (and apparently some foreign men) on the grounds that foreign things did not so easily proclaim their price (p.28). To Erica, entering junior high school in a mood of Ballad-for-Americans patriotism, the foreign clothes, foods and even accent, foisted upon her by her affected Mama, were entirely hateful. She resolved to become as all-American as possible, to avoid and suspect everything and everyone foreign. (p.30). Indeed the desire for all-American isolation is at least partly responsible for her marriage to Brian, a long-established WASP whose field of study is American Government.

The background to Brian's affair is equally significant. Apparently fated from birth for a brilliant career, descended from illustrious ancestors and exceptional in every way, Brian is dissatisfied with his academic career. "Why," he asks himself sourly, "is he speaking on foreign policy instead of helping to make it?" (p.35). On the one hand he feels that his ideas have been misunderstood, just as George Kennan had been misunderstood (p.37). More prosaically, Brian fears that the main reason for his failure to become a great man may be his height – he is five foot five. Perhaps his public image implies a lack of real stature? He is also anxious that he is diminutive in other, more intimate, areas, despite the reassurance of the girlfriends of his youth. "But what if they had been politely lying?" he wonders. "Or what if he had shrunk, in fifteen years?" (p.52). Approached by the erotically-smitten Wendy, Brian gets the chance to check out both his anxieties. Essentially he sparks off the "war" on behalf of his own self-image, the need to restore the vision of himself as distinguished, impressive, a man of weight and substance.

Initially Brian tolerates Wendy's attentions on the grounds that she is in a separate sphere, a student of Social Psychology, not in his own department of Political Science. He also reassures Wendy that her interest in mystical communities, pooh-poohed as examples of social pathology in her own department, is a legitimate study of groups in the mainstream of the American Utopian tradition. In addition Brian enjoys the information which Wendy brings him from the other side, the students. As his "Native Informant" Wendy enables Brian to impress his colleagues with his "intuitive" grasp of student politics. Alternatively disguised as a squaw or a Hindu, in mock-ethnic garb, "Native" Wendy pursues Brian relentlessly. Even when she is not physically present, "the waves of her passion reached him like the vibrations of a distant bombardment." (p.49), the more so after she collapses on his office floor with maximum display of transparent tights. Eventually Brian convinces himself that he should sleep with her, out of pity and to cure her of her obsession. The political analogy is overtly drawn. As Zed later comments, Wendy gets what she wants from Brian by going into his office and falling apart.

> Weakness can be a strategy like any other ... The battle isn't always to the strong ... The weak have their weapons too. They come and collapse on you, like defeated nations, and you have to take care of them." (p.210).

If the Tates are the representatives of the American state, Wendy, the staff-student go-between, is fairly clearly related to the South Vietnamese, collapsing for support onto an ally who will pick her up and get her back on her feet, an ally who is all too ready to prove his greatness in a display of strength and male, even phallic, power.

Unfortunately for Brian's peace of mind, however, Wendy does not subscribe to the Kennanite notion of separate spheres. While Brian, confronted with her pregnancy, congratulates himself on his separate bank account, which will finance an abortion, Wendy proceeds directly to Erica's house to apologise. (Wendy feels responsibility for everything.) Once again, in a reprise of her tactics with Brian, she falls apart, revealing the pregnancy by means of morning sickness in Erica's sink and collapsing onto Erica, who is not slow to see the implications.

> Sometimes a miserable refugee cat or dog, abandoned by its owners, appears in your yard. If you keep your door shut until it goes away, nobody will blame you. But suppose instead you take it into the house, feed it,

> find it a place to stay.   From then on you are
> responsible. (p.165).

Erica accepts this responsibility, intervening directly into Wendy's life, attempting to find her a safe abortionist, and then when she changes her mind, deciding that she must divorce Brian so that he can make an honest woman out of Wendy. Yet although her refusal to leave mother and child in a separate sphere contrasts with Brian's lack of responsibility, Erica's motives are none the less similarly governed by the desire to protect her own self-image, to be seen to do the right thing. When she tells Brian to divorce her she is fanatically certain of her mission:

> I don't agree that it's not my concern ... That's what
> the "Good Germans" said. After all, Wendy came to
> me: I have to help her. I don't want to be like those
> people in Dante who did neither good nor evil, but
> were always just for themselves. (p.177).

A self-appointed moral policeman, Erica has thrust herself into events, in the desire to appear noble and good, as a supremely self-sacrificing wife, who puts the good of Wendy's child before everything else.

Throughout the novel characters repeatedly go to war on behalf of their own self-image, or in order to destroy that of another character – frequently by means of a dehumanising objectification. Erica reduces Brian to "That Thing" (his penis) and turns Sanford into an ostrich. Later she characterises Brian as an alley cat, like the one who twice impregnated the Tates' Flopsy, before they had her fixed. Wendy, knowing of Erica only that she is tall and cool, forms the impression of her as a "frozen lady giant eight feet high." (p.139). Erica, realising that Brian has been deceiving her, and that his infidelity with Wendy has been continuous, feels like "an animated cartoon cat" (p.136) presented with only one small pathetic mouse. Erroneously she had imagined three different mistresses. Now "Like a cartoon character she sits frowning, watching the stars and asterisks fade; three images blend into one." (p.135).   Meanwhile Brian imagines Wendy as the subject of a Fragonard painting, passive, docile and pink.

When Erica intervenes with Wendy, to maintain her own noble image, Brian at first responds in Kennanite terms of containment: "he must separate his opponents," (p.181) he thinks, after which he will reoccupy his territory and pacify the natives (p.183). In one respect he is successful. When he takes the initiative and arranges Wendy's abortion, Erica is quite outflanked. Up to this point she has figured as a moral heroine; "now, with one stroke, he had turned her into a character in a cheap farce." (p.234) – a deceived wife. When Brian returns to the marital home, however, it is to discover that the domestic sphere is no longer his to command. Earlier, when Brian attempted to look more impressive by giving up shaving, he was defeated by a student cartoonist who portrayed him as a very small man, attached to a very large moustache. Now, too, he finds that the images have escaped from his control. It is the evening of Halloween and the streets are full of monstrously disguised trick-or-treaters. At home, his daughter Matilda stands before her mirror, transmuted into "a fat witch" (p.187) hideously painted. Jeffrey, now considerably larger than Brian, is slumped on his plastic spine reading Plastic Man Comics. The horrible suspicion dawns on Brian that his children's monstrous appearance is not a temporary disguise:

> that the scowling adolescent hag upstairs is Matilda's true self, just as Jeffrey is in some profound sense a plastic man; that all the monstrous children he passed this afternoon on his way home, dressed as devils, ghosts, Dracula, etc., have merely made their real natures visible, this one day of the year. (p.190).

It is as if the characters in a hall of mirrors had stepped out of their frames.

Earlier in the novel, the war between parents and children had been characterised in terms of the war in Vietnam. Originally when Brian drew the parallel, he identified with the South Vietnamese. In his view, the conflict, begun a year or so ago as a minor police action, intended only to preserve democratic government and maintain the status quo, has escalated steadily and disastrously against his and Erica's wishes. Now Jeffrey and Matilda have turned the house into occupied territory, slowly taking it over, filling it with rock music and destroying its original culture. For Jeffrey and Matilda, however, the North Vietnamese sympathisers, Brian and Erica are the invaders, the large, callous Americans, vastly superior in material resources and military experience and with powerful allies in the local school. Despite their wish for self-government the children remain dependent on Erican aid and are subject to Erican propaganda. As a result they refuse to negotiate and retreat "into the jungles of their rooms ... where they plan guerrilla attacks." (p.101). As this war escalates, in tandem with the Vietnam war, Brian, rather than fight on, follows Kennan's advice and disengages; he moves in with Wendy. As a result he is able to de-escalate the war with Jeffrey and Matilda, to meet them only on neutral ground, and therefore to establish friendly, or at least neutral, diplomatic relations with his own children. In contrast, Erica has had to stay on the ground, fighting a losing battle and maintaining "a precarious puppet government, with only very minimal and intermittent air support from her former ally." (p.256).

With her own interventionist tactics defeated Erica finds the tables turned. She is now forced into isolationism and a high moral tone, but not in a manner of her own choosing. Increasingly isolated socially, less from choice than from necessity, invited to fewer social events, she also finds that her separated status forces her to act the moral angel, to wear highnecked dresses and behave with circumspection, to avoid giving the impression of sexual availability. Dressing for one party, Erica realises that, like Brian, her relationship with mirror images, has also changed. Formerly as an acknowledged beauty, she enjoyed seeing her reflection. Now her mirror gives her back a woman whom she hardly recognises, thin, careworn and ageing. Only when she backs off to a considerable distance does her familiar self-image re-form. At the party she is therefore careful to keep a precise distance (two and a half feet) from everyone, to avoid close observation of her heavy makeup. (Since the party is dominated by members of the foreign language departments, it is a nice image of isolation.) Indeed, she realises that over the last months she has learned to keep her distance with everyone, "a distance not only physical, but psychological." (p.271). As the scene implies, in her desire to hold on to her attractive moral self-image, to protect the status quo, Erica is in danger of losing all real contact with others and all feeling for reality. In contrast her friend Danielle, dressing for the party in front of her glass, announces that she intends to remarry (with a carefully negotiated marriage contract) and move, and "steps out of the mirror frame" (p.269).

It is not surprising therefore that in her isolation Erica should turn to Sanford Finkelstein, on whom she had modelled her ostrich. As the proprietor of the Krishna bookshop, Sandy espouses a vague Eastern mysticism, reflected in the eclectic literary works on his shelves, which is the polar opposite of Brian's political writings. Immortalised as an ostrich in Erica's books, Sanford has changed his name (to Zed) but not his opinions. At first he appears as an entirely praiseworthy quietist, pacifist vegetarian. Although he has desired Erica for twenty years he has never made a move in her direction, nor has she suspected his desire, given the fashion in which she has dehumanised him. To Erica's eyes, he resembles "a large scrawny wounded bird, shot out of season" (p.299). Just like Brian, however, Erica responds out of pity to this lame duck. She decides to give him

a present – of herself. Moreover she intends thereby to accomplish a
good moral action:

> to deconvert Sandy, to bring him back into the world
> in every way and show him that it was real and good,
> so that he would give up his pathetic empty
> asceticism. (p.330).

Unfortunately for Erica Sandy's role as an ostrich extends to his
sexual activities: he has a tendency to shrink away from involvement.
On the one occasion when, under the influence of L.S.D., he does take
the initiative, Erica herself, afraid of pregnancy, disengages at the vital
moment, and their affair remains unconsummated. The L.S.D. trip
also confronts Erica with her own subjective isolation. At first Erica
had believed Sandy's mystic assertions that "the world is what you
say it is" (p.342), that language creates reality. But his bathroom
mirror tells her otherwise. Catching a glimpse of an old woman's
face, "blank, white, creased" (p.344) Erica breaks down and weeps.
"Somebody's crying," she remarks. "I think it's me." (p.345). From
this point on, Erica draws back from an isolation which has
culminated, damagingly, in a dissociation from her own feelings
which verges on breakdown. She rejects Sandy's invitation to join
him on "the spiritual path" and is next seen, once more amidst people,
at a large social occasion – the Peace March.

If Erica's neo-isolationism is finally brought to a close,
Brian's desire for an active political career comes to an even stickier
end. Where the Erica/Sanford plot underlines the deficiencies of the
Utopian, detached idealist, Brian's involvement with the radical
feminists emphasises the problems of political pragmatism. Earlier, at
the Frick Museum, Brian had contemplated the Holbein portraits of
Sir Thomas More, the ultimate idealist, and his Machiavellian
opponent, Thomas Cromwell, the unrivalled pragmatist. In his youth
Brian had copied out the words from More's Utopia: "For it is not
possible for al thinges to be well, onles al men were good. Whych I
thinke wil not be yet thies good many yeares." (p.220). On his way
back from the Frick, Brian picks up Sara, a feminist hitchhiker, whose
tirade against male objectification of women so infuriates him, that in
a moment of Machiavellian malice he recommends to her his
reactionary colleague Donald Dibble's course in Constitutional Law.
(Dibble's sexism is such that he informs the class that women's IQs
do not develop beyond the age of twelve.)

In the ensuing conflict, Brian pictures himself as only the
adviser to the feminists, suggesting that they pack the course with
sympathetic women, shout Dibble down, amass evidence of Dibble's

sexism. When this evidence is produced, Brian enjoys an intoxicating sense of power. Almost without effort,

> he had set the two people in Corinth he most disliked upon each other. He had chosen their battlegrounds and their weapons; now he could sit behind the scenes and hear them attack each other, saying things he would have liked to say himself. (p.307).

Unable to influence foreign policy, Brian has brought the war home to its bases in male/female relationships.

Regrettably, Brian's status as adviser proves no more durable than that of the U.S. "advisers" in Vietnam. Women can also go to war. When the feminists hold Dibble hostage, Brian goes to the rescue: "It was time to return to the policy of containment." (p.308). In the scene which follows, which involves farcical activity with a large rope, Brian's role as would-be Top Cat to his colleague's Officer Dibble reduces· him to caricature. His plan backfires when the feminists catch him and he is featured in the New York Times in a photo which becomes

> a classic image of the women's-liberation threat, at once comic and symbolic: a small middle-aged man, his face expressing fear and outrage, being wrestled to the floor by long-haired Amazons. (p.324).

Brian's public image has now been defined to the entire world. Like Kennan, he finds himself the recipient of a deluge of mail, much of it abusive hate mail, the rest hysterical misogynist tracts: "after trying for forty-seven years he has become a famous man." (p.326). His attempt to intervene in politics ended in disaster in the kidnap of Dibble; his attempt to contain the consequences, by helping Dibble to escape, has also been a failure. In contrast, the radical feminists win their case by violence; the university concedes their demands for a non-sexist speaker. Wearily Brian recognises that "Other wars end eventually in victory, defeat, or exhaustion, but the war between men and women goes on forever." (p.326).

If by this point it appears as if the Tates have been royally taught a few lessons by the activists (in Brian's case) and the pacifists (in Erica's) the reader should not necessarily assume that Lurie lends Zed and Wendy her full approval. At the end a series of minor aftershocks places both in an ambiguous light. Brian now discovers that Wendy (like Flopsy) is pregnant again. (She had deceived him into thinking that she was still on the pill, and has concealed the results for several months.) Even worse, in Brian's terms, it transpires that just as Erica gave herself to Sandy, just as Brian slept with Wendy out of pity, Wendy has been charitable to Ahmed, an engineering student from Pakistan. Wendy felt sorry for Ahmed in his lonely isolation and so gave herself to him for Christmas. Ironically, having destroyed his own child, Brian is faced with the prospect of supporting someone else's, a child whom he envisages as probably "brownish is colour and interested in machines". (p.361). So much for Brian's oft-reiterated principle of putting the wellbeing of "The Children" first. Earlier Wendy had declared that she would always belong to Brian completely.   Now she solves his problems by departing in the company of yet another man, to a primitive commune in Northern California. Ominously her last words concerning her child are "I'll always belong to him completely." (p.368). It is weak, defenceless, collapsing Wendy, entirely bereft of moral principles, who gets exactly what she wants, a child and life in a commune, by classically manipulative, old-fashioned methods.

Nor does pacifist Zed emerge unscathed.   Ostensibly Zed exemplifies the most complete detachment and disengagement from ordinary life, and yet it transpires that he has known all along about Wendy's baby and has been using mysticism to self-serving ends. He has quoted the Prophet to Wendy – "Lo, your children are not your children, but the sons and daughters of God." – in order to convince her that the precise paternity of the infant in question is unimportant, so that she will pass it off as Brian's, Brian will have to marry her, and he will have more chance with Erica.   If Brian lives on Kennanite instructions, if Erica is isolationist, suspicious of foreigners and yet obsessed with her own moral vision, Zed represents the force of Utopian idealism as opportunism, a force which almost involves everyone in disaster. Utopian passivity can also fuel conflicts. Zed, who has never taken part in any political activity, never written to his Congressman, nor even voted since 1954, is the only major character not to participate in the Peace March that closes the novel.

It is at this march, which brings the war home to Corinth, that Brian and Erica reunite, drawn back together less by any resurgence of love, than for base financial reasons. Brian thinks that it will be better for all of them economically. Erica has plans for a cleaning lady and a three-week vacation. From a revisionist point of view, the mainspring of their relationship has been redefined from moral vision to the requirements of their joint domestic capital. Neither, however, admits to this motivation.   Brian plans to be diplomatic to Erica at their projected meeting.   In his imagination he thinks that he must be generous enough not to point out that all that had happened was in a way Erica's fault. Erica is also planning to occupy the moral high ground. In her view

> She will have to make up her mind never to say anything that might remind Brian of how selfish and irresponsible and ridiculous he has been. (p.376).

This moralistic approach, as Kennan suggested, dooms them to failure. The precariousness of their truce may be imagined from the fate of the march itself. Ostensibly a fine, peaceful, praiseworthy demonstration, to good idealistic ends, it has in fact been organised by Brian largely in an attempt to restore his Liberal image.   His motivation is thus entirely pragmatic.   Indeed he has attempted to prevent the Maoists from taking part – ironic given the context. Brian and Erica's belief in their own exceptionalism is also belied by the March itself.   Already, as it begins, the purity of the marchers' message has been diluted. The march has been hijacked for various economic purposes. Among the anti-war signs can also be read "Eat at Elaine's Country Cooking", "George Brampton for School Board", "Noel Lee and the Gnomes in Concert", and "Boycott Grapes". When the novel closes with a small child asking, "Mummy will the war end now", the question is marked out as purely rhetorical. Unknown to themselves the marchers (like Brian and Erica Tate) are on a collision course:

> In a few moments, as they pass a bar called The Old Bavaria, all hell is going to break loose. Empty beer bottles and other garbage will be thrown, fist fights will break out; there will be the sound of smashing plate glass and popping flashbulbs and police sirens. (p.378-9).

As the suggestions of the Second World War (implicit in the Old Bavaria) imply, an action replay of preceding violence appears to be on the cards. Although the novel ends before this point, in a display of apparent social unity which includes all the disparate social and political groupings in Corinth, it leaves little room for optimism, whether on the domestic front – or abroad.

Chapter Seven
The Uses of Enchantment: *Only Children*

Prompted in part by the horror which greeted her portrait of the Tates' children, Lurie's next novel turned the tables on the adults. *Only Children*, largely narrated from a child's viewpoint, constitutes an unfolding story of adult education during the Independence Day weekend of 1935, as two couples and their nine-year old daughters pay a visit to Anna King's Catskill farmhouse. Anna is headmistress of Eastwind, a progressive school reminiscent of Windward, the school run by socialists which Lurie attended as a child. Anna's Utopia stands as something of a counterweight to the runaway capitalism which has led America into Depression. Her ideals are representative of a return to an older, less commodified America, rendered symbolically here by a weekend roughing it amidst mock hardships (no indoor plumbing and a wood stove) down on the farm. In Anna's Utopia, however, sooner or later, everyone regresses into infantile behaviour. Echoes of events in Europe rumble menacingly in the background; one family is of Jewish extraction. Both couples are also representative in terms of American politics. Dan Zimmern, a failed writer and would-be socialist, now an ad-man, is a prime example of the forces which create illusory needs, to fuel an overheated economy. Huckster Dan has himself been overtaken by the desire for the new – a new car, a new wife, and potentially this weekend, a new mistress in the shape of Honey Hubbard. Bill Hubbard, a New Deal Democrat of unimpeachable moral earnestness, works as a social welfare administrator. Yet financially Bill depends upon the prolongation of economic misery: the more the Depression bites, the more secure his own job. The Second New Deal of 1935-7 saw the beginnings of the creation of a welfare state. In 1934 thousands of new social work jobs had been created.[1] Lurie's title unpacks in several different directions. In the climactic bout of fisticuffs, Bill describes Dan as

> Treating the American people like children. Like little kids that want cheap toys, and can be fooled by cheap lies.[2]

---

[1] See John H. Ehrenreich, *The Altruistic Imagination* (Ithaca: Cornell University Press, 1985).

[2] Alison Lurie, *Only Children* (London: Heinemann, 1979), p.181. All subsequent references are to this edition of the novel and follow quotations in parentheses.

For Bill, Dan is peddling illusions, "convincing some poor sap that can't even keep up his mortgage payments to buy a new Buick on time." (p.181). Dan, however, maintains that it is Bill's welfare mentality which has infantilised Americans into a state of dependency.

> It's you and your pals that treat people like kids. You take away their jobs with chicken shit regulations and taxes, and then you make them line up and beg for handouts, and that makes you feel oh so generous. (p.181).

Which of the two political alternatives comes closest to responsible government? Lurie's only historical novel, *Only Children* also has a fairly obvious reference to the debates of its year of publication (1979) when Reaganomics, which fostered similar laissez-faire arguments to Dan's, was on the horizon.

The novel also extends to debates of the 1970s concerning feminism, the nature of sexual relationships and particularly, distorted male perceptions of women.[3] In their domestic economies Bill and Dan are not so very distinct. For Dan, a devotee of conspicuous and vicarious consumption, the greatest luxury is to have a non-working wife, Celia, a beautiful (and wretched) object of display, who revolves moth-like around Dan's flame. In contrast Honey Hubbard, to all intents and purposes a stereotypical Southern belle, has managed to negotiate a degree of autonomy for herself by consciously playing the little-girl role. For all their political differences Bill and Dan are in complete agreement on the roles of women (or "babes" in Dan's terminology). Bill puts it directly:

> See, the women we know, they most of them grew up before the Eighteenth Amendment. They're usually pretty irrational, like children really, because that's how they were brought up to be. When they got the vote, and short skirts, and all that, it was too late for them. (p.106).

In contrast, their wives, furiously picking vegetables, boiling water and slaving over a wood stove, unassisted by the males, agree that "men are such babies" (p.98), hopelessly dependent on women for every practical purpose.

In their two daughters, Lolly Zimmern and Mary Ann Hubbard, both "only children", Lurie articulates a satire on adult life

---

[3] See Joyce Carol Oates, "Honey and Bill and Dan and Celia," *New York Times Book Review* 84 (22 April 1979), p.7, p.27.

from a child's perspective. As the weekend wears on, adults and children change places. As Mary Ann observes,

> They play kids' games and don't even stick to the rules. They tell lies ... They shout and get dirty and are rude to each other (p.115).

For the reader with hindsight, the image of thoughtless Americans at play is sharpened by one particular conversation. Lolly overhears the adults discussing events in Europe and puzzling over the fate of Dan's second cousins in Strasbourg, who no longer reply to his letters. On making enquiries Dan found that "The whole family had disappeared. They had a little girl, a few years younger than Lolly, named Danielle." (p.123). In overheard snatches ("threatening calls" "attacked in the street" "No better than murderers") the horrors of the Holocaust are briefly evoked, together with the incredulity of innocent Americans. ("I don't get it. You mean they could have killed ..." p.124). From a European perspective the Americans, fiddling while Rome burns, are "only children" in terms of international – as well as national and gender – politics.

In some respects, therefore *Only Children* looks back to (and extends) the debate of *The Nowhere City*, in its concern with the 1930s as a formative decade, the role of the masses, and the power of consumerism. In articulating her satire on the hapless Hubbards and Zimmerns, Lurie employs fairy tale motifs to underline the adult idiocies which result from romantic paradigms and wish-fulfilment fantasies. The contrast between the ad world of America and the nightmare of totalitarianism inevitably recalls the arguments of Walter Benjamin, and his end, dead by his own hand on the Spanish frontier, to avoid a worse fate from Nazi pursuers. Benjamin has a special relevance for Lurie's novel, particularly in relation to its major narrative framework: the fairy tale. In Benjamin's argument industrialisation had brought about a reenchantment of the social world at an unconscious "dream" level, with myth alive everywhere, in, for example, posters advertising "toothpaste for giants";[4] in the consumer dream worlds of shopping arcades; and in labyrinthine cities like enchanted forests. Benjamin saw the collective imagination as mobilising its forces for a revolutionary break from the recent past, by evoking a cultural memory reservoir of mythic and Utopian symbols from an Ur-past, offering the possibility that the imagination can cut across the continuum of technology and historical development, and

---

[4] Susan Buck-Morss, *The Dialectics of Seeing. Walter Benjamin and the Arcades Project* (Cambridge, Mass.: MIT, 1989) p.254.

evoking the potential for revolutionary rupture.[5] For Benjamin, the purpose of the ad was to blur the commodity character of things,[6] purveying dream images, collective wish symbols. In the opening pages of Lurie's novel, Mary Ann transforms herself in imagination into Princess Miranda, with a magic wish-box;

> she wished for a big red horse with wings like on gas stations that could fly up in the clouds. (p.1).

The conjunction of Pegasus with the Amoco symbol immediately evokes Benjamin's focus upon the relationship of consumerism to myth, and thus to the redemptive power of the human imagination. Importantly, Benjamin was interested in children, and in their games, rhymes and stories, apparently perceiving in the consciousness of the child the unsevered connection between perception and action which also distinguished the revolutionary consciousness in adults. In the child he saw a creative spontaneity of response that bourgeois socialization destroyed. His major (uncompleted) work, the Arcades project, has been read in terms of revisionist fairy tale, as a Marxist retelling of the tale of Sleeping Beauty, an attempt to wake the masses from the collective dream of the commodity phantasmagoria. In his 1936 essay "The Storyteller" Benjamin describes fairy tale as a mode of cultural inheritance, that keeps alive the promise of liberation by showing that nature (animals, animated forces) is aligned with human beings against myth.[7]

Contemporary critics, however, have been rather less certain of the value of fairy tales. In "Fairy Tale Liberation" Lurie recalled that in her own childhood, in "high-minded progressive circles"[8] fairy tales were considered unsuitable for children. As one child education expert, Lucy Sprague Mitchell, put it

> Does not Cinderella interject a social and economic situation which is both confusing and vicious? … Does not Jack and the Beanstalk delay a child's rationalizing of the world and leave him longer than is

---

[5] Buck-Morss, p.116.

[6] Buck-Morss, p.184.

[7] Walter Benjamin, "The Storyteller," in *Illuminations*, ed. Hannah Arendt (London: Fontana/Collins, 1973). First published as *Schriften* (Frankfurt: Suhrkamp Verlag, 1955).

[8] "Fairy Tale Liberation," *New York Review of Books*, XV, 11 (17 December 1970), 42.

desirable without the beginnings of scientific standards?[9]

Lurie received Mitchell's *Here and Now Story Book* – designed to provide simple realistic stories that would prepare children for the real world – for her fifth birthday. It was less than enthralling. "The children and parents in these stories were exactly like the ones I knew, only more boring."[10] Today Mrs Mitchell reads like a particularly demented embodiment of agitprop. "The Farmer Tries To Sleep" owes its position in the volume to her decision that children should realise the incessant nature of farm work, before they learned about that of the factory. Few readers can have been persuaded by Mitchell's belief that "The world of industry holds possibilities for adventure as thrilling as the world of high-colored romance."[11] Even worse, in Lurie's view, the stories failed lamentably to prepare anyone for the real world. Later she discovered that

> The fairy tales had been right all along – the world was full of hostile, stupid giants and perilous castles and people who abandoned their children in the nearest forest. To succeed in this world you needed some special skill or patronage, plus remarkable luck. And it didn't hurt to be very good-looking. The other qualities which counted were wit, boldness, stubborn persistence, and an eye for the main chance.[12]

Lurie also defended the classic fairy tales as potentially liberatory for women. In Mrs Mitchell's stories men drove engines, ran factories, built houses; women did nothing but look after children and go shopping. In contrast traditional tale-tellers were often women, portrayed women as competent (e.g. Gretel not Hansel defeating the witch) and often as embodying real power (whether benevolent as fairy godmothers, or sinister as witches and stepmothers). Men, on the other hand, tended to be dumb giants or malevolent dwarves. Lurie recommended Andrew Lang's *Blue Fairy Book* among other collections, concluding that the traditional folk tale was "one of the few sorts of classic children's literature of which a radical feminist could approve."[13]

---

[9] Lucy Sprague Mitchell, *Here And Now Story Book* (London: J. M. Dent, 1972), quoted by Lurie in "Fairy Tale Liberation," p.42.

[10] "Fairy Tale Liberation," p.42.

[11] Mitchell, p.21.

[12] "Fairy Tale Liberation," p.42.

[13] "Fairy Tale Liberation," p.42.

Not all feminists, radical or otherwise, agreed. In 1972 Marcia Lieberman took specific issue with Lurie. Lieberman did a close study of Lang's *Blue Fairy Book* and argued that the stories were inherently sexist, involving passive heroines, helpless and submissive, who functioned largely as the prize for the handsome prince.[14] Other critics were in broad agreement, noting such features as the beauty contest (beauties always win), the association of meekness and good temper with beauty, the subtle promotion of jealousy and divisiveness between girls, and the sparsity of active heroines. In "The Goose Girl", for example, the princess is submissive to ill treatment to a masochistic degree and is saved only by outside intervention. The victimized girl (e.g. Cinderella) is always rescued and rewarded. In other words, suffering goodness can afford to remain meek and need not strive to defend itself. Marriage is the ultimate goal. Most powerful women are evil. In short, fairy tales teach girls to "play dead across the path of some young man who has been led to believe that he rules the world."[15] In *Only Children* pretty Lolly and plain Mary Ann, on a visit to Anna the powerful wise-woman in her mother's cottage in the woods, are characters modelled on the archetypes of the fairy tale. The same is also true of their mothers. In *The Second Sex* Simone de Beauvoir commented that

> Woman is the Sleeping Beauty, Cinderella, Snow White, she who receives and submits. In song and story the young man is seen departing adventurously in search of a woman; he slays the dragon, he battles giants, she is locked in a tower, a palace, a garden, a cave; she is chained to a rock, a captive, sound asleep: she waits.[16]

Madonna Kolbenschlag considered such passivity representative of a "sleep" of the self, and drew connections to concretely narcotic expression in women's behaviour – drugs, reading a lot, napping. "Daytime sleeping is a form of suicide. Amazing numbers of women

---

[14] Marcia Lieberman, "'Some Day My Prince Will Come'. Female Acculturation Through the Fairy Tale," *College English* 34 (1972) 383-95. Reprinted in Jack Zipes (ed.), *Don't Bet on the Prince. Contemporary Feminist Fairy Tales in North America and England* (London: Gower, 1986). For an important essay which comments on attempts by Lurie and Bruno Bettelheim to promote fairy tales as pyschologically healthy for children see Rosan A. Jordan and F. A. DeCaro, "Women and the Study of Folklore," *SIGNS* 11, 3 (1986), 500-518.

[15] J. Waelti-Walters, "On Princesses," *International Journal of Women's Studies* 2 (1979), 180-88. (Quoted p.180).

[16] Simone de Beauvoir, *The Second Sex* (New York: Bantam, 1970), p.272.

resort to it," she reported.[17] Consumerism or invalidism are similar tactics, offering an escape from a half life, and a response to personal invalidation. In *Only Children*, Celia is rarely fully awake; she drifts dreamily about, reading continually and frequently needing a nap. Prevented from working by Dan, often ill, she is a locked away princess who admits at one point that she would give anything to sleep for "days and days. Or months ... years. If it wasn't for Lolly, I sometimes think I'd ... You know." (p.202). In contrast to Celia's deathwish, Honey Hubbard is distinctly non-suicidal, adopting the strategy of a "little girl" persona, and a continual flirtatiousness which keeps her handsome prince on his toes. In "Witches and Fairies: Fitzgerald to Updike" (1971) Lurie had herself drawn attention to the passivity of the fairy tale princess, and the attraction of her entranced quality for men, whether the trance is physical virginity, psychic virginity (unaroused sexuality), or a politically or intellectually unawakened character (Gwendolen Harleth or the Princess Casamassima).[18] Lurie went on to consider the persistence of fairy tale motifs in contemporary fiction, dwelling particularly on *Tender is the Night*. In Fitzgerald's novel Nicole escapes from the evil spell (in her case insanity following paternal incest) but is only able to become completely cured once she stops being dependent on her husband. In her little girl role, Honey is very clearly modelled on the adult Nicole Diver, the archetypal Southern belle, with the role of father-as-sexual threat reserved by Lurie for Dan Zimmern.

In response to criticisms of fairy tale there has been an outpouring of revisionings to feminist ends, notably in the works of Anne Sexton and Angela Carter, and including Lurie herself, whose 1980 collection, *Clever Gretchen* promoted active heroines by its selection of tales. The collection none the less drew fire in some quarters. Brigid Brophy was withering. "I would as soon give a child a ticket for *Psycho* as a collection of such tales."[19] Brophy shifted the ground back to politics and class to attack Lurie: "A reader of the type she seems to expect would conclude from the majority of her chosen stories that the world is supposed to be divided into absolute rulers and peasants or very rich and very poor."[20]

---

[17] Madonna Kolbenschlag, *Goodbye Sleeping Beauty: Breaking the Spell of Feminine Myths and Models* (London: Marion Boyars, 1979), p.18.

[18] "Witches and Fairies: Fitzgerald to Updike," *New York Review of Books*, XVII, 9 (2 December 1971), 6-10.

[19] Brigid Brophy, "Feminist Folk Tales," *Times Literary Supplement*, 4034 (18 July 1980), 808.

[20] Brophy, p.808.

What Brophy had clearly missed was Lurie's own preceding engagement with the issues of both class and gender in fairy tale, in *Only Children*. Mary Ann's story of the wish-box which frames the action offers a child's version of the American Dream, and of the consequences of unchecked materialism and fulfilment of consumerist desires. The tale takes off from the Amoco gas-station symbol, a winged horse, aligning the Pegasus of the American imagination with conspicuous consumption, as Mary Ann wishes for a swimming pool, jungle gym, and candy store, among other objects of desire. Later when she overhears her mother's description of her as an "ugly duckling" Mary Ann takes up the fantasy again. As in all such fairy tales the wishes granted by the wishbox rebound upon the wisher. The queen (mother) wishes for strawberry soda and peach ice cream to issue from the faucets, and is promptly engulfed with the king in the ensuing flood.

> So they drowned and were dead. And a little thin
> voice came out of the hole in the top of the wish-box,
> and it said 'Nyah nyah. You asked for it.' (p.158).

As a metaphor for American greed, fed by rags-to-riches stories (the Hubbards' car is named for Benjamin Franklin) the tale suggests that America got what it asked for in the Thirties, in more ways than one. Bill Hubbard may denounce fairy stories as irrational and superstitious (p.27), but his daughter knows better and is able to use them. At the close of the novel, the tale of the wishbox is reprised, and the novel returns with it, as in all good fairy tales, to the status quo. This time Mary Ann offers a revision of the original, restoring her run-over dog Woozle to life, reincarnated not as an ugly mutt but as a handsome prince who sprouts wings, flies over the drowning pair, and plucks them from danger with his paws. A less than mythic Pegasus, more like the friendly animals of Benjamin's vision of folk tale, he turns off the flood from the wishbox and wishes everything back to rights: "and they all lived happily ever after." (p.219). In imagination, Mary Ann has turned the clock back, rescued the characters from the consequences of their own greed, and at the same time taken full possession of her own imaginative powers, no longer symbolised by Amoco, but by her very own Woozle.

Mary Ann is similarly adept in her restaging of one of the classic fairy tales. When Lolly and Mary Ann play princesses, climbing trees, Lolly proceeds rather circumspectly, afraid that her underwear will be visible, whereas Mary Ann explores dangerously close to the thin, upper branches. Lolly (aka Princess Elinore of the White Meadows) describes her tree as a castle, though not her principal castle which is "on a mountain in the middle of a forest surrounded by a howling desert" (p.67) an uncomfortable image of defensive isolation. Mary Ann (aka Princess Miranda of the Larch Mountains) transforms her tree into a sailing ship, the Flying Horse, with herself as the captain in the crow's nest, spotting sharks and whales and bellowing "Thar she blows!" p.67. The fantasy owes more to Captain Ahab or to Hornblower than to Grimm or Perrault. Lolly's story concentrates on looking out for the arrival of a prince, a tale which Mary Ann dismisses as "sort of dull ... because nothing much ever happens." (p.73). Her own plans do not involve marriage but hordes of suitors who will "help me go and fight armies and kill horrible giants and build towns in one day." (p.73). Mary Ann is a far cry from passive subservience.   Where Lolly is attractive, and repeatedly complimented by adults on her meek, biddable nature, plain and skinny Mary Ann has a temper and displays it frequently. When the girls decide to stage a play she rejects Sleeping Beauty in favour of the Brothers Grimm's "The Goose Girl" in which she plays a variety of roles and triumphantly usurps the place of her prettier friend. This particular tale, generally understood in terms of the need for the female to gain autonomy, stand up for herself and recognise that neither mother nor money can protect her, is an apt choice for toughminded Mary Ann, who finds handsome princes distinctly boring.[21] The children's play demonstrates how a child can use fairy tales creatively, in this case to reverse capitalist and sexist conventions. In the tale, the old queen (dying) sends her daughter to marry a far away prince, accompanied by her maid, a magic charm, and Falada, the talking horse. When the princess loses the charm, the maid takes over and becomes the bride, while the princess becomes a goose girl. Falada is decapitated. When the real princess's identity is finally discovered, the maid-pretender is put in a barrel of nails and rolled to and fro to her death. On one level the tale epitomises the nefarious example offered by fairy tale of passive suffering and division between girls. The reader may recall Lurie's own comment that whenever she read tales in which one daughter was ill-tempered, spiteful and plain and the other gentle, kind and pretty, she knew that the latter was her sister, who was

> as good as she was beautiful, [and] would grow up to marry the prince, while I would be lucky if I didn't end up being rolled downhill in a barrel of nails.[22]

---

[21] Bruno Bettelheim, *The Uses of Enchantment* (London: Penguin, 1978).

[22] "Witches and Fairies", p.6.

In the play Lolly remains a passive Princess. Mary Ann, however, translates art into life and life into art with a vengeance. The damage to her pigtail, chopped off onstage to make the magic charm, is as nothing compared to Celia's misery as she sees the relevance of the play's theme of usurped affections to her own life. (Honey has absented herself for a rendezvous with Dan.) When Falada (headless, but not voiceless, and also played by Mary Ann) declares that if the princess's mother could see her fallen condition "her heart would break in two" (p.113), the play world and the frame world coalesce as Celia breaks out sobbing and exits sharp left. As a result the play breaks off before the Princess can regain her rights, leaving the rich girl reduced to penury and the maid in the ascendancy, having seized prince, money and power by her own efforts. Rather as Benjamin suggested, Mary Ann, chopping off her pigtail, deposing an aristocrat and taking on a whole variety of male and female roles, has demonstrated a capacity to connect her imagination to action. In this version of the story, the status quo – whether economic or gendered – is never restored.

"The Goose Girl" also acts as an analogy, or play-within-the-play, to the events of the main plot. Dividing her novel into five acts (one for each day) and situating events in the classic greenwood and holiday location, Lurie also reproduces the magical transformations of festive comedy. In this *Midsummer Night's Dream*, not all of them are reassuring. Glimpses behind the scenes (e.g. to Anna's secret love for Dan) convert the apparently solid family relationships into illusion and pretence. Imagination can nevertheless turn ugliness into power. Mary Ann hears Honey describe her as an Ugly Duckling, but uses art to transform herself. Her pretty mother, however, ducked in the creek by Dan, undergoes a reverse transformation from swan to duck. Honey's revenge on Dan illustrates the way in which stories can spill over into life. In *Only Children* women who tell stories gain access to power: Mary Ann, Anna and Honey. Celia, however, only reads. In the first chapter of the novel Honey firmly establishes her credentials as femme fatale in the tale she tells of Landon Clay, an adolescent beau who abducted her teddy bear ostensibly because he was "jealous of Teddy, sleeping up so close to me in mah bed every night" (p.31). Honey volunteered the story as a riposte to Bill who had declared that Mary Ann was too old to be clutching her teddy bear, that her behaviour was childish. Honey turns on him: "Why in tarnation shouldn't Mary Ann act childish? She's a child isn't she?" (p.31) and goes on to recall that she had kept her teddy until she was at college. There is nothing childish, however, about the story which she tells, which scores points over men in general and both Bill and Dan in particular. Honey's tale both leads Dan on while at the same time warning him to be circumspect. Honey refused to pay the ransom for her teddy (a late night rendezvous in a romantic location) on the grounds **not** of physical timidity but of her public role.

> Ah wasn't worried about mah virtue, Ah could take care of that; Ah was worried about mah reputation (p.31).

Mock childishness here conceals an erotic subtext (in the terminology of the period a "teddy" was a garment worn close to the skin) and sentimental immunity. The teddy ended up in France with the American forces and Landon, whose fate is merely an aside to that of the bear: "Ah just hope the Huns didn't get him, like they did silly old Landon". (p.32). Honey communicates her real indifference to men indirectly through story. Dan, however, is not a clever enough reader to see that she is unlikely to succumb to him. Later, when Dan vents his frustration by ducking Honey in the river (turning her from swan to ugly duckling in a nastier revision of fairy tale) Honey ostensibly forgives him, and offers to trim his hair, all the time telling the tale of Eddie Rose, a "down home" barber, and the haircut he gave to Frank Ferguson. Frank had jilted Eddie's sister, and on the morning of his wedding to another girl, had his hair trimmed and anointed by Eddie. Colour blind, Frank admired the result in the mirror and departed for the wedding ceremony – with bright green hair. Snipping, combing, cooing and fluttering around Dan, Honey weaves a tale which conceals her own intention to carry out a similar tonsorial revenge. As the laughter subsides, she comments that "there's more than one way to cook a goose" p.168 and taking her cue from Mary Ann's amputated pigtail in "The Goose Girl", accidentally-on-purpose cuts off one half of Dan's luxuriant moustache. Both the Hubbard women appear to demonstrate the empowering nature of tale-telling, deploying it to their own advantage, if only in a relatively comic mode.

It is, however, Dan's transformation which reminds the reader that there is a darker side to fairy tale. For all its creative pleasures, imaginative life has its concomitant dangers. Lurie went on to edit *The Oxford Book of Modern Fairy Tales* (1993) and in her introduction has this to say of these stories of magic and transformation.

> The fairy tale survives because it presents experience in vivid symbolic form. Sometimes we need to have

the truth exaggerated and made more dramatic, even fantastic, in order to comprehend it.[23] As an example she cites the fancy dress party, where we suddenly recognise that one of our acquaintances is essentially a dancing doll. In *Only Children* Dan originally features as a dashing cowboy. When he visits the local store he adopts a gunslinger role, offering to "clean out your store" (p.51) and "set this town on fire tonight". The country store keeper remains impassively dignified, surrounded by sacks of beans, oats and rice, in surroundings which are a very far cry from the world of advertising products. Mary Ann remembers Dan appearing at Lolly's birthday party as a Wild West outlaw threatening a stick-up, who then handed out candy from his sack. But the image also suggests that in some sense, for all his free spending and entertaining ways, Dan is fundamentally a bit of a cowboy, intent on robbery on a broader scale, and careless of damage. Somehow, in the Fourth of July celebrations that evening, Dan's son Lenny does get quite badly burned. Lenny is reading *Dracula*, and shows Lolly the cover, depicting "a tall handsome man in fancy party clothes, with shiny black hair and two thin black lines of moustache on his lip" (p.161) carrying off a woman in a nightgown. When Lolly sees her father later that night wearing a shiny party hat, the image recreates Dan to Lolly as Dracula, a man intent on sucking some poor woman dry. Like a children's writer whom Lurie admires, Edith Nesbit (whose 1907 novel *The Enchanted Castle* also involves a wish ring and a children's play which goes badly wrong) Lurie reminds her readers that stories release images into the mind which may have delightful – or disastrous – results.[24] Fairy tales cannot be envisaged as unchanging mythic reservoirs of stable pre-bourgeois values. Tale tellers (and listeners) can interpret the script to very different ends.

Language behaves in similar fashion for the literal-minded children, continually offering uncontrollable quasi-Freudian slippages of meaning. Where Mary Ann moves from Amoco to Pegasus and then to Woozle, Lolly sees a more fearful potential in commercial products. The picture of the "Dutch Twins" on the scouring powder packet horrifies her because the bonneted twins appear to have no faces. (p.37). Nesbit's novel featured the Ugly-Wuglies, faceless dolls

---

[23] Alison Lurie (ed.), *The Oxford Book of Modern Fairy Tales* (Oxford: Oxford University Press, 1993), xi.

[24] See Edith Nesbit, *The Enchanted Castle* (London, Ernest Benn, 1956). For Lurie's own discussion of Edith Nesbit see "Riding the Wave of the Future," *New York Review of Books*, 25 October 1984, pp.19-22. Reprinted in Alison Lurie, *Don't Tell the Grown Ups. Subversive Children's Literature* (London: Bloomsbury, 1990).

which came to life with horrible results. For Lolly the stories in the family maid's copy of *Journal-American*, a scandal sheet, are taken literally, along with their illustrations of gangsters and criminals

> with their heads bent down or covered with hats to hide their awful-to-see faces. Or no faces at all because they are FACELESS CRIMINALS with nothing under their hats but a horrible smooth grey space (p.90).

Loss of firm identity is a constant anxiety for Lolly, who thinks of her mother as "unsafe, watery ... her face ... all wet and melting" (p.91), and is frequently in the grip of sexual terrors and nightmares about ghosts and monsters. Imagination, for all its enchantments, may prove a snare and a delusion. At one point Lolly hears Dan described as a "parlour pink" and a "skirt chaser ... always trying to get into some girl's panties" (p.127). Remembering the admonition of her Aunt Helen (confusingly not a real aunt, according to her mother) against the dangers of sex-pests (they could look like anyone's father, according to Helen p.91) Lolly is consumed with panic:

> Vulgar dirty words. Things suddenly are called a different name that makes them change invisibly ... Or other times the word holds still and the thing changes behind it and some ordinary safe word is wrong and awful (p.127).

"Parlour" and "pink" slide together to mean something unpleasant. "Ass" (the Biblical animal) suddenly means "behind". With the phrase "Ants in your pants" Lolly goes into associative free fall. The school word game ("How many words can you make out of --?") accelerates the process. The sequence of 'ants – aunties – pants – panties' renders Lolly's whole world unstable and threatening.

> Because you must never let any strange man or boy see your panties. It is a terrible magic that can turn even good safe ones into monsters. Like fairy tales where the handsome prince is changed into a bear or a hungry ravening grey wolf, and he has to have his head chopped off before he can change back. And you can never tell which ones will be bears. (p.128).

Lolly also overhears talk of events in Europe. The ambivalent nature of the imagination is expressed in the fantasy which she elaborates while half listening to the grownup discussion. For Lolly "Moosy Leeny" and his brownshirts promptly conjure up an attractive image of a mouse called Leena, royal, bejewelled and sleekly furred in grey, surrounded by more ordinary brown mice who follow their

Princess everywhere "with fanatical obedience and every other kind of obedience" (p.123). Imagination can return us to Ur-images in questionable fashion. In response to slippages of meaning, strange transformations and images apparently moving from books to life, Lolly is drawn to the image of the fanatical leader and followers. One way to halt threatening transformations – of words, people, things – is to yield to the lure of authoritarian fantasies which can apparently make everything hold still. (The connection to the social chaos of pre-Fascist Germany needs no elaboration.)

In the denouement of the novel, strange metamorphoses, confrontations and crises culminate in a drunken brawl, in which the adults' childish bad behaviour is watched by their scandalised children. Pragmatic Mary Ann emerges unscathed from the weekend; she is able to revise her vengeful fantasy of death by peach soda and restore the status quo, effectively using story to correct story. Her example suggests that the evils released by the imagination can only be fought by counterbalancing good from the same source.[25] Indeed, later she adopts the name Miranda for her own – featuring as Miranda Fenn in *Love and Friendship*. Women may establish their autonomy through story, despite the perils of hegemonic language. Although Mary Ann's story also supplies the last line of Lurie's novel, "and they all lived happily ever after." (p.219), readers of her later works are aware of the ironies. Defensive Lolly shows every sign of incipient psychological damage (as *The Truth About Lorin Jones* was to confirm). And in all the implied discussion of the effects of story in acculturating girls, one child has been left conspicuously out of the argument. Stepson Lenny, his mother's "only" child, remains the outsider in the family group. For him all the masculinities remain in place, and his only resource is a bitterly ironic detachment, as his later career as a sharp-penned literary critic in most of Lurie's other novels, makes clear. In Lolly's mind all the normal barriers between reality and imagination have come down, confronting her with an uncontrollable world. Something of the same happens in Lurie's novel, as art crosses over into life, as in the examples of Mary Ann's pigtail and Dan's moustache. Mary Ann sees her inmost fantasy acted out as her mother becomes the Ugly Duckling. Dan, superficially charming and generous, is revealed in his true colours, as the handsome prince/Dracula who is sucking Celia dry, and is a threat to

---

[25] I am much indebted here to Julia Briggs' astute analysis of the work of Nesbit. Julia Briggs, *A Woman of Passion. The Life of Edith Nesbit 1858-1924* (London: Hutchinson, 1987), p.220.

Lolly's development. Dan does not, of course, follow the example of Nicole Diver's incestuous father. But he becomes a similar image of horror to his daughter. Perhaps the worst example of the dangers of story is the romance, the degenerate fairy tale fantasy of gaining the prince which has caught Celia in its web. In contrast Anna stands out firmly against romantic love which she describes as "philosophically comforting. Like all illusions. When you're in love the world seems to make sense for a little while" (p.176). Just like authoritarian political systems, romantic love merely offers an illusory way out of chaos and confusion. Yet Anna is not let off lightly. There is a sting in the tail for the rationalist reader. As Celia comments, Anna is also "like a child", emotionally immature. "It's easy to be decent," she adds, "If you don't care about anybody too much." (p.198). In short, even the rejection of romantic love can itself be an illusion – as Lurie's next novel was to confirm.

Chapter Eight
Paleface into Redskin: *Foreign Affairs*

> A critic once divided American writers into two
> camps, the Palefaces and the Redskins. The Redskins
> looked west, toward the frontier, responded to the
> more physical and natural aspects of life, and often
> wrote in a style which expressed raw experience
> rather than literary form. The Palefaces looked east,
> wrote of those peculiarly elusive areas in American
> life, society and manners, and were preoccupied with
> craft and formal brilliance.[1]

With these words, Malcolm Bradbury opens his review of Alison
Lurie's *Foreign Affairs*. Following in the footsteps of Philip Rahv,
the critic in question,[2] Bradbury designates Lurie as a Paleface, noting
the enthusiastic reception of her work by the British (Palefaces to a
man) as indicative of her true forte as a novelist of manners in the
mould of Henry James and Edith Wharton. Rahv's paradigm of the
schizophrenic nature of the American literary artist is also, of course,
a close approximation to the conventional opposition between
America and Europe, and between nature and culture, as it is
commonly expressed in American fiction in the "International
Theme", the encounter in one novel between representatives of the
two cultures, which is coincidentally also the plot of *Foreign Affairs*.

Since ideas of what is characteristically American or
European, definitions of a national culture, stem as much from
literature as from life, the notion of intertextuality is once again
relevant here. If we define "text" as a system of signs, a text may
extend to include folklore, movies, the language of dress, symbolic
systems, and the constructions of cultural – or even, if we accept
Lacanian notions of the primacy of language – individual identity.
The "International Theme" may be defined as itself an intertext, a set
of plots, characters, images and conventions to which a particular
novel refers. Moreover, its central situation, in which characters are
physically translated and transformed, as a result of crossing from one
culture, one set of signs, to another, itself thematises intertextuality.

---

[1] Malcolm Bradbury, "The Paleface Professor", *The Times*, 19 January 1985, p.6.
[2] Philip Rahv, "Paleface and Redskin", in *Literature and the Sixth Sense* (London:
Faber, 1970), pp.1-6.

Transposition from one intertext to another necessarily brings into question the autonomy of the individual. In interview Lurie described the germ of the novel as an idea which "came to me at the Opera. I noticed that when the scene changed behind someone they looked different."[3] The theatrical context is appropriate. If individuals are passive to change, altered by a different cultural scene, they may be considered as acting within a social fiction, a text which is socially evolved, playing a role in a story which is directed elsewhere. In this sense, human experience may generate literature but such experience has already been filtered through forms of artistic organisation which may militate against - or even taboo - certain forms of experience. As Lurie's own collection of feminist folktales suggested,[4] too many women have waited around for a handsome prince, to the detriment of creative experience. Fifty-four year old Vinnie Miner (the *major* heroine of *Foreign Affairs*) risks the opposite fate, giving up all hope of an erotic existence because "in English literature, to which in early childhood Vinnie had given her deepest trust – and which for half a century has suggested to her what she might do, think, feel, desire, and become – women of her age seldom have any sexual or romantic life."[5]

Conversely the notion of life as imitating art opens the way for a dramaturgical concept of the self, continually creating itself through role play. Vinnie Miner's *alter ego*, Rosemary Radley, a British actress, escapes from type-casting only to undergo a series of rapid transformations which pass well beyond the bounds of creative adaptivity and into the realm of madness. Where Vinnie is more attentive to a past script than to present reality, Rosemary risks the collapse of a self which is already shifting and permeable at the boundaries. In translating characters from one cultural frame (America) to another (London) Lurie investigates whether the result is the regeneration of an ossified individual in a creative rewriting of the scripted self, or merely a defensive adaptation to different defining norms. By employing the International Theme, Lurie exposes her characters to a variety of intertextual frames, creating comic, ironic, or even tragic effects, as characters who have scripted themselves in

---

[3] Christopher Tookey, "The witch guide to literary London", *Books and Bookmen*, 352 (January 1985), p.25.

[4] Alison Lurie, *Clever Gretchen and Other Forgotten Folktales* (London: Heinemann, 1980).

[5] Alison Lurie, *Foreign Affairs* (London: Abacus, 1986), p.75. Subsequent page references follow citations in parentheses.

accordance with one acculturated model undergo slippage into less exalted or more challenging roles.

The International Theme has been a staple of the American novel from Hawthorne's *Dr. Grimshawe's Secret* to Twain's *Innocents Abroad* and Edith Wharton's *Roman Fever*. Broadly defined, the situation involves the encounter between the moral consciousness of an American and the rich cultural atmosphere of Europe, with the ensuing clash of values demonstrating either the provincialism of the American, at sea in a European world of established customs and sophisticated manners, or the precarious moral footing of the experienced European. The American innocent abroad may feature (positively) as democratic, spontaneous, natural and sincere, or (less attractively) as crude, vulgar and ignorant, while the European sophisticate is alternatively representative of all that is aesthetic and civilised in culture, or conversely of a decadent world of deceit, artifice and aristocratic corruption. Henry James, past master of the theme, gives it classic expression in *The American* (1877) in which Christopher Newman, thwarted in his love for Claire de Cintré by the machinations of the corrupt Bellegardes (who include a murderer within their aristocratic ranks) nobly eschews revenge, out of the American generosity of his spirit, thus revealing a natural nobility of worth rather than birth, which is opposed to the false nobility of the Bellegardes. It is something of a fixed fight, as highly idealised American virtue does battle with stereotypical European villainy.[6] In less clearcut fashion, in *Daisy Miller* (1878) the eponymous heroine falls foul of her fellow American expatriates in Rome, her innocence recognisable only to a young Italian. This shift towards the Europeanised American as villain is also marked in *The Portrait of A Lady* (1881) where Isabel Archer becomes the prey of the self-centred expatriate Gilbert Osmond. By *The Ambassadors* (1903) the American himself is culpable. Chad Newsome pursues a love affair with Madame de Vionnet only as a temporary diversion from his business interests. His countryman, Lambert Strether, despatched to fetch Chad home to America, ultimately crosses to the lady's side, transferring his allegiance to the ostensibly corrupting European mistress, whose love for Chad is real. James therefore offers a range of possibilities, from the stereotypical American

---

[6] For a comprehensive and accessible discussion of the International Theme in James see Christof Wegelin, *The Image of Europe in Henry James* (Dallas: Southern Methodist University Press, 1958) and Tony Tanner, *Henry James. The Writer and His Work* (Amherst: University of Massachusetts Press, 1985). The rapid sketch here owes much to them both.

innocent, corrupted by sinister Europeans, to the vulnerable European, exploited and about to be betrayed by the New World.

Americans do not, however, feature very effectively in James as redemptive of Old World corruption. Ironically, for that particular variation, the reader must turn to a less exalted version of the International Theme, by a British writer, Frances Hodgson Burnett's *Little Lord Fauntleroy* (1886). A bestseller in its day, when the distinctions between adult and children's fiction were elastic, the novel was much admired by Gladstone who told its author that "the book would have great effect in bringing about added good feeling between the two nations and making them understand each other."[7] Despite addressing her as "noblest of neighbours and most heavenly of women"[8] James was somewhat jealous of Burnett's success,[9] unsurprisingly, perhaps, given that in *Pilgrimage* Dorothy Richardson's heroine recommends that one should read "as Anglo-American history, first *Little Lord Fauntleroy* and then *The Ambassadors*."[10]

Although the novel involves a persistent criticism of adult values from the child's standpoint, Burnett is relatively evenhanded in her treatment of the two cultures, depicting illness and unemployment among the New York working poor as well as poverty and squalor in Britain. Cedric Errol, a child living in straitened circumstances with his widowed mother, is suddenly transplanted to the home of his rich grandfather, the Earl of Dorincourt, a thoroughly selfish English aristocrat, whose heir he becomes. Little Lord Fauntleroy (as he now is) promptly humanises his grandfather by the force of love, bringing out the good in him simply by assuming that he **is** good, and scripting him into that role. In the comic plot, a false claimant to the title is bested with the help of Mr. Hobbs, an American grocer of pronounced democratic views, initially scathing about the aristocracy, who finally becomes ancestor-mad and settles in England. As Alison Lurie notes[11] the appeal of the book depended upon its combination of the

---

[7] Ann Thwaite, *Waiting for the Party. The Life of Frances Hodgson Burnett* (London: Secker and Warburg, 1974), pp.107-8; Frances Hodgson Burnett, *Little Lord Fauntleroy* (London: Puffin, 1981).

[8] Thwaite, p.xi.

[9] Juliet Dusinberre, *Alice to the Lighthouse: Children's Books and Radical Experiments in Art* (London: Macmillan, 1987), p.30.

[10] Dusinberre, p.30.

[11] Alison Lurie, "Happy Endings: Frances Hodgson Burnett", in *Don't Tell the Grown-Ups: Subversive Children's Literature* (London: Bloomsbury, 1990), pp.136-43.

"long lost heir" plot with the International Theme, and a form of secular conversion story, involving the regeneration of an older person through the influence of an affectionate and attractive child. Cedric is also the embodiment of republican virtue, whereas his grandfather represents England, the past, age, rank and selfish pride. Lurie herself draws the analogy with *The Portrait of a Lady* "which also features the confrontation between a charming, eager, natural young American and representatives of an older and more devious civilization"[12] – though Burnett, unlike James, provides a happy ending.

It is perhaps unsurprising that a writer whose second (unpublished) novel despatched its heroine, Chloe Newcome, to discover crime, poverty and despair in post-war Europe[13] should direct her attention to the International Theme. In *Foreign Affairs* two American academics, on sabbatical in London, provide the focus for an exploration of the special relationship, as it obtains in the present, as created by past literary models and, by extension, as an example of the fashion in which literary models may function for good or ill. When Vinnie Miner, sceptical and worldly wise rather than innocent, and in her devout Anglophilia a close approximation to one of James's Europeanised Americans, encounters Chuck Mumpson, an Oklahoma "cowboy", she learns a lesson in morals. In the more mannered companion plot, Fred Turner, an all-American hero, has an affair with an English aristocratic lady of a certain age and experience, and feels as if he has got into the pages of a James novel, though whether *The American* or *The Ambassadors* is a moot point. Any easy binary oppositions of American innocence to European experience are subject to revision in a novel which interrogates the nature of the relationship by setting it within a variety of intertextual frames. Paradigms of innocence are thematised by Vinnie's research topic (children's play-rhymes) and undergo radical transformation in the interplay of dramaturgical and folk motifs, literary texts and intertexts, as the four main characters move from American to British intertexts, from Alcott and James to Burnett, Gay and Dickens, and from literature to folktale.

The characteristic note is struck from the beginning. Vinnie Miner is explicitly signalled as the creation of fiction by a series of authorial asides. The reader is informed, for example, that "In less time than it takes to read this paragraph" (p.2) she has installed herself comfortably on the flight to London, an experienced transatlantic

---

[12] "Happy Endings", p.140.

[13] Private interview with Alison Lurie, Key West, Florida, 19 February 1991.

traveller. The image of a character creating her own cultural reality, enhanced by the capsule effect of air travel which suspends her between two worlds, also reflects Vinnie's Anglophilia. Her dearest fantasy is that she may one day live permanently in London and become an Englishwoman. In advance of her first visit, England had been "slowly and lovingly shaped and furnished out of her favourite books" (p.15) so that when she eventually reached "the country of her mind" (p.15) she found it almost akin to entering the pages of English literature. The opening chapter recapitulates the process of approaching England through framing fictions. Entry into a different world is also entry into a series of texts. Vinnie can hardly wait to get away from the aptly named *Atlantic* in which a slighting reference to her research from a critic (Leonard Zimmern) has filled her with fantasies of revenge. Instead she takes refuge in the "cosily confiding" (p.8) pages of British *Vogue*, and is calmed by *The Times*, compared here to the "voice of an English nanny" (p.11). Finally "the shadows of war darken over Singapore" (p.15) as she flies on, engrossed in *The Singapore Grip*. Briskly classifying her seatmate, Chuck Mumpson, from the semiotic indicators of his tan suit and rawhide tie as "a Southern Plains States businessman of no particular education or distinction" (p.11) she fends off his conversational overtures by lending him *Little Lord Fauntleroy*, mentally casting him as the democratic grocer, Mr. Hobbs, whom he slightly resembles.

Vinnie's casual dismissal of Chuck rebounds upon her however. While she is haunted in the London Library by "the portly, well-dressed spirit of Henry James" (p.59), and entertains erotic fantasies about writers and critics (starring roles go to Lionel Trilling, M. H. Abrams, and John Cheever, *inter alia*) Chuck allows the fantasy of the long lost heir to take hold. Predictably his quest ends in apparent disillusion when he discovers that his ancestor, the Hermit of South Leigh (a legendary troglodyte clad in animal skins) was in fact an illiterate pauper acting in someone else's fantasy: Old Mumpson was hired to impersonate a hermit in an eighteenth century aristocrat's decorative grotto. Later, however, Chuck realises that illiteracy need not preclude wisdom: "There's a hell of a lot of learning that isn't in books." (p.167). It is a lesson which Vinnie is about to learn. Unwillingly she begins to detect an uncomfortable resemblance between Chuck's fantasy of being an English lord and her own of becoming an English lady. She is slower, however, to recognise that she is as unable as Leonard Zimmern to see the relevance of her field of research – oral folklore – to her own life. While she casts Chuck as Mr. Hobbs, he is actually functioning within a very different intertextual frame. With his ancestry, his leathery tan and his garb of animal skins (a cowboy hat trimmed with feathers, a fleecy sheepskin coat and a leather jacket) Chuck figures as the "animal groom" of folk tale. Typically such tales centre on the shock of recognition when what seemed vulgar, coarse or "beastly" reveals itself as the source of human happiness.[14] (*Beauty and the Beast* is a representative example.) Originally Vinnie had found sexual activity embarrassing (one relationship foundered on the excessively hirsute nature of her lover) and is now poised to abandon "the foamy backwash and weed-choked turbulence of passion" (p.76).

The metaphor is subconsciously revelatory. Chuck's greenish waterproof outer layer (a semi-transparent plastic raincoat of repellent design), his pearl studs and habit of slow blinking, identify him as the Frog Prince.[15] Even his occupation – as a sanitary engineer conversant with drains and wells – fits the bill, though he has now been "flushed out" (p.123) by his company's redundancy scheme. Vinnie, like the princess in the story, fails to spot his potential, even when he covers her with green slime (avocado and watercress soup). Eventually, however, she admits him to her table and her bed, and discovers that nature has its points over culture. With the destruction of the loathed outer skin (in favour of a Burberry) Chuck is transformed from frog to prince, revealed as "One of nature's noblemen." (p.276). The phrase, used by James in *The American*,[16] and something of a cliché of American literature, is given a fresh resonance by the folklore motif. As a frog prince, Chuck does come into his own in Europe, in Vinnie's arms, rather than as heir to a fortune. He also negotiates a more objective and productive relation with the past, using his engineering expertise to drain a sunken archaeological site.

Vinnie had read *Little Lord Fauntleroy* without absorbing its message, that it is never too late for change and regeneration.

---

[14] Bruno Bettelheim, *The Uses of Enchantment. The Meaning and Importance of Fairy Tales* (London: Penguin, 1978), pp.277-310.

[15] Maureen Corrigan is the one reviewer who drew attention to this motif, reviewing the novel in *Village Voice Literary Supplement*, October 1984, p.5.

[16] Christof Wegelin notes that James used the phrase in the New York edition of *The American* (p.91) as a revision of "a noble fellow" (Rinehart edition, p.63). Emerson wrote in his *Journal* of "Nature's Gentlemen, who need no discipline, but grow straight up into shape and grace and can match the proudest in dignified demeanour and the gentlest in courtesy." Thoreau, Margaret Fuller, Howells and Melville all make conspicuous reference to the concept of natural nobility. (*The Image of Europe in Henry James*, p.178).

Through Chuck she too is transformed, realising that she has allowed the defining voices of English literature to overdetermine her existence. Now, "English literature … has suddenly fallen silent … because she is just too old." (p.199). In the world of classic British fiction, Vinnie sees, almost the entire population is under fifty (as may have been true of the real world when the novel was invented) and the few older women are cast in minor parts as comic, pathetic or disagreeable. It is assumed that nothing interesting can happen to them. Influenced by Chuck's transformation Vinnie refuses now to become a minor character in her own life. For years, she has accustomed herself to the idea that the rest of her life would be "a mere epilogue to what was never, it has to be admitted, a very exciting novel." (p.199). Now, however, she realises that beyond the frame of fiction life has its own horizons:

> this world … is not English literature. It is full of people over fifty who will be around and in fairly good shape for the next quarter-century: plenty of time for adventure and change, even for heroism and transformation. (p.199).

Vinnie, whose research into children's rhymes is largely a product of her own nostalgia for childhood, has also to learn that age and experience have their merits. In a particularly unpleasant encounter with a grasping child, who regales her with obscene verses, she realises that innocence is not the preserve of youth, and that her thesis – that British rhymes are more lyrical and literary than their cruder American counterparts – is untenable. If the child in question has come a long way from Little Lord Fauntleroy, Chuck, however unprepossessing his initial impression, fulfils the role to a tee. Although he, too, is no stereotypical innocent (driving while intoxicated he was responsible for a boy's death) Chuck's persistent vision of self-centred Vinnie as a good woman eventually scripts her into the role. Much as the Earl lived up to Cedric's expectations, so Vinnie fulfils Chuck's. Like Christopher Newman, when the opportunity for revenge on the hated Zimmern occurs (by proxy through his daughter) Vinnie allows her better impulses to triumph, attentive to the inner voice of Chuck. Appealed to by Ruth (nee Zimmern) to deliver a message to Fred Turner which will reunite these star-crossed lovers, Vinnie hesitates. Fred is on Hampstead Heath observing the solstice: "most people Vinnie knows certainly wouldn't expect her to go to Hampstead Heath. But one person would … Chuck Mumpson." (p.244). At the end of the novel, heroically braving the muggers, the latter day heirs to Gay's *Beggar's Opera*,

Vinnie does bear the message to Fred. Rejecting a false model in classic British fiction, she adopts a better one, the product of the interaction of folklore and children's literature.

More importantly she recognises the variety of human existence, and the potentially coercive nature of literary models. At a symposium on "Literature and the Child", the lecturer declares that "The Child's" moral awareness must be awakened by responsible literature. Vinnie is now in no mood to look to literature for guidance. "There is no Child," she wants to shout, "only children, each one different, unique." (p.235). The realisation cuts two ways. Though Vinnie has shed her passivity to the discourses of literature which previously wrote her, it is in fact to children's literature that she owes that transformation. Moreover, if the stereotypes of age and youth have been comprehensively revised, the novel none the less appears to conform to the paradigms provided by Burnett and James, as a Europeanised American is redeemed by love, and American virtue triumphs with nature over the rigid forms of European culture. Under Chuck's influence, Vinnie concludes that doing things for others may have caused most of the trouble of her life, "but it has also caused most of the surprise and interest and even in the end joy." (p.270).

The novel does not end, however, on such a potentially schmaltzy note as *Little Lord Fauntleroy*. Although Vinnie finally wakes up to the fact that Chuck loves her and she him, it is very much a case of too little, too late. Because of her dogged attachment to her image as English lady, Vinnie fears cultural redefinition by proximity to Chuck. When she is juxtaposed with him, her British friends are likely to equate them as each "rather simple, vulgar, and amusing – a typical American." (p.206). As a result she fails to join him in Wiltshire, where he dies of a heart attack. Vinnie's story is also only part of the novel, doubled, and its implications to some extent reversed, by that of her fellow expatriate, Fred Turner. Lurie's novel practices what it preaches, offering a choice of outcomes to the International Theme, weaving a plot in one direction and then, Penelope-like, unpicking the threads in the companion plot, so that *Foreign Affairs* resists reinforcing any one literary model.

Even more than Vinnie, Fred sees himself within a literary frame, thinking of John Gay's *Trivia* as he walks the streets of London (Gay is his research topic) and imagining himself as a character in a

Henry James novel (p.87).[17]   Others, however, envisage him in a variety of less prestigious roles, as the hero of a Gothic romance, as an actor in *Love's Labour's Lost*, a character in an American detective series, or "the guy who fought the giant man-eating extraterrestrial cabbage in *The Thing from Beyond*" (p.25).   Nobody connects him with light comedy or game shows; his brooding good looks militate against certain parts.   Quite the reverse of Chuck, Ivy League Fred, an American aristocrat in terms of entitlement psychology, is recognised as her handsome prince by his wife Roo (Ruth Zimmern).   The latter, now surnamed March in homage to "tomboy" Jo in Alcott's *Little Women*, whom she closely resembles physically (a long chestnut braid) and in character, unwittingly follows the fate of her chosen model, forfeiting her trip to Europe, like Jo, as the result of independence and frankness.   Very much a female version of Chuck, Roo is at home in nature and initiates her relationship with Fred outdoors, following a riding excursion.   Just as Vinnie found her world transformed by Chuck, so Fred under Roo's influence sees it as "naked, beautiful, full of meaning." (p.44).   Fred's story, however, is a replay in reverse of Vinnie's, from frankness, sincerity and natural sexuality in America to the constricting European world of manners and culture.   Appropriately, as an artist, Roo draws her effects from the juxtaposition of nature and culture, often with satiric results.   Her exhibition, "Natural Forms" includes a shot of two overweight politicians next to a pair of beef cattle, for example.[18]   Fred, however, is discomfited by a photograph of his own penis in juxtaposition with a large and beautiful mushroom, and even less delighted by the presence of two other unidentified male organs – even if one is juxtaposed with an asparagus stalk, and the other with a rusty bolt.   In the ensuing marital fracas, Fred concludes that Roo is not a lady, and exits sharply for Europe.

In Rosemary Radley, however, he appears to have found the real thing.   Herself the daughter of an earl, Rosemary specialises in acting highborn ladies, particularly in *Tallyho Castle*, a television series of snobbish appeal, which paints a fake picture of upper class country life.   The contrast between the two cultures is expressed for Fred by his two women.   Where Ruth flung herself into his arms, Fred has to court Rosemary in traditional fashion.   She is sophisticated

---

[17] Readers familiar with Lurie's work will note a further irony.   Fred is already a character in a novel – Lurie's first, *Love and Friendship* – a scene from which is referred to in *Foreign Affairs*, p.43, to establish Fred's obtuseness.

[18] Similar juxtapositions were a feature of the British magazine *Lilliput*. See Kaye Webb (ed.), *Lilliput Goes To War* (London: Hutchinson, 1985).

where Roo is naïve, graceful where Roo is coarse, reticent where Roo is outspoken, "Just as, compared with England, America is large, naïve, noisy, crude, etc." (p.81). Fred's revision of his mental image of Roo is a pompously textual operation, an example in his mind of "retrospective influence" (p.81). Just as Wordsworth forever altered our reading of Milton, "so Rosemary Radley has altered his reading of Ruth March." (p.81). Roo's previous natural, free behaviour, her rapid sexual surrender, now seems less a warranty of passion and sincerity than "hardly civilized" (p.82). Significantly, where he and Roo came together out of doors, he and Rosemary meet at the theatre, in a world of artifice and illusion. Fred, the expert on Gay, ascribes his conquest of Rosemary to eighteenth century virtues of civility and boldness. By politely remaining at Vinnie's party he was able to meet Rosemary, a congenital latecomer, and he subsequently pursues her as a challenge "undertaken in the same spirit that makes other Americans expend energy and ingenuity to view some art collection or local ceremony that is out of bounds to most tourists." (p.79).

In Rosemary's world – specifically, spending a weekend in an English country house – Fred revels in the sensation that "by some supernatural slippage between life and art, he has got into a Henry James novel like the one he watched on television" (p.87). In cold fact the televisual metaphor is more apt than the fictional. Rosemary is not just typecast on celluloid as an English lady, but also in life. Although she complains to Fred that she longs to play the classic parts ("I know what it is to feel murderous, coarse, full of hate." pp.88-89) he pooh-poohs her, refusing to envisage her in any character other than that of cultured aristocrat. When, however, the assembled house guests play charades, the childish game reveals raw experience beneath its formal surface. Presumably inspired by Dorothy Parker's dictum that "You can lead a whore to culture but you can't make her think" Rosemary's team chooses to dramatise the word "horticulture", breaking it down into three component parts, to reveal a coarse subtext beneath the surface cultivation. In the first, to Fred's horror, Rosemary appears as "whore". Since her costume is the identical nightgown in which she has just slept with Fred, the distinction between art and life almost dissolves. In the second ("Tit") she is part of a cow, and in the third a sulky schoolchild (reminiscent of Vinnie's ghastly informant) resisting the efforts of a schoolmaster to lead her to culture. The emphasis on language is also significant. Vinnie had previously described Rosemary's conversation as mere musical noise: "Words don't matter to actors as they do to a literary person. For them, meaning is mainly in expression and gesture; the text is just the libretto." (p.64). Gleefully Rosemary acts on this assumption, transforming her text in order to act out the parts denied her in life. In the charades, her homosexual friend Edwin actually seems more natural as a fortyish matron, than in real life as a male. Role play reveals the multifaceted nature of the self in creative ways. The arrival of the hostess's husband, however, reveals even more, as her lover has to be whisked into hiding. Faced with the visible evidence of upper-class corruption, Fred's Jamesian frame of reference wavers:

> only an hour ago he thought it was all beautiful, the real thing. James again, Fred thinks: a Jamesian phrase, a Jamesian situation. But in the novels the scandals and secrets of high life are portrayed as more elegant; the people are better mannered. Maybe because it was a century earlier; or maybe only because the mannered elegance of James' prose obfuscates the crude subtext. Maybe, in fact, it was just like now. (p.101).

Briskly excluding Rosemary from these speculations, Fred readjusts his James, determined to rescue his innocent beloved from these evil influences, and electing himself as the sterling young American champion James himself would have provided. "For the second time that day Fred has the giddy sense of having got into a novel." (p.101).

Ironically, however, Fred has once more got into the wrong fiction. To become Rosemary's true champion, he should have been less intent on stereotyping her as a lady, and paid more attention to the subtext, as the reference to "the real thing" indicates. In James's story of that title a well-bred couple offer themselves as an artist's models on the grounds that it would be good for him to use "the real thing; a gentleman ... or a lady."[19] When, however, the painter employs the lady he finds her so lacking in adaptive plasticity and expression that she is inferior as a model to his servants: "She was always a lady, certainly, and into the bargain was always the same lady. She was the real thing, but always the same thing."[20] As a result, the real thing turns out to be less valuable for artistic purposes than the fake; art depends upon the transformation of reality rather than reflecting the thing itself. Ultimately the real thing is the product of the creative imagination of the artist, just as, paradoxically, Rosemary is more

---

[19] Henry James, "The Real Thing" (1982), in Christof Wegelin (ed.), *Tales of Henry James* (New York: W. W. Norton, 1984), p.246.

[20] "The Real Thing", p.249.

herself when she demonstrates the power of her creative adaptation of words to role.

Where Vinnie finds a new role by accepting a "lower" subtext, in vulgar Chuck, Fred is determined to expunge it in favour of genteel forms, editing out any aspects of Rosemary's behaviour which he considers out of character. He even insists that she set an appropriate scene for their affair, badgering her to engage a charlady to clean up her grubby house. Meeting the pair at the Opera, Vinnie reflects that the dusty chaos of Rosemary's house seems an unsuitable backdrop for their love affair. Indeed, in the outcome it appears that Fred's arguments have carried the day. Rosemary hires Mrs. Harris, a cockney char, and as a result creates a scene that resembles "a commercial for some luxury product: the perfectly elegant party." (p.137). Surveying his surroundings, Fred congratulates himself that his rush of moral indignation during the country weekend was merely priggish and provincial, misled by a too-vivid memory of the novels of Henry James into condemning an entire society. Although Roo has now contacted him, and convinced him that she is innocent of adultery, and guilty only of bad taste, his standards are now those of European manners rather than American morals: "in Rosemary's world bad taste is not nothing: it is the outward and visible sign of an inward and spiritual flaw." (p.134). Unsurprisingly when Fred meets Chuck at the party, he assumes that someone so inappropriate to the elegant occasion cannot be real, but must be one of Rosemary's actor friends, trying out a role. Commenting on Chuck's origins, he quips that he has never been to Oklahoma, but that he saw the movie. In contrast, although he has yet to meet her, Mrs. Harris "sounds like the genuine article" (p.140). With his taste for Gay, Fred welcomes the crudity of Mrs. Harris's manners (as reported by Rosemary) as if she were a character out of eighteenth century literature, "a figure from the subplot of some robust comedy illustrated by Hogarth or Rowlandson." (p.142). As the alert reader may already recognise, the joke is very much on Fred, who finds himself starring in a rather different fictional role in the outcome, scripted in part by the character of Mrs. Harris.

The party ends in disaster when Fred's friend Joe Vogeler inadvertently reveals Fred's intention to return to America, on schedule, to teach summer school. Rosemary draws the conclusion that "it was only an act with you" (p.149) and breaks off the relationship. Fred is less a Christopher Newman or a Lambert Strether, than a Chad Newsome. He has encouraged Rosemary to love him unconditionally while intending to love her only as long as it was convenient. Although Fred pleads poverty as his motive for returning, he refuses Rosemary's offer of a loan, on the Victorian moral principle that a man cannot take money from a woman. Although the offer is made on the set of a television historical drama, with Rosemary in full makeup it is Fred, in her opinion, who is caught in a rigid role: "You think you're in some historical drama; it's you who ought to be in costume." (p.181). Accordingly, despite his American accent, Rosemary offers him a film role: "you could be a silent brooding undergardener or gypsy tramp." (p.181). Fred, however, can accept nothing less than heroic status. Instead, he swiftly reclaims the moral high ground by redefining Rosemary. The idea that he has fallen into a Henry James novel recurs, "but now he casts Rosemary in a different role, as one of James's beautiful, worldly, corrupt European villainesses." (p.194). Like his Australian friends, who describe their convict ancestors as adventurous and risk-taking, "Moll Flanders not Oliver Twist" (p.187), Fred is quick to cite chapter and verse of a supportive literary model, making an opportunistic choice of literary frame.

Where Vinnie learned the need to escape from overly constricting models, Fred has gone to the other extreme, and gets his comeuppance as a result of his belief that he can pick and choose freely between them. Rosemary also operates intertextually, with tragic results, breaking out of her role as English lady and shifting the frame of reference once more, from America to Britain and from James to Dickens. Once again truth comes into being through role play. Sharing a taxi with Vinnie, Rosemary takes the opportunity to complain about Fred; her speech alternates between her own upper class drawl and an accent so vulgar and coarse that "if they hadn't been alone Vinnie would have looked round to see who else was speaking." (p.209). She goes on alternating between being pathetically ladylike and a low comedy voice, slips into tenor to imitate a male friend, and concludes – to Vinnie's horror – by insulting the latter in a caricature of her own intonation and accent. On one level, of course, the scene appears to confirm Fred's estimation of Rosemary's fundamental falsity. Yet, crying over Fred, Rosemary's face is "distorted in a way it never becomes when she weeps on camera." (p.211). Rosemary believed that Fred loved her for herself alone, as the real thing: "He'd never even heard of *Tallyho Castle* ... He never even saw the show, he loved me anyhow." (p.211). Where Vinnie had been chary of introducing Chuck to her British friends, afraid of being redefined as of similarly American character, Rosemary actively sought role revision by contact with

Fred. She has been over-defined, as an English lady, and the cultural definition has constricted her life. Ironically, the fate which Vinnie so feared is actually visited upon her by her association with Fred. Gesturing at souvenir shops and hamburger joints, Rosemary accuses: "I've had it with all you fuckin' Americans. Why don't you stay home where you belong? Nobody wants you comin' over here, messin' up our country." (p.212). Uneasily Vinnie recognises the low comedy stage character as that of Mrs. Harris, whom Rosemary has taken to imitating. For Vinnie the episode reveals that there is "something unnatural, really, in the ability of certain persons to assume at will a completely alien voice and manner." (p.213); the practice "overturns our belief in the uniqueness of the individual." (p.213). The comment extends also to Vinnie, who has been acting the alien role of English lady and sacrificing her own uniqueness to the scripts of British fiction. When Rosemary uses her histrionic talents to become Vinnie Miner, she indicates that the two have more in common than Vinnie would care to concede.

If Vinnie's encounter with "Mrs. Harris" leaves her shaken, Fred's has even more bruising consequences. Entering Rosemary's house in search of his *Oxford Book of Eighteenth Century Verse*, Fred finds Mrs. Harris, a drunken slut, in the darkened basement drinking Rosemary's gin. Upstairs he recoils in horror at the dirt and disorder. Rosemary's bathroom is "littered and foul – the toilet, for instance, is full of turds." (p.226). When Mrs. Harris makes a pass at him in a drunken imitation of Rosemary's voice, he calls her a "dirty old cow" (p.228) and shoves her forcibly aside. Giving an edited account of the scene later to his friends, Fred converts it into comedy, "a scene from Smollett ... a cartoon by Rowlandson," (p.229). But as the alert reader may have guessed[21] Mrs. Harris is not so much an eighteenth century character as a modern one. In a moment of dreadful revelation Fred recalls the charlady's telltale birthmark, identical to Rosemary's: Mrs. Harris and Rosemary are one and the same. While Fred wandered the pages of James, Rosemary has adopted a character from another novel of transatlantic encounter, Dickens' *Martin Chuzzlewit*, in which Mrs. Harris features as Sairey Gamp's imaginary friend.

---

[21] Some of the most alert were Ferdinand Mount, "The lonely American", *Spectator*, 26 January 1985, p.24; Walter Clemons, "Lovers and Other Strangers", *Newsweek*, 104 (24 September 1984), p.80; Lorna Sage, "Adventures in the old world", *Times Literary Supplement*, 1 February 1985, p.109; Marilyn Butler, "Amor Vincit Vinnie", *London Review of Books*, 21 February 1985, pp.5-6.

> A fearful mystery surrounded this lady of the name of
> Harris, whom no one in the circle of Mrs. Gamp's
> acquaintance had ever seen ... There were conflicting
> rumours on the subject; but the prevalent opinion was
> that she was a phantom of Mrs. Gamp's brain.[22]

Thwarted by typecasting, Rosemary has created in life the part denied
her on stage. Fred had allowed the idea of her as cultivated, refined
and aristocratically English to become so fixed in his mind that
anyone who did not conform to the model could not be Rosemary.
Although her roleplay has now tipped her over into Gothic delusion –
her repressed self finally emerging, if not as the madwoman in the
attic, at least as the charwoman in the basement – Fred does little to
save her, though he nobly offers to see her once more in the *twenty
minutes* which he can spare before his flight departs.

Cultural transformations can work both ways. Where Vinnie,
the stereotypical sexless crone of British fiction, is transformed by
love, Rosemary evolves from beauty to hag, in the "loathly lady"
motif of folklore.[23] Chuck transforms himself from beast to prince,
Fred from prince to brute. The parallels are emphasised in the action.
In a reprise of the folklore motif, Fred is seen walking by Regent's
canal with the Vogelers. The latter equate his passion for Rosemary
with their infant's desire for an old rubber ball, its cracked surface
patterned with a dirty Union Jack. (They have been discussing
Rosemary's advanced age.) As the ball bounces into the "frog-green
water" (p.189) "surrounded by waterlogged crap" (p.190), the image
is associated with the foulness of Rosemary's house, and takes the
reader back to the starting point of *The Frog Prince*, when the
princess's ball is lost, and rescued by the frog. Earlier Vinnie had
reminisced about her husband, who had married her when, on the
rebound from another woman, he had "like a waterlogged tennis ball
... rolled into the nearest hole" only to regain his elasticity, "bounce
about" at parties, and "hop" into the arms of another. (p.74). The ball
metaphor (with its connections to an even cruder subtext) suggests
that Fred is unable to reconcile the "beastly" elements of Rosemary's
character with his ideal, or to love anyone who is not young and
beautiful. It dawns upon him – too late – that his chosen role of
Jamesian hero is altogether less convincing than that of a British rogue

---

[22] Charles Dickens, *The Life and Adventures of Martin Chuzzlewitt* (London:
Chapman and Hall, 1858), p.423.
[23] In which either a hag turns into a lovely lady, or vice versa. See Chaucer's Wife of
Bath's Tale, *Sir Gawain and the Green Knight* or Spenser's *Fairy Queen*, Book One.

– Macheath in Gay's *The Beggar's Opera*. If his academic work now appears as a mere patching together of ideas from other people's books, his love life is no better. "Like Macheath's, it follows one of the classic literary patterns of the eighteenth century, in which a man meets and seduces an innocent woman, then abandons her." (p.255).

Lurie, however, like Gay, is merciful. At the end the two plots unite on Hampstead Heath. Clad in a romantically draped coat, a gift from Chuck, Vinnie looks like one of the "Druids" celebrating the solstice, derided by Fred as examples of mummery and phoniness. Yet it is Fred, the American champion, who is rescued by Vinnie, braving drifters, tramps and thieves to deliver the vital message which will reunite him with Roo. As the dramatic mummery of the Druids indicates, Fred's rescue and Vinnie's regeneration both depend to some extent on contacts with an artificial world in which a new self can be fashioned. Neither Vinnie nor Fred have survived with their illusions about England intact. Vinnie sees a different, potentially violent, London on her way to the Heath; Fred decides that "London in Gay's time was filthy, violent, corrupt – and it hasn't changed all that much." (p.249). In a last, ironic turn of the plot, however, the cycle of illusion reopens, as the Vogelers declare their enthusiasm for the country: "It's like being in the nineteenth century, really. Everybody in the village is so friendly ... and they're all such perfect *characters*." (p.250).

This chapter began from a consideration of Lurie as a "paleface" writer. Whereas the relation to James may appear to confirm Malcolm Bradbury's hypothesis, it is worth noting that in this novel Chuck and Roo – the cowboy and the Alcott girl – come up trumps, while Jamesian Fred and Vinnie are led intertextually astray. Moreover the robustness of the folklore plot, the directness of its crude subtext, impose different conclusions. Teasingly, Lurie includes as the climax to the romantic plot a scene in which Vinnie (pale but not very interesting as the result of a heavy cold) is contrasted with Chuck in the role of redskin. The latter, minus his clothes on which he has spilled soup, is transformed by a fringed, homespun bedspread into "a comic oversized pink-faced Red Indian" (p.172), who promptly seduces Vinnie against the backdrop of a singularly inappropriate watercolour of New College, Oxford. Although paleface and redskin – the two halves of the American character – come together for once, the national stereotype does not remain fixed. Confusingly, the couple consume a (British) Indian takeaway, and reference is made to Gandhi.

As these examples of cultural slippage indicate, there can be no real return to nature, nor to some primary state of childlike innocence of language or culture. Culture is textuality. Even Roo is an artist, and in her chosen surname as consciously intertextual as Rosemary. Each of us is always to some extent a role player; only Fred is so naïve as to consider Roo sincere, Rosemary false. Yet although cultural models cannot be ignored, Lurie indicates that wiser choices may be made between them. When Chuck is informed that he is descended from the aristocratic De Mompesson family – of which Mumpson is a contraction – he wisely discards the idea as irrelevant, a sensible contrast to the father of Tess Durbeyfield. *Little Lord Fauntleroy* turns out to be more productive of happiness for Chuck and Vinnie, than Dickens and Gay are for Rosemary and Fred. The fact that he is an expert on *The Beggar's Opera* does not prevent Rosemary from beggaring Fred. On the other hand ignorance is never bliss, as Fred's inability to recognise Mrs. Harris, and Vinnie's to spot her frog prince amply demonstrate. Although Roo features, like Daisy Miller, as the American Girl, Chuck's daughter Barbie, introduced at the close, acts as a corrective to any anti-intellectual glorification of a state of nature. Barbie commits every form of vulgar Americanism, from describing her father's "cremains" while shovelling down a cream tea, to subsequently wishing Vinnie "Have a nice day." (p.270). So much for the Jamesian heiress of all the ages.

While the novel demonstrates the dangers of looking to literature for guidance, it therefore also indicates the very real advantages of a sophisticated knowledge thereof. Both British and American heroines, for all their differences, are almost equally victimised by literary and cultural stereotypes. Rosemary's English lady reveals depths of feeling, while Chuck, emblematic of "Oklahoma crude", proves a sensitive lover who enables Vinnie to grow and change. Chuck may be said to civilise Vinnie, whereas Fred comes close to ruining Rosemary altogether. The deconstruction of the fiction of The Child and the stereotype of The Lady is part and parcel of the deconstruction of the stereotypes of national and literary character. As the novel indicates, works of literature are flexibly bound to each other despite national divisions. As a result *Foreign Affairs* is not merely a novel about two cultures clashing, but about all culture as intertextual, changing and created by individuals, and continually undergoing slippage, reversals and revision. Just as its meaning is constructed and revised, built up or shifted by slippage between intertextual frames, the novel's overall structure allows one plot to form a paradigm, a guide through the labyrinth, which the other is simultaneously unravelling. Even as culture is revealed as a continual process of creative transformation, so *Foreign Affairs* is careful to preclude the possibility of establishing a single, normative voice. In its imaginative transformations, it may therefore be characterised as in itself very much the real thing.

Chapter Nine
Truth, Secrets and Lies: *The Truth About Lorin Jones*

> There are four ways to write a woman's life: the
> woman herself may tell it, in what she chooses to call
> an autobiography; she may tell it in what she chooses
> to call fiction; a biographer, woman or man, may
> write the woman's life in what is called a biography;
> or the woman may write her own life in advance of
> living it, unconsciously, and without recognising or
> naming the process. (Carolyn Heilbrun)

Alison Lurie tends to be categorised as an essentially realist
(or neo-realist) writer. Notions of realism, however, have always been
problematic for the female subject. Although it is a truth well
recognised that "Realism has little to do with reality"[1] but is rather a
critical construct developed in response to a particular social and
ideological climate, realism none the less rests its premises on the
assumption of a direct correspondence between art and life. Its
attendant methods of criticism therefore involve charting the
similarities and differences between experiential reality and the artist's
transcript, as if "experience" were common to all. George Eliot's
stated aim, however, "to give a faithful account of men and things as
they have mirrored themselves in my mind"[2] is not quite so easily
realised in the case of women. As Rachel Brownstein memorably puts
it

> Female, a Quixote is no Quixote at all; told about a
> woman, the tale of being caught in a fantasy becomes
> the story of everyday life.[3]

In this feminist argument reinscriptions of experience in literature are
actually organisations – or fantasies – of the dominant male culture.[4]

---

[1] Alison Lee, *Realism and Power: Postmodern British Fiction* (London: Routledge,
1990), p.3. Lee's succinct discussion of realism deserves to be more widely known.
On the relation of women to postmodernism see Patricia Waugh, *Feminine Fictions:
Revisiting the Postmodern* (New York and London, 1989).

[2] George Eliot, *Adam Bede* (London: Penguin, 1980), p.221.

[3] Rachel Brownstein, *Becoming a Heroine* (New York: Viking, 1982). Quoted in
Carolyn Heilbrun, *Writing A Woman's Life* (London and New York: W. W. Norton,
1988), p.76.

[4] Nancy K. Miller, *Subject to Change: Reading Feminist Writing* (New York:
Columbia University Press, 1988), p.43.

Because women are not always mirrored in culture in ways that provide adequate self-definition, the creation of full-blooded, substantial identities and strong female representations remains an important project for the woman writer. In contrast, in its concern to decentre humanist notions of individuality and of universal and essential selves postmodernism has tended to fragment identity, to reveal it as a flux of differently contextualised selves, or as the product of a system of differences. Women, however, may be forgiven for considering that they are too often already portrayed as fleeting, evanescent or silenced to wish to figure as postmodernist deconstructed selves. As a result, with a few honourable exceptions, postmodernist fiction has tended to offer only games for the boys.

At the risk of a minor digression, the extent to which these are live issues may be gauged by the parallels between Lurie's *The Truth About Lorin Jones* and Mary Gordon's *Men and Angels*.[5] In the latter novel the heroine, Anne Foster, investigates the life of a neglected American painter, Caroline Watson. Caroline, a loose amalgam of Suzanne Valadon, Cecilia Beaux, Mary Cassatt and Paula Modersohn-Becker, is a figurative painter, known for her studies of women and children, flowers and landscape – a fairly typical set of subjects for the female artist. Historically women have tended to be cut off from the "high" public realm of history painting – with its grand scale and rigorous anatomical demands, and have opted instead for the still life, portrait and genre painting, and hence often for the realistic depiction of everyday life.[6] On one level therefore, Caroline's paintings are necessary representations of the lives of women, offering "a universe exclusively female" (p.6) and recording how women's lives have been constructed by domestic society. As such, their non-idealised iconography has a clear political value. Annette Kuhn has identified the very real benefits of realist modes of representation in dealing with women's issues, as a product of the transparency which marks all forms of realism:

---

[5] Mary Gordon, *Men and Angels* (London: Penguin, 1986). Subsequent references follow quotations in parentheses. See also Judie Newman, "Telling A Woman's Story: Fiction as Biography and Biography as Fiction in Mary Gordon's *Men and Angels* and Alison Lurie's *The Truth About Lorin Jones*" in *Neo-Realism in Contemporary American Fiction*, ed. Kristiaan Versluys (Amsterdam: Rodopi and Antwerpen: Restant, 1992), pp.171-192.

[6] Linda Nochlin, *Women, Art, and Power and Other Essays* (London: Thames and Hudson, 1989), p.86.

> Articulated within a mode of representation that does not foreground its own processes of signification, political issues can stand out clearly.[7]

On the other hand Caroline's realism has tactical disadvantages, not least in the opportunities it provides for the reductive comment. To the unsympathetic her works are dismissed as grossly material, documenting the flesh: "Pictures of fat mothers with fat babies." (p.47).

In writing about Caroline, Anne faces a dilemma. Should she ignore Caroline's personal history, to focus on the history of art?[8] Or should she yield to her intuition that it is important to represent Caroline as fully as possible: "People were hungry for details of the lives of women." (p.71). Anne is aware, of course, that the equation of women with the flesh, matter or nature is a stereotypical one, and has its own perils:

> people who were interested in the achievements of women wanted the grossest facts: Whom did they sleep with? Did they have any babies? Were their fathers kind to them, cruel to them? Did they obey or go against their mothers? Infantile questions, yet one felt one had to know. It gave courage, somehow. (pp.71-2).

Alison Lurie's biographer-heroine, Polly Alter, faces the same dilemma in *her* quest for the truth about another female painter, Lorin Jones (aka Lolly Zimmern). Jones, however, has adopted different aesthetic tactics; her paintings are vague, elusive and fragmentary. Barely representational at all, constantly revised, with blank unfinished areas, floating figures and hermetic titles, they are designed (recognisably after the school of Larry Rivers) to mystify by absences and gaps. In little, the two painters demonstrate two possibilities for the woman artist; to make statements, as Caroline does, and risk being derided as mere "flesh", or to create postmodernist selves, deconstructed, oblique and therefore vulnerable to evanescence. As analogues to the work of the writer, the artist at the centre of each novel confronts the reader with a choice of alternate models for the

---

[7] Annette Kuhn, "Real Women," in Judith Newton and Deborah Rosenfelt (ed.), *Feminist Criticism and Social Change: Sex, Class and Race in Literature and Culture* (London: Methuen, 1985), p.270.

[8] Feminist art-historians have argued that the individual biographies of women artists have been overemphasised to the detriment of serious consideration of their art. See Rozsika Parker and Griselda Pollock, *Old Mistresses* (London: Routledge and Kegan Paul, 1981), p.xix.

female subject. Lorin's paintings create no danger of stereotyping, but she is perhaps too shadowy to be a useful model; Caroline's solid representations are too easily dismissed as gross materialism.

Importantly neither Lurie nor Gordon tell the tale of the artist directly. In each case a biographer intervenes between reader and artist. Recent commentators have suggested that biography – unlike literary criticism – remains in a state of relative innocence.[9] Just as third person narrative best produces the illusion of pure reference, so biography tends to sustain an illusory reality, as the genre most dependent upon notions of an essential self, continuous through time. For any biographer, however, there remains the awareness that (to quote Roland Barthes) biography is "a novel that dare not speak its name"[10] and that the author faces similar choices to the painter. Indeed, the metaphor of the biographer as portrait painter is one which crops up frequently in biography. Psychological realism may demand a transformative attitude to the subject. Conversely, the subject of the biography may transform the life of the author – as in the famous example of André Maurois, who saw in Shelley a mirror of his own youthful emotions and wanted to tell the story of Shelley's life in order to liberate himself. Freud had this to say of biographers:

> Frequently they take the hero as the object of study because, for reasons of their personal emotional life, they bear him a special affection from the very outset. They then devote themselves to a work of idealization which strives to enrol the great man among their infantile models, and to revive through him, as it were, the infantile conception of the father.[11]

Freud might equally well, of course, have described the opposite case (chain-saw biography, after the school of Kitty Kelley) in which the biographer selects a subject on whom to vent his spleen and exorcise unhappy memories. Alternatively biographers can simply be surprised by unpleasant facts – as Lawrance Thompson was by Robert Frost, or as Polly Alter is by Lorin Jones.

But what of female biographers? For the feminist – and both Gordon's Anne Foster and Lurie's Polly Alter fit the bill – there are

---

[9] Stephen Logan, "Uncluttered by cloisters," *Observer*, 14 April 1991, p.63; Ira Bruce Nadel, *Biography, Fiction, Fact and Form* (London: Macmillan, 1984).

[10] Quoted by Heilbrun, p.28.

[11] Sigmund Freud, *Leonardo da Vinci. A Psychosexual Study of an Infantile Reminiscence* (London: Routledge and Kegan Paul, 1948), pp.115-6. Interestingly Freud's discussion centres on Leonardo as marked by the absence of a father but doubly mothered by a biological and a step-mother.

additional problems. Bell Gale Chevigny, the biographer of Margaret Fuller, has described her own anxieties about her sense of identification, and has related them to contemporary neo-Freudian concepts of the relation of mothers and daughters. Chevigny granted that biography offered a psychological intersection between the personality of biographer and subject, and therefore accepted that "it is nearly inevitable that women writing about women will symbolically reflect their internalised relations with their mothers and in some measure recreate them."[12] In addition, however, Chevigny recognised the danger of introducing a fresh mode of distortion, a feminist fallacy, by projecting her own fantasies onto Fuller:

> The validating stress that feminist theory has laid on the personal, the confusions about the role of the personal in our theory, the urgency and the fervour associated with a movement to redress historical and current injustice – all make feminist biographers of women more susceptible to uncritical identification.[13]

On the positive side, identification may produce a deeper understanding. Just as Margaret Fuller may have felt that her mother was elusive, so that Fuller's *Woman in the Nineteenth Century* may have been a reparative text, so Chevigny felt that in exploring Fuller, in her turn, she had created a "mirroring self":

> when I sought to explain her, especially her confusing behaviour, I was generating analogous explanations or partial sanctions for aspects of my own behaviour. At the same time I was working as such a sanctioning mirror for her. To put it another way, I had created a "mother" of sorts for myself at the same time as I was acting as one for Fuller, "mothers" of the sort that would nurture the difficult and unsteady growth of autonomous selves in us.[14]

Obviously, women who are trying to make a different life for themselves from their biological mothers can benefit from supplementary models. Chevigny needed to recreate a feminist "mother" who could sanction what she herself wanted to become. In short she needed to create a sanctioning precedent.

---

[12] Bell Gale Chevigny, "Daughters Writing: Toward A Theory Of Women's Biography," *Feminist Studies* 9 (1983), p.80.

[13] Chevigny, p.81.

[14] Chevigny, p.94.

Although such an enterprise may involve projection, Chevigny argues that the fantasy element can be constructively experienced. In the biographical process there is a stage at which author and subject become, in effect "surrogate" or "foster" mothers, offering maternal nurture to each other, in a relation of reciprocity. Whether foremothers are famous and their stories distorted (Virginia Woolf perhaps) or (as in the case of the fictional Caroline Watson and Lorin Jones) neglected and unknown, writing about them is likely to be, on some level, an act of retrieval which is experienced as rescue. When the work is most intensely experienced as rescue, the fantasy of reciprocal relations is likely to be activated. Thus in rescuing a forgotten or misunderstood woman, the author may be seeking, indirectly, to rescue herself. The process is therefore a double-mothering; both "mothers" nurture not an infant but a woman, and for both nurturing is a sanctioning of their autonomy. In other words, as biographers, women recreate "mothers" with whom they can integrate – and separate – more effectively than from their biological mothers. As they enter – and separate from – the lives which they present, so the individuality of both "foremother" and "author" may be more firmly secured.

It is against this psychoanalytic understanding of the biographer's project that *Men and Angels* and *The Truth About Lorin Jones* demand to be read. Both heroines envisage their researches as a rescue mission, a process of mothering. Polly Alter, an unsuccessful painter, is intent on recreating Lorin Jones as the victim of the male establishment – thereby implicitly sanctioning Polly's failure – and as a child to be rescued. Polly's maternal fantasy even extends to a trip back in time to the 1960s, to find Lorin Jones alive and well in Key West:

> "God damn it", Polly would say to her, "You've got to take more care of yourself. You've got to quit smoking, get more sleep, eat better, see a doctor about that cough. You can't give up now; you're a very great painter. You're going to be in art history."[15]

Baulked in this maternal enterprise by Lorin's death, Polly resolves to find out all the facts and publish: "Then the truth would be known, and not only Lorin's life but Polly's too would be justified and made whole." (p.4). In the light of this fantasy of reciprocal relations, it is clearly no accident that while writing about Lorin, Polly acquires the

---

[15] Alison Lurie, *The Truth About Lorin Jones* (London: Michael Joseph, 1988), p.4. Subsequent references follow quotations in parentheses.

liberated, nurturing Jeanne as a supplementary mother and model. Or, that Anne Foster's pursuit of Caroline, carried out in order to create a nurturing foremother, and thus, in reparative fantasy, a nurtured child-self, involves the employment of Laura Post, a miserably undernurtured childminder, as surrogate mother to Anne's children. The feminist rescue mission is attended with ironies, comic in Lurie's case, tragic in Gordon's. Just as Anne sets out to save Caroline from being written off as merely "flesh", so Laura, a religious fanatic, believes that she can save Anne from the lusts of the flesh, in a dark mirroring of Anne's own activities, which culminates in her suicide. Gordon's dead female artist is lovingly investigated and recreated at the price of a living girl. In a lighter mode, Polly Alter's pursuit of the truth about her *alter ego* is doubled by her Lesbian friend Jeanne, who in less highminded but equally committed fashion pursues Betsy, a vapid and infantile student. Lurie's two pairs of seekers and sought strike a series of variations on the central psychoanalytic thesis, culminating in the separation by Polly from both Lorin (a more ambiguous subject than she had imagined) and Jeanne. The novel therefore sets up a series of mirrorings and doublings, in order to investigate the means by which a woman's story may best be told, the utility or otherwise of models and precedents, and the status of realism in such telling. Although the major plot strand puts foremothers and daughters first, the main plot is shadowed by the ghost of a male story – an Oedipal one – which, like the backing to a mirror, sets the feminist rescue mission in sharp relief.

In *The Truth About Lorin Jones* Lurie continues the investigation of women's relation to artistic and social structures, already the topic in different ways of *The Nowhere City, Real People* and *Only Children*, and examines the fashion in which pre-existent psychological patterns shape the ways in which we order the world. The focus on biography is perhaps unsurprising. Lurie's career began with biography, the memoir of V. R. Lang which eventually launched her career as a novelist. V. R. Lang was therefore considerably more than a sanctioning precedent. Writing her biography kickstarted Lurie's own stalled career. Polly Alter's biography of Lorin Jones is also, potentially, a means of restarting her career as a painter. Newly divorced and a recent convert to Lesbian feminism, Polly searches for the truth about her *alter ego*, and is buttressed, in practical terms, in her fantasy of reciprocity, by her friend Jeanne. In recoil from a history of abuse at male hands, Jeanne has become an incongruously fluffy Lesbian separatist, given to needlework, cooking and cats, and adopts a maternal stance to Polly. Polly's early abandonment by her father and lukewarm relation to her exceptionally unliberated mother, make her as vulnerable to Jeanne as she is to an idealisation of Lorin as sanctioning precedent. Duplicitous Jeanne takes over Polly's life, her bed, and her apartment, very nearly ousting her son, Stevie, in the process. Meanwhile Polly is too busy mothering Lorin-as-fantasy-child to defend herself or her offspring. Overtly Jeanne, as a Marxist-feminist historian, disapproves of individual biography as a genre, on the grounds that writing about atypical "heroes" and the lives of the great is merely playing the game by male rules. Indeed Jeanne (herself fixated on Betsy) even counsels Polly that she is becoming obsessed by Lorin: "I think you're falling in love with your subject." (p.66). But she is more than happy to take advantage of Polly's obsession to advance her own.

As events unfold, Polly succumbs swiftly to a "magical sense of identity with Lorin" (p.131), imagining that she has been following the same path as her predecessor all her life. Both painters share similar suburban childhoods, schools and colleges and even lived at one point on the same street in the West Village. Polly had been immediately struck with admiration by the first painting of Lorin's which she saw, despite the fact that, in her pre-feminist incarnation, she assumed that "Lorin" was a man's name. The sense of identification nearly extends to seduction by Garrett Jones, Lorin's husband. Immersed in a fantasy of acting as Lorin's proxy, "pardoning him in Lorin's name" (p.114) Polly almost succumbs. Significantly Garrett approaches her in extremely paternal terms, calling her "child" (p.108), feeding her from his own cutlery in a restaurant, and declaring that passion always involves falling in love with "the child in the other person" (p.102). Confronted, however, with Garrett Jones in seduction garb of white silk pyjamas and red damask robe, Polly comes sharply to her senses and repels his advances. "I'm not your darling, she thought. I'm not Lorin." (p.113). Despite her rebuff, Garrett none the less presents Polly with one of his wife's paintings as a gift, and lends her copies of a mass of research material. (His pride is salvaged by the belief that Polly is a Lesbian.) He also passes on the unwelcome information that Lorin had cleaned out their joint bank account when she left him for her lover. As a result Polly begins to separate from Lorin.

> Though Polly still loved Lorin Jones, she no longer admired her unreservedly ... the hovering presence of Lorin's spirit appeared to her now as a kind of false, fleeting enchantment; or, in more prosaic psychological terms, a temporary delusion. (p.131).

As Polly pursues Lorin through a series of interviews with the latter's friends, lovers and associates, the image of her as exploited by the male establishment begins to crumble in the face of the evidence – that Lorin lived off men, sacrificing everything and everyone to the demands of art. Far from resembling Polly, Lorin saw her paintings as her children and was as possessive about them as Jeanne is of Betsy. Unwelcome revelations about Lorin are accompanied by equally unpleasant discoveries about Jeanne. In a moment of revelation Polly realises that the all-female household which she has constituted for herself masks a reinscription of the pattern of her childhood.

> And now it seemed to Polly that the scene in the apartment was like a caricature of a traditional marriage. She was the cross husband, in worn jeans and baggy sweater, owner of the house and its main economic support, working late. The tactful, charming manipulative wife [Jeanne/Polly's mother], in a flowered apron was making supper and the spoilt stepdaughter [Betsy/Polly] was pretending to help. (p.279).

As Polly's idealised image of Lorin corrects itself, so she is set free from manipulative Jeanne, and the infantile Betsy, and recognises the need to safeguard real rather than imaginary offspring, in the shape of her son Stevie. Jeanne is ousted – though interestingly the reader does not witness her defeat directly. Recounted at second hand in somewhat summary fashion, it is the great missing scene of the novel, suggesting that getting rid of "Mom" (even in metaphor) still presents special obstacles to the writer. Although grey areas remain, knowledge about Lorin is accompanied by self-knowledge. In a comic and symbolic moment, her father's present of an Etch-A-Sketch toy, desired since her childhood, reveals to Polly her father's love for her. The revelation immediately precedes her decision to commit herself anew to a man, specifically Hugh Cameron. The transparently Oedipal overtones here – Cameron is the ex-lover of Lorin, Polly's chosen foremother – are teasingly recognised and belied in the Etch-A-Sketch toy. An Etch-A-Sketch involves a magnetised screen on which drawings can be made with a wand. A shake of the screen and the drawing disappears. In short it allows a picture to be both produced and erased, reproduced and corrected, rather than being fixed for all time. Polly has earlier recognised that Cameron (his identity as Lorin's lover at that point concealed) fulfils most of the specifications for her fantasy ideal male:

a stupid false adolescent idea of the desirable male –
the Gothic myth of the Dark Stranger: reckless,
wilful, undependable (p.13).

In Key West, amidst hot tropical scenery and plants, where "the very
air ... smelt of sex" (p.193) she finds the fantasy of the Romantic
Hero "recurring like some persistent tropical weed." (p.223). By
setting the affair in the stereotypical romance situation of the
Caribbean location Lurie both recognises the strength of the fantasy –
and underlines the fact that it is a fantasy. The reader's own
identification is deflected – not least by the interruption of the
couple's clinch by Polly's fears of herpes, gonorrhoea and genital
warts – not the usual inward thoughts of the Mills and Boon heroine at
the moment of rapturous surrender.

Just as Polly corrects her picture of Lorin, and draws strength
from a fantasy without being imprisoned within it, so the reader is
actively involved in the same process. In *The Truth About Lorin
Jones* it is not a revelation of some external truth which functions as
the corrective to fantasy, but the reader's own input. In the novel,
third person narration alternates with transcriptions of taped
interviews, which reveal a woman as multifaceted as a Cubist
painting, alternatively shy, spiteful, generous, unscrupulous, schizoid
or grasping, according to the vested interests of the person telling
Lorin's story, the interviewee. The interviewees are also using Lorin
to buttress their own autonomy; they tend to embark on long
anecdotes about their own lives, or use Lorin to portray themselves in
a flattering light. Like Polly, when apparently recreating Lorin they
are also mirroring themselves. Grace Skelly, for example, reportedly
struck Lorin as so philistine that when she bought one of Lorin's
paintings, the artist asked to buy it back, giving her reasons. In
interview, however, Grace describes a perfectly friendly relationship
between fellow-aesthetes, and emphasises the fact that she "spotted"
Lorin first. (Though the painting was never hung and merely
remained in the Skellys' vaults, appreciating in value.) Importantly
the interviews, apparently perfect transcriptions from life, lack a vital
element. Only responses are given. The reader is left to second-guess
Polly's questions and therefore to take on her interrogative role. In
some cases (the initial interview – of steadily escalating hostility –
with Paolo Carducci, Lorin's dealer) it is not difficult to supply a
rough version of the questions from the answers. ("No. As a matter
of fact, in my honest opinion, there's never been a woman artist of the
very first rank" (p.21), is one response.) In others the reader is much
less constrained. Broadly speaking, the interviews tend to progress

from those which support Polly's image of Lorin-as-victim (Paolo, Mary Ann Fenn, Grace Skelly) to more hostile accounts (Kenneth Foster, Marcia Zimmern) which undermine Polly's hypotheses. The reader is also confronted with a question concerning the method of interrogation. Jeanne suggests to Polly that in order to lull her subjects into a state of security and catch them off guard, she should avoid confrontation lest they guess her intention of writing a feminist exposé of the art world. (It seems wise advice in the case of Paolo who breaks off the interview in a fury and is then taken ill and unable to provide further, vital details.) Polly demurs however. "Women have been smiling and lying to men for centuries." (p.7), she objects. But when she yields to Jeanne's advice when interviewing Garrett Jones, she plays the passive admiring female so completely that he jumps to the wrong conclusions and makes a pass at her. The reader is left to assess the respective merits of the different interview techniques – reenacting them by supplying the questions, and thus acting out Polly's role. Just as Lorin's paintings left blank spaces, absences, incomplete areas, so Lurie's text replicates her mystery. As Lorin's paintings made viewers project themselves into the vision, as Polly has projected herself into Lorin's life, so the reader becomes an active presence within the novel and must struggle to maintain an independent view. Narrative method therefore dramatises the uneasy relation of nurturance and autonomy which is its major concern. Lorin is less a "real" female subject than a discursive construct, co-produced by author and readers, a process which clearly privileges the construction of meaning over the raw event. It is perhaps Danielle Zimmern who draws the moral: "Events happen to you, sure, but it's up to you to decide what they mean." (p.189).

A further complicating factor also affects the quest for truth. Since most of Polly's interviewees are "carry-over" characters from Lurie's other novels, the reader also has *their* fictional biographies as available information, often ironising or undercutting their accounts of Lorin, sometimes implicitly supporting their truths. As readers of her other novels, we see some of the characters in terms of very different "lives", in other fictional worlds, and in alternative "stories". When Janet Belle Smith, for example, describes Lorin as so`odd that she would scarcely be a credible fictional character, the wise reader may remember how extremely conventional Janet is, and find her views suspect. Sara Sachs Vogeler (presumably the Sally Sachs of *Real People*) is a more sympathetic figure, and generous in her assessment: "she was way ahead of me." (p.77). Kenneth Foster describes Lorin as single-minded and unscrupulous, in taking Garrett Jones from his first wife, Roz: "The only things Laurie Zimmern ever loved were herself and painting, in that order" (p.144). But when he tells Polly "I loved them both" (p.143) (meaning Garrett and Roz) before describing Garrett as hopelessly weak where women were concerned the reader recalls Janet's suspicion that Kenneth is gay. Later it transpires that Kenneth only married Roz himself, to free Garrett to marry Lorin, in return for which Garrett, an influential critic, made Kenneth famous.

Quite clearly, the characters' own experiences shape their accounts of Lorin and of her pictures. Reinscriptions of experience are often tinged with fantasy. Garrett Jones declares to Polly that what appears to be an abstract actually portrays a pond with romantic associations for him. When Mary Ann Fenn recognises the title of one of Lorin's' paintings ("Princess Elinore of the White Meadows") and realises that Lorin is the Lolly of her childhood (*Only Children*) the reader is encouraged towards Mary Ann's interpretation of the painting. What had seemed an abstraction is suddenly revealed as a landscape, involving daisies, clouds, and a tree-as-fairy-tale-castle, recalling a precise scene in the earlier novel. Thus when Mary Ann says that Lolly had been frightened in childhood by some form of abuse ("some sexual thing" p.39) the reader is inclined to believe her. Leonard Zimmern, however, rebuffs the suggestion, "If you're expecting some sensational tale of child abuse, forget it." (p.26). For Leonard it is too early for an analytic biography. He counsels Polly to stay off the life and focus only on the work. In his view (quite the reverse of Polly's idealizing rescue mission) the current fashion for exposing the private lives of artists is the product of envy of their gifts. As a result, though readers may need heroes to idealize, they also want them to suffer from awful childhoods, alcoholism, emotional misery or illness. Danielle Zimmern Kotelchuk (reappearing from *The War Between the Tates*) remembers a minor incident at a picnic where Lorin was found without her panties (scared but otherwise unmolested) but argues, as this robust survivor would, that "I don't believe that people are ruined by one bad childhood experience". (p.189). (Danielle was a Jew in Nazi Germany.) Danielle describes Marcia, Lorin's stepmother, as fundamentally good-hearted and excuses Lorin's economic dependence on men, on the grounds that she had been brought up by a patriarchal father and passive mother. Marcia Zimmern is less forgiving: "Laurie Zimmern wasn't a nice person" (p.168). She sees Lorin's paintings entirely in relation to her own experience. "Who Is Coming?" is in her view a picture of the late Celia Zimmern, given to Dan purely to remind him of his deceased first wife. The painting features "wispy bug kind of things" (p.165) and a figure which in Marcia's view is either a moth or a woman in a chiffon nightgown. The reader who has not read Lurie's preceding novels will tend to write Marcia off as a philistine unable to appreciate abstract art. Conversely the reader who recalls Lolly's bughunting in *Only Children* in which Celia, rather given to floating garments, is also frequently characterised as moth-like, may conclude that Marcia is more perceptive than she knows. When Hugh Cameron admits that Lorin lived entirely off him, and that her death was considerably hastened by drug abuse, Polly becomes almost entirely disenchanted. By this point she has already begun to see Lorin as responsible for halting her own career (when Polly saw her work and was beset by the anxiety of influence). Yet the final interview with Ruth March makes a crucial point, since it establishes that Lorin was an active nurturer of another woman's talents. When Roo was frustrated at her inability to draw a horse exactly, Lorin gave her a camera (and later, a collection of serious studies of photography as an art form) and launched (as *Foreign Affairs* establishes) a successful career.

Polly is left with a dilemma. Should she write an orthodox analytic biography, aimed at the art world? Or a feminist exposé? Should she draw a flattering portrait – or one with "warts and all"? And what kind of life and career will she choose *for herself* by the kind of book which she composes? In her mind's eye Polly envisages a series of visions of her future self, as a figure of power and importance in the art world or alternatively as an impoverished feminist, in full awareness that she was "about to choose, not only a version of Lorin Jones' past, but also her own unattractive future." (p.290). In characteristic fashion, Lurie leaves Polly (and the reader) poised on the brink of decision. It seems clear, however, that just as Lurie employs a postmodernist method in which the truth about Lorin becomes many different truths, so Polly will opt for a metabiography in which all her findings, contradictory or otherwise, will be pluralistically presented. A suggestive example exists in the biography of Edie Sedgwick, Sixties pop star, which juxtaposes comments quoted, without linking narrative, from various sources who speak with – and against – each other through quoted transcripts. The narrator is almost entirely removed from the text.[16]

> What she'd really like to do, Polly thought ... was to write a book that would tell the whole confusing

---

[16] Jean Stein, *Edie: An American Biography* (London: Cape, 1982).

contradictory truth. She'd like to put in all the different stories she'd collected. (pp.290-291).

In so doing she also opts for Hugh Cameron (the novel ends as she lifts the receiver to telephone him) and a renewed career as a painter. (In *The Last Resort*, she is mentioned preparing for her own show.) Lorin, like Larry Rivers, tended to emphasise the process of constant revision through which her images developed. She is seen at one point scrubbing at a painting which is already on display. Another painting, "Aftershocks" has a hole torn through its centre. Unfinished or only partly painted areas are left on the canvases, or motifs scribbled on them, with prominence given to floating objects and figures, sketchy lines and suggested forms. The allusive titles (some drawn at random from the dictionary, others entirely hermetic) recreate at the verbal level the areas of mystery in the canvas. Larry Rivers argued that by using blanks he allowed the spectator to play a role in the decision-making (he distrusted too much "finish") and allowed the paintings to figure as arrested metamorphoses, coalescing or dissolving before the spectator's eyes.[17] In a sense therefore, Polly's implied decision to leave the mysteries as mysteries is her greatest homage to (and imitation of) Lorin. And Lurie's refusal to tie up all the ends at the close has the same effect.

Lorin's ambiguity, therefore, is in the end more fruitful for her biographer than Caroline Watson's solid representations. Because Lorin's life is almost as mysterious as her paintings, Polly has to choose her own life-story and authorize herself. Lorin can be at best only a partial model, and paradoxically that is the source of Polly's freedom. As Polly corrects a fantasy of Lorin-as-innocent-victim, so the novel invites the reader to participate in – and separate from – the fantasy, to form the picture and to correct it. In consequence, as Lurie privileges postmodernist or metafictional discourse over transcriptions of "reality", so she privileges fiction over biography, and story over lives. Where Gordon's Anne Foster found only a partial and unreliable sanctioning foremother in Caroline, Polly finds in Lorin – because fragmented, because a construction – a means to script her own life and take control of her own plot. Lurie therefore moves away from biography and towards fiction as the preferred enhancer of a woman's autonomy, and she is in good feminist company. To quote Carolyn Heilbrun

What matters is that lives do not serve as models; only stories do that. And it is a hard thing to make up

---

[17] See Helen A. Harrison, *Larry Rivers* (New York: Harper and Row, 1984).

> stories to live by. We can only retell and live life by the stories that we have read or heard. We live our lives through texts.[18]

Although Lorin's actual life may not be rewritten, Lurie argues none the less for a sense of alternative destinies, that to choose a story is to choose a life. Fiction becomes biography – and biography fiction. Polly's biography of Lorin will be metafictional but it will script Polly's life thereafter. As lives become stories, so stories become lives. Polly Alter therefore sets out to construct both a life for Lorin Jones and for herself.

---

[18] Heilbrun, p.37.

Chapter Ten
The Gay Imaginary: *The Last Resort*

In *The Truth About Lorin Jones*, Hugh Cameron, seated in a bar in Key West, lifts his glass to toast Polly:

> "Here's to your stay in the last resort."
> "The last resort?"
> "That's what we all call it."[1]

Ten years later Lurie published her ninth novel, which exploited the phrase to the full both in its title and in its theme. On a banal level, Key West is both a resort (for vacationers) and the last (the southernmost) resort in America, located at the end of the chain of islands which make up the Florida Keys. In addition, as one character explains in the later novel, it is so called

> Not just because it was at the end of the Keys, but because it was where you went when other places hadn't worked out.[2]

In this respect two groups of characters are juxtaposed in *The Last Resort*: on the one hand ageing "snowbird" retirees, fleeing the rigours of the Northern winter, represented primarily in the novel by Wilkie Walker, a retired naturalist in his seventies, and Molly Hopkins, even older and stricken with crippling arthritis; and on the other the island's sizeable gay community, represented by Perry Jackson, Lee Weiss and the longterm partnership of Dennis and Tommy. Key West thus appears as both a tropical paradise, a place where "everything seemed designed to recommend and encourage sensual pleasure" (p.152) and as a place of death. Inevitably it is a place where AIDS sufferers come to die.

> At the end of their lives they returned to the place where they had once been happiest – and where, quite probably, they had been infected and infected others. (p.164).

As a fictional setting, therefore, Key West offers a reworking of Lurie's interest in the Utopian/dystopian opposition, and once more focuses upon a small, and somewhat artificial community.

In this case, however, a third term needs to be added to the familiar dichotomy: heterotopia. Lurie's setting conforms to

---

[1] *The Truth About Lorin Jones*, p.209.

[2] Alison Lurie, *The Last Resort* (London: Vintage, 1998), p.67. All subsequent references are to this edition of the novel.

Foucault's definition of a heterotopia, as a place which is both real and imaginary, nature suffused with culture. Foucault coined the term in 1967, when it appears in a collection of his lecture notes, which were finally published more than twenty years later, first in the French journal *Architecture-Mouvement-Continuité*, then in translation in the English journal, *Diacritics* as "Of Other Spaces". The term heterotopias, which translates as "places of difference", has been widely used to discuss gay or lesbian communities. Where Utopias are fundamentally unreal, either as presenting society in perfect form, or as society turned upside down, heterotopias are

> real places ... which are something like counter-sites, a kind of effectively enacted Utopia in which the real sites, all the other real sites that can be found within the culture, are simultaneously represented, contested and inverted.[3]

Like a mirror, heterotopias can be both real and unreal at the same time, reflecting an image of a perfect world but at the same time reconfiguring it. Containing their own contradictions, they also expose the illusions and delusions of the so-called "real" world. As Foucault argues.

> The heterotopia is capable of juxtaposing in a single real space several spaces, several sites that are themselves incompatible.[4]

Heterotopias thus have a function in relation to all the space that remains, "to create a space of illusion that exposes every real space, all the sites inside of which life is partitioned as still more illusory".[5] The argument has an obvious reference to the gay enclave, often a real geographical location which has an undeniable physical form (the Castro, for example, or Sydney's Oxford St.) yet is also an "imagined community". As Affrica Taylor comments, there is more to a community than a spatial location – "we dream up communities as utopias of belonging",[6] in gay terms as places of tolerance and

---

[3] Michel Foucault, "Of other Spaces," *Diacritics* 16 (Spring 1986), p.24. (First published as "Des Espaces Autres," *Architecture-Mouvement-Continuité*, October 1986. English translation by Jay Miskowiec.)

[4] Foucault, p.25.

[5] Foucault, p.27.

[6] Affrica Taylor, "A Queer Geography," in Andy Medhurst and Sally Munt (ed.), *Lesbian and Gay Studies: A Critical Introduction* (London: Cassell, 1997), p.10. On the concept of the heterotopia see also Edward W. Soja, "Heterologies: A Remembrance of other spaces in the Citadel-LA," in Sophie Watson and Katherine Gibson (ed.), *Postmodern Cities and Spaces* (Oxford: Blackwell, 1995), pp.13-34.

freedom of expression, without homophobia or heterosexism. To enter this space of the gay imaginary, however, is to discover contradictions, fissures in the apparently unified gay community, for the heterotopia is capable of juxtaposing in one real place several different spaces, several sites which are themselves incompatible or foreign to one another. At the same time these "other" spaces maintain their function of destabilizing "normal" territories of meaning; they are "disruptive sites which displace centres". "What they reveal threatens to displace all that might be taken for granted as 'real'."[7]

In fairly obvious terms Lurie's Key West represents a real space where several imaginary spaces converge and get entangled, particularly in the juxtaposition of homophobic Wilkie Walker and the gay community. Foucault included in his discussion of heterotopias both heterotopias of deviance (prisons, psychiatric hospitals, rest homes) and heterochronic sites, representing specialised spaces of time (festival sites, fairgrounds, leisure villages, resorts). For Wilkie Key West is "a tropical version of Skytop" (p.43) the exclusive "elder community" back home in Corinth, where he has no intention of ending his days. For the tourists who frolic temporarily on the island, it is a place without responsibilities, unrelated to normal time. If, however, they stay on, as permanent residents, as Molly and Lee have done, it changes aspect. As they acquire local interests and commitments, and abandon tourist habits, "Key West was no longer a playground. It had become the real world." (p.18). Lee now runs a women-only guest house: tourists are her bread and butter. If **she** wants a holiday she has to leave Key West and go somewhere else.

The idea of conflicting sites is embodied most powerfully in 909 Hibiscus Street, Wilkie Walker's temporary holiday home. In the course of the novel ownership of the house – outrageously camp in its décor and furnishings – passes from Alvin (dead of a stroke) to his erstwhile lover Perry Jackson (Jacko), its caretaker. Unknown to Wilkie, Jacko has been recently diagnosed as HIV positive. When this news reaches his mercenary Aunt Myra, a realtor from Tulsa, she descends immediately to assess the value of the property, which to her is interesting only in so far as it is "realisable" in cash terms (as three good condos, with pool and space for more.) As Myra barges around the house dropping such real estate phrases as "contemporary island kitchen" and "en suite luxury master bath" (p.161) the real nature of the location becomes a sliding kaleidoscope of images, a place

---

[7] Taylor, p.8.

simultaneously of unfettered gay fantasy and (in Oklahoma terms) of absolutely real material assets.

It is no accident that this particularly inappropriate habitat is reserved for Wilkie Walker. Lurie's novel, originally entitled "Endangered Species",[8] draws upon Foucault in another sense. In Foucault's argument previous ages may have known of various sexual acts and practices but did not extend the practice to categorise the individual. There were thus no "homosexuals" in Ancient Greece, only people who engaged in same-sex practices. Changes in the way society constitutes the individual have led to the invention of "the homosexual".[9] As Stein puts it,

> A sodomite had been a temporary aberration; the homosexual was now a species.[10]

Just as Lurie invents characters, so society makes up homosexuals as a separate species. The practice is exposed and mocked in the person of Wilkie, an unrepentant homophobe whose career as a natural scientist allows Lurie to engage powerfully with debates concerning homosexuality, and AIDS, and specifically with the arguments of sociobiology, particularly the often expressed view that homosexuals are "unnatural" or, at best, left over from some previous evolutionary state.

Wilkie's wife Jenny plays devil's advocate to her husband's view that homosexuality is unnatural. In that case, she wonders, why have homosexuals not died out, by the process of natural selection? Wilkie's response is a textbook restatement of the "kinship selection hypothesis", the classic explanation of the survival of gays, as propounded by E. O. Wilson, the father of sociobiology.[11]

> "Of course it's a genetic anomaly darling," Wilkie replies. "But it probably had survival value in the past among primitive people. A tribe or family which

---

[8] I am grateful to Derek Johns for facilitating the opportunity to read the novel in typescript.

[9] Michel Foucault, *La volonté de savoir* (Paris: Editions Gallimard, 1976.)

[10] Edward Stein (ed.), *Forms of Desire. Sexual Orientation and the Social Constructionist Controversy* (London: Routledge, 1990), 18.

[11] Edward O. Wilson, *Sociobiology. The New Synthesis* (Cambridge, Mass.: Belknap Press of Harvard University Press, 1975), p.555. On altruism see Edward O. Wilson, *On Human Nature* (Harvard University Press, 1978), p.143. See also Don Smith, *Why Are There "Gays" At All? Why Hasn't Evolution Eliminated "Gayness" Millions Of Years Ago?* (London: Quantum Jump Press, 1978); Michael Ruse, "Are There Gay Genes? Sociobiology and Homosexuality." *Journal of Homosexuality* 6, 4 (Summer 1981), pp.5-34.

included extra adult men, men who didn't reproduce, had a competitive advantage. There would be fewer children to care for, and more adult males to hunt and fight for them. If some of these males were sexually attracted to each other, they would be less likely to fight over the women, or to leave the group and form families of their own." (p.236).

Warming to his topic and assuming his lecturing voice, Wilkie expands the argument to include gay women (available to care for their siblings' children, giving the tribe a better chance of survival) and such contemporary social practices as late marriage or the responsibility of unmarried siblings for their nieces and nephews. He does not include American society in the equation, however. In his view "homosexuals in America today are pretty useless" (p.237), mostly abandoning their families in favour of extravagant spending on themselves. He indicates the lavish décor of the holiday home, replete with gold taps and massive statuary as evidence.

"Homosexuality isn't as useful to the species as it once was. It may even die out eventually, but genetic change is slow. Still the numbers are declining even now. Partly as the result of AIDS and other diseases, of course. Nature can seem cruel, but she balances her books." (p.237).

With breathtaking insouciance, Wilkie leans back, the lecture concluded, quite unaware that the joke is on him. Indeed, Wilkie is the butt of a book length joke. For all the grimness of Lurie's subject matter, which includes terminal illness, chronic disease, sudden death, an assisted suicide, seriopositive diagnosis, marital and financial betrayals and the spectre of ecological disaster, *The Last Resort* is a comedy at the expense of homophobia. Its fictional spaces reflect back ironically upon the assumptions of the "straight" world. In the course of the novel Wilkie goes through a process which converts him into a quasi-gay. Caught in the illusion that he is dying of an incurable disease, Wilkie unwittingly finds himself mirroring the behaviour of the closet seriopositive, residing in a gay community, and even, in the denouement, unintentionally propelling his beloved wife into the arms of a Lesbian lover, Lee Weiss, the very person whose early life had been ruined by reading Wilkie's homophobic theories. As a result *The Last Resort* is probably Lurie's most daring and risky novel to date. Writing a comedy about old age and dying has its own pitfalls. Lurie goes out onto even thinner ice to write a comedy about AIDS. By focussing upon a straight individual, only afflicted in metaphoric terms, she sidesteps the major pitfalls, turning the tables on the homophobe, and placing the straight world squarely in her target range. Wilkie enters the gay imaginary with a vengeance – he becomes a form of imaginary gay, a shadow or double to Jacko. As a result Lurie's novel exposes straight illusions in terms of sociobiology, scientific discourse, and the body politic.

Metaphors drawn from sociobiology run through the novel, with almost every human character compared to an animal at some point – or anthropomorphizing animal into human. The technique extends from style and characterisation to the essential engine of plot. From the outset Wilkie is established as irremediably on the nature side of the nature/nurture argument, with a tendency to see people as animals, determined by their instincts. In almost all respects he is a classic sociobiologist, committed to a belief in the biological basis of human behaviour. Interestingly almost all sociobiologists are male, with a general tendency to a "his and hers" view of human nature,[12] as distinctly male or distinctly female. Sociobiology depends upon the belief that the traits of human nature were adaptive during the time in which the human species evolved. Adaptiveness may be defined as behaviour which increased an individual's chances of seeing his or her genes represented in the next generation. "Greater genetic fitness" would thus involve enhanced personal survival, enhanced personal reproduction, and the enhanced survival and reproduction of close relatives with the same genes. Nonreproductive human behaviour therefore comes into question. As Jeffrey Weeks notes, in his overview of sexual behaviour and theories,

> Nowhere has the sanctification of the premature biological hypothesis inflicted more pain than in the treatment of homosexuals.[13]

Weeks points out that homosexual activity is common in most cultures, and may be an important beneficent form of behaviour:

> Homosexuals may be the genetic carriers of some of mankind's rare altruistic impulses.[14]

In the 1960s there was a spate of sociobiological works which claimed to describe man's "real" or natural behaviour in ethological terms. Robert Ardrey's *The Territorial Imperative*, Desmond Morris's *The*

---

[12] See Clifford Geertz, "Sociosexology," *New York Review of Books* XXVI, 21-2 (24 January 1980), 3-4.

[13] Jeffrey Weeks, *Sexuality and its Discontents* (London: Routledge and Kegan Paul, 1985), p.142.

[14] Weeks, p.143.

Human Zoo and *The Naked Ape*, and Konrad Lorenz's *On Aggression* all became popular bestsellers. Wilkie is the author of *The Naked Animal* which according to Lee made homophobia respectable and supplied abundant ammunition to "Family Values creeps" (p.20). She continues:

> I read how I was sick and unnatural, because animals aren't queer. According to Walker, whatever animals do is natural and good. Homosexuality is a disease; it's got to be treated and wiped out. (p.20).

When he himself begins to ail, however, Wilkie does not find it quite so easy to accept his fate. "He was an animal and animals suffered and died" (p.12), he reasons. But having spotted fresh blood in his stool and strongly suspecting bowel cancer, Wilkie determines to avoid a slow lingering death, if only to spare his wife Jenny, to whom he has always been intensely protective. He describes Jenny as "a creature of the woods and wild places" (p.13) whom he married in a spirit of ecological knight-errantry, intent on restoring "this beautiful unique primate" from the polluted environment of California to her natural habitat, an unspoiled area of New England. It was Jenny (a decidedly unliberated mouse of a woman) who suggested the name Salty for the animal hero of Wilkie's bestseller *The Last Salt Marsh Mouse*, a classic account of a species doomed to extinction, a fate considerably accelerated by the popularity gained by the unfortunate rodent as a result of the book. Wilkie's attempt to alert the world to an endangered species led to the kidnapping of salt marsh mice as pets and for zoos. Though bad news in many respects for Salty, his book was very good news, professionally and financially, for Wilkie. As he reflects somewhat sourly, "I preserved the species Wilkie Walker", p.10. Although Wilkie dissociates himself from the cultural artefacts which flourished in Salty's train (posters, t-shirts and Disneyesque toys) his books none the less propagated a whole species of noisy, sentimental amateur naturalists, destructive in their numbers and behaviour. He visualises them as "half-human Yahoos" p.10, tramping heavily over the fields and forests of North America in large packs, crushing the flora and frightening the fauna.

The same destruction follows from Wilkie's attempts to protect and preserve his wife. In order to kill himself without arousing suspicions, Wilkie agrees to spend a winter in Key West, a good locale in his view for a staged drowning accident. In his determination to conceal the awful facts from Jenny (he is desperate to tell all and constantly tempted to spill the beans) he becomes silent, cold, unresponsive and angry, and manages both to kill his marriage stone dead, and to propel Jenny into Lee's arms. The ironies of this particular situation need not be belaboured. The site of Wilkie's imaginary disease, and the nature of his symptoms, bring together anal blood and cancer in an all-too-suggestive fashion. Indeed, if the reader did not know better, it would be easy to assume from the opening of the novel that Wilkie is a closet gay. Before meeting Jenny, Wilkie had been married twice, both times briefly and disastrously, and is described as extremely wary of women, whom he treats almost as a separate species. Now, affected by the symptoms of what appears to be a terminal disease involving a bloody anus, he conceals the facts from both his doctor and his wife, avoids going for tests, and settles on suicide in a gay enclave. He also gives up sex. The novel opens with Jenny's observation that for nearly a month Wilkie had not suggested making love (p.4) and when he does make one final, farewell attempt, the result is sexual failure. (p.64). Whenever Jenny asks him if anything is wrong with him he responds with resentment, "Why do you keep asking that?" (p.33). Meanwhile all Jacko's friends are scrutinising him night and day for signs of disease. Because of the juxtaposition of the pair in the same heterochronic site, Wilkie, like an invisibly seriopositive person, appears to mirror the behaviour of the closet gay.

Imitation and mirroring are also the key features of the plot. Wilkie finds himself surrounded by imitators getting in his way, rather as if he were in a hall of mirrors. One such is Gerry Grass, reappearing from *Real People*, still a poet, but flawed by his fatal tendency to imitate other artists (p.149). Gerry is also occupying the site at Hibiscus Street, in a flat over the garage. A nature poet of pronounced heterosexual orientation, Gerry has published a book on the men's movement entitled *Men of Oak*. (p.158). An ersatz Robert Bly, he is given to chanting and to accompanying his poems with drumming, emphasising a "primitive" or tribal quality. He has also (in the classic sociobiological scenario of males seeking younger mates to impregnate) exchanged his wife for a succession of younger women. Fate has not been particularly kind to him, however. He is clearly on his way down professionally in the opinion of Wilkie, whose sociobiological eye also notes the apelike placement of Gerry's thumb, suggestive of a throwback. Comically Wilkie's first suicide attempt is foiled by Gerry. When he joins Wilkie, uninvited, on what was to have been the latter's last swim, Wilkie is so infuriated that he considers drowning Gerry with him: "Let him find that unity with nature he was gabbling about last night." (p.80). Ironically, however, Gerry, the apparent throwback, is much more likely to survive than

Wilkie. He is younger and fitter. Recoiling from the prospect of being rescued by "this fuzzy-minded anthropoid ape" (p.80) Wilkie reluctantly regains the shore.

Wilkie's other imitators are even less "fit" than Gerry. A second try at killing himself is foiled by a more successful suicide, a meticulously planned attempt in which Tommy (confined to a wheelchair and in the last stages of AIDS) rolls his wheelchair off the boardwalk into the sea, after one last embrace with his devoted partner Dennis. Shortly before this event Wilkie had learned of Jacko's diagnosis. His reaction is panic and fear:

> the man had been in and out of their house, cleaning every week. It was quite possible that he had left some smear of blood, some secretion (p.115).

After Tommy's death, once the immediate confusion of rescue attempts and police statements has dissipated, Wilkie considers whether to go through with his own attempt. But he realises that, given the confusing effects of synchronicity, the two deaths would become irremediably linked. People would wonder whether Wilkie's accident was also suicide, whether he and Tommy "had once been intimate" (p.107), whether in fact he was also an AIDS victim. Occupying the same site leads to a confusing mirroring and mimicry. The scene of contamination by association also exposes the central mechanism of Lurie's novel, in which AIDS is seen as an analogy to the straight world's view of gays. As several commentators have demonstrated, AIDS often was seen as if it gave physical form to the normative view of deviance. When AIDS was a disease of gays, the world scarcely noticed. When it showed signs of infecting others the world began to wake up. Wilkie's homophobia exposes him to all his worst fears, as if he had somehow caught AIDS in metaphor. As David Black argues, any account of AIDS is not just a story about the gay community but also a story about the straight community's reaction:

> it's a story about how the straight community has used and is using AIDS as a mask for its feelings about gayness. It is a story about the ramifications of a metaphor. The traditional straight fear that gayness is somehow catching has found its ideal expression in the equation of homosexuality with disease. Gay = AIDS.[15]

---

[15] David Black, *The Plague Years. A Chronicle of AIDS, The Epidemic of Our Times* (New York: Simon and Schuster, 1985), p.30.

In writing about AIDS in an oblique mirrored fashion through the vehicle of the straight Wilkie, Lurie avoids making AIDS a ghettoised gay story, and insists that it is a human story. Wilkie's metaphoric illness draws him into the gay imaginary while exposing the illusions of the straight world. Wilkie fears contamination by Tommy's death in the sense that his "story" – the eventual biography on which he had planned to collaborate – would be fatally altered by sharing the site of his death with an AIDS victim. This connection between viral and linguistic contamination underlines the dangers posed by metaphor to the scientist's discourse. Catherine Waldby has argued that in scientific discourse metaphors may form chains of analogy which travel across system boundaries, contagious and uncontrollable.

> They infect each other, forming chains of association
> which can link different texts and narratives together
> in complex ways without regard for the nature/culture
> distinction. They create intertextual relations which
> complicate the simplicity of referential chains, and
> assimilate the authoritative discourse of science
> towards the less certain status of literature.[16]

Lurie's own discursive space is similarly traversed by illness-as-metaphor linking the different sites of her heterotopia in unexpected ways. As the heterotopia mirrors the "normal" world in distorted fashion, so Wilkie's fictional disease undermines straight assumptions, intermingling nature (the sociobiologist's foundational value) with culture. There is thus a general lesson implicit in the character of Wilkie – that scientific discourse may find that metaphor destabilises its own claims to transparency of language, and to the derivation of its knowledge in a direct way from the naturally given object. In scientific discourse every metaphoric performance is the text's point of vulnerability to an irreverent reading. Wilkie Walker is walking proof. As a scientist Wilkie is quite capable of extending his arguments from animal to human, when it suits his own purposes. But once the comparison has been made it may be extended in other directions, and to other ends.

One example will bring the point into sharp relief. Wilkie, killing time before the weather conditions improve sufficiently for him to kill himself, agrees to accompany Jacko's mother and his tiresome cousin, Barbie, on a trip to a dolphin sanctuary. Wilkie's

---

[16] Catherine Waldby, *AIDS and the Body Politic. Biomedecine and Sexual Difference* (London: Routledge, 1996), p.30. See also Paula Treichler, "AIDS, Homophobia and Biomedical Discourse: an epidemic of signification," in Douglas Crimp (ed.), *AIDS: Cultural Analysis, Cultural Activism* (Cambridge, Mass.: MIT Press, 1988), 31-70.

mind is swift to connect human and animal. When Barbie creates a
sentimental fuss, cooing over injured animals, Wilkie describes it as a
performance which is almost as automatic in her case as that of a
performing dolphin. Itself a heterotopic site, the dolphin sanctuary is
an ambivalent locale, both a necessary refuge and place of rescue, and
uncomfortably akin to a theme park or zoo. Its economy is not unlike
the macro economy of Key West, dependent on a constant supply of
damaged specimens for its own survival.

> When the supply of damaged individuals fell off,
> there would be a natural tendency to keep them in
> care as long as possible, to sentimentalize them and
> treat them as pets. (pp.110-11).

Wilkie is swift to seize the parallel to his own ageing state. Just as
Lady Edna, an old dolphin, can no longer be released into the ocean
where she could no longer survive, he feels that he "couldn't make it
on my own in the wild any more" (p.112) and is reinforced in his plan
to "go back to the ocean" and drown (p.112). The old have become,
in his view, sacred cows, useless but preserved into a dismal old age
which would never have occurred in the natural state. Despite the
sensible comment from the tour guide (Glory Green, older and wiser)
that we cannot extrapolate from human to animal, that we can never
really know what animals feel, Wilkie continues to anthropomorphise
animals and to animalise human beings. The reader, however, is swift
to extend the human-animal comparison in a different direction, to a
group for whom Wilkie has less compassion. When the tour group
suddenly spot a manatee the question of the survival of the apparently
useless comes into focus from a rather different angle. Slow moving,
easily injured by motor boats, the Florida manatee has also recently
become the victim of a mysterious disease, affecting its ability to
breed and the health of its offspring.[17] "The pups get sick and die,"
(p.114) the guide explains. Jacko's mother, thinking at once of her
own sick pup, slumps forward in tears. Wherever one endangered
species is referred to, notions of other endangered groups come into
play, in the slippery translations of metaphor.

It is no accident that Lurie transports Wilkie as a metaphorical
gay from one site to another within the Key West heterotopia. The
connection between heterotopia and metaphor is a close one. Just as
"other spaces" destabilise the grounds of meaning, so metaphor
unsettles our assumptions. As Eric Cheyfitz reminds us, Aristotle's

---

[17] Kurt Kleiner, "Mystery Malady Claims Florida's Gentle Giants," *New Scientist* 150 (20 April 1996), p.11.

basic definition of metaphor involved transporting a term from a familiar to a foreign place, from its proper significance to a figurative sense, with the idea of resemblance or similitude determining the decorous limits of such transportation. (Wilkie's categorisation of his overrefined first wife as a Persian cat and his feisty second wife as an Alaskan husky would fail the test for most readers.) "Metaphora" derives from the verb "metaphero", to carry across. In the *Poetics* Aristotle describes metaphor as

> The application of an alien name by transference either from genus to species, or from species to genus, or from species to species, or by analogy.[18]

As Cheyfitz argues, theories of metaphor are inseparable from ideas of place, and of the frontiers between domestic and foreign, self and "Other". When vigorously policed by the agents of rhetorical politics, metaphor may come under suspicion as the foreign – "far-fetched" comparisons are the frontier of metaphor, only dubiously acceptable. They have gone too far, taken the reader to "other places". They threaten the assumption that the domestic should dominate the alien, the different be sacrificed to similitude. On the positive side, however, as in Lurie's translation of the scientific discourse of sociobiology into literature, and of one species into another, metaphor opens up a space for interpretation, allowing a simultaneous perception of likeness and difference. Jacko and Wilkie are in most respects diametric opposites. Yet they share their endangered status and the same animal reference. Just to reinforce the point, Barbie Mumpson describes the manatee – tubby, brownish grey and bewhiskered – as rather like Professor Walker (p.120).

As a result wherever one endangered species features (e.g. the ageing, the salt marsh mouse) the reader translates the reference to a gay application. Given the straight world's initial impassivity to the fate of endangered gays, Wilkie's concern for *Reithrodontomys raviventris* becomes distinctly questionable. Turning the comparison around, if non-reproductive, uselessly extravagant gays, are surplus to the requirements of the species, what of senior citizens? It is the final irony of the novel, perhaps, that Wilkie ends up lecturing to a large audience in Key West, made up of wealthy retirees,

> also an endangered species – endangered by age and illness and irrelevance – but most obviously and

---

[18] On the connection between metaphor and place, in an imperialist context, see Eric Cheyfitz, *The Poetics of Imperialism: Translation and Colonisation From The Tempest to Tarzan* (Oxford: Oxford University Press, 1991). Quoted p.35.

immediately by death. When Wilkie declared that an aquatic mammal, though not productive or attractive or well-adapted to its present environment, was still very valuable, interesting, and worth preserving, they naturally felt better. Because by analogy, so were they. (p.244).

If any character, however, appears least well-fitted for survival, it is Barbie Mumpson, repeatedly described by all around her as clumsy, impractical, and a booby. Childless, and the hapless victim of a philandering husband and scheming mother, Barbie enters the novel as companion to Jacko's mother, to Jacko's ill-concealed horror. She continually repeats to all who will listen to her that she has never served any useful purpose in life, and is good for absolutely nothing, and she swiftly decides that her best course would be to drown herself. Wilkie is infuriated by yet another mirror self ("Was everyone in Key West planning to imitate him in this farcical way?" p.201), another distorted reflection of his own intentions, and visualises Barbie (slow, fleshy, harmless but not very bright) in her turn as a manatee. It is Barbie, however, apparently surplus to all requirements, who rearranges the lives of every character, to the benefit of them all. When Barbie gives Wilkie a spontaneous hug, Jenny, invisible in the gloom, assumes that an affair is in process, and after months of hesitation, throws herself into the arms of Lee.   As Wilkie later realises, it was not at all irrational for Jenny to assume that he was in love with Barbie.

> Statistically, genetically … a man of his age was supposed to wish to discard his ageing wife and impregnate younger and presumably more fertile females. His selfish genes were said to be urging him to produce more and more children so that they, the genes, could be sure of survival. (p.231).

As a result, far from staging a perfect exit, he realises that he would have left behind a miserable and embittered wife who believed he was having an affair with a brainless bimbo. And he has only his own much vaunted sociobiological views to blame. That Wilkie is alive to make this realisation is also thanks to Barbie's intervention. Wilkie is saved from death fortuitously (while choking on a sandwich in the midst of a gallstone attack) by Barbie who gets him to hospital and insists on immediate treatment for the famous naturalist. Here, in perhaps the most galling of Wilkie's realisations, he discovers that he is suffering only from gallstones and hemorrhoids and is at no more risk of death than any other seventy year old. When he actually **is** sick (the gallstones attack) he discovers that he never **was** sick – real illness replaces the imaginary and the metaphoric.

In terms of the kinship selection hypothesis, Barbie's relation to Jacko is even more revealing. In the novel the gay characters at first appear to support the vision of altruism offered by some commentators. Lesbian Lee is a thoroughly admirable character, often providing free board and therapy to various women in crisis, humane and deeply concerned for the welfare of others. She makes her first appearance in terms which are almost too symbolic when she rescues Jenny from drowning as a result of a painful jellyfish sting. Appropriately the species is the man of war. The antidote is papaya – conveniently carried by Key West residents as meat tenderizer. With the comment "I have what you need" (p.37) Lee tenderizes Jenny's injured thigh in a scene entirely proleptic of the various *tendresses* to come. Tommy and Dennis feature as absolutely devoted longterm partners, firmly in the romantic mould. When Tommy arranges his suicide he first makes Dennis promise (shades of Ingrid Bergman and Gregory Peck in *For Whom the Bell Tolls*) to go on living for both of them, playing their Callas records, eating artichokes and hollandaise sauce, and drinking Dubonnet. Dennis has cared for Tommy to the very end and is devastated by his death. Clearly both Lee and Dennis espouse a creed of romantic love which makes them easily assimilable to the heterosexual norm. Lurie is no sentimentalist, however, whether the species is animal or human, and Jacko is characterised rather differently, in order to give full weight to more radical positions in gay politics. Unlike Dennis, Jacko favours casual sex with strangers, preferring never to learn such personal details as last names or family background. As he expresses it, pungently, to Lee:

> The better I know somebody, the less he excites me. Pretty soon he isn't a great fuck any more, he's just some guy I know. (p.173).

Jacko never sought an AIDS test; he was tested without his knowledge when he cut himself mending a greenhouse. And he regrets having the knowledge. Though he recognises that the having the disease is rather like "carrying a concealed weapon" (p.175) and that he has been "walking around in my sleep, killing people without knowing it, like some zombie in an old horror flick" (p.175) Jacko still cannot bring himself to regret the past.

> Even now, when I think of some of the fantastic times I've had, I can't make myself wish they'd never happened. Sometimes I think it was worth it, those

years. That I was lucky to have been born when I was. (p.175).

If Tommy and Dennis represent the new post-AIDS emphasis on monogamy, romantic love and stable partnerships, Jacko is more akin to the image of the "fast-track gay", for whom more sex is automatically equated with more freedom. Some gay activists have welcomed anonymous promiscuity as a means of ridding themselves of the earlier image of the gay male as effeminate, mooning romantically over some pale youth. The orgiastic excesses of the San Francisco bathhouses, for example, feature in some accounts as a radical validation of free emotion, as opposed to the sin and guilt laid upon gays by a repressive society. If others view this argument as encouraging the worst stereotypically male behaviour – fear of emotion, lack of commitment, aggressive scoring and cruising – it is none the less equally arguable that Jacko espouses a politics of romanticism where desire exists to disrupt order and where transgression is a key to pleasure.[19]   His gay community is a heterotopia which vigorously undermines the standards of the straight world, in a fashion which can never be the case with Lee's altruism or Dennis's romantic pair-bonding, both much more easily seen as assimilationist positions. It is a measure of Lurie's achievement that she does not fight shy of presenting the contradictions within the gay heterotopia, that she resists any easy categorisation of gays as a monolithic species, and that she gives Jacko a fair run for his money.

Nor is it easy to envisage Jacko as endorsing the kinship selection hypothesis. After breaking with most of his family back in Oklahoma Jacko has maintained contact only with his mother, with whom he shares a keen love of gardening. There is no love lost between him and Barbie, whom he remembers from family events as always "striking out on the team" (p.84). Because Jacko was gay ("It's not as if you had a steady girlfriend" p.84) his aunt saw him as a spare male and repeatedly forced him to partner Barbie to assorted social events, with the result that, far from feeling altruistic kinship, he cordially detests her. Yet it is Barbie who saves Jacko from the machinations of her mother – and saves his fortune from being diverted into the coffers of homophobic politicos. Politics per se enters the novel in the person of Barbie's husband, congressman Bob Hickock. In the name of kinship, Myra has descended on Key West,

---

[19] For accounts of the division in the gay community between orgiasts and celibates in reaction to the AIDS crisis see Randy Shilts, *And The Band Played On. Politics, People and the AIDS Epidemic* (London: Penguin, 1988); Dennis Altman, *AIDS and the New Puritanism* (London: Pluto, 1986).

partly to make Barbie go back to her husband, partly to enquire into Jacko's condition – medical and economic. Myra is virulently homophobic, using the term "pansy" freely, originally suggesting that Jacko be "cured" of the disease of gayness by psychiatry, and now unable even to shake his hand, lest she catch AIDS. As a Bible-thumping, anti-abortion Republican she roundly condemns Key West as a place of loose perversions, on the ground that she has seen two men kissing in public. Myra's political views underline the degree to which Wilkie's sociobiological views, and much official discourse concerning homosexuality, are complicit with a phallocentric human order in which only the heterosexual male is fully human, and can represent the body politic. As Myra's actions suggest, it is assumed that the sex of the body politic is masculine, and that those who represent it (like Barbie's husband) by standing for its interests, also represent it in the sense of producing the right image.[20] The health of the heterosexual male body can therefore stand for the health of the body politic. Barbie's husband is exceptionally good-looking, six foot five, deep-voiced and photogenic. Unfortunately he takes the heterosexual logic to a philandering extreme. Although his infidelity is indisputable, Myra tells Barbie that she must remain with her husband for the good of his political career.

> It was her job to be her husband's helpmate, especially in politics where the wife was an important part of the public image. (p.144).

Barbie's oldfashioned role as wife mirrors Jenny's anachronistic submission to her husband's career. It is appropriate therefore that Barbie's flight from her husband is a major factor in Jenny's liberation – another mirroring between rather different characters.

Barbie also thwarts her mother's political intentions in more specific fashion. For Myra, Jacko is prey. She has every intention that his childlessness will benefit his kin group. After his death she plans to seize his property from his weak-willed mother and pass the proceeds right along to the Republican party. Myra is entirely scornful of her daughter's environmental enthusiasms and dismisses the manatee as "not fitted for the modern world" (p.135). Yet it is Barbie who foils her plans. Despite (or almost because) of her clumsiness and his ill-will, it is Barbie (last seen in a Save the Manatee t-shirt) who saves Jacko's bacon. When she drops a tray of plants and tactlessly tells Jacko (recovering from a bout of viral pneumonia) that he is too sick for the heavy work of gardening, he

---

[20] Waldby, pp.83-94.

erupts and tells her that she is merely her mother's mouthpiece, parroting Myra's views as always. Infuriated, Barbie spills the beans – that Myra does not want to take him back to Tulsa for the good of his health, or to sell the house for his medical treatment, but that she will take the property for her own, just as she has already induced her sister to sell her house in order to finance Bob's political campaign. In the upshot, the wicked sister is defeated – though as a result she decides to run for office herself rather than propping up the political careers of various males by her fundraising efforts. Though she is clearly on the wrong side as far as Lurie is concerned, it looks as if she will prove highly effective despite her gender. When Myra takes Molly Hopkins to lunch in an attempt to pump her for details of Jacko's condition, a row erupts in the restaurant as a drunken tourist castigates Dennis as a "dumb little chink" in a "goddam pansy place" (p.141). It is Myra who comes to his defence, and (with a certain amount of incidental damage) sees the rowdy unceremoniously ejected. While the vision of Myra with political power may give the reader pause, it is none the less her daughter who has made it possible for her to fulfil her own ambitions.

In short, through the intervention of Barbie, the least obviously useful character in the novel, Jenny finds love with Lee and part-time employment in her own right to boot, Jacko's house is protected from Myra's rapaciousness, Wilkie is saved from an ignominious death and sees something of the error of his ways, Myra emerges from the political shadows, and Barbie herself divorces her husband and finds a new career as an environmentalist, incidentally becoming the salvation of the crippled Molly Hopkins, who offers her room and board in exchange for all the little household tasks which Molly can no longer carry out. Supporting the manatee with one hand and Molly with the other, Barbie has struck a balance between the claims of animal and human. A complete klutz, and an apparent disaster in sociobiological terms, she is actually the lynchpin of the plot and is instrumental in engineering a beneficial new set of human arrangements, likely to enhance the survival and the happiness of all concerned. Importantly, the heterosexual pair bond is almost entirely absent from the new social settlement. Lurie's novel moves away from the initial focus on Wilkie and Jenny, sidesteps the possibility of a new partnership in Jenny and Gerry (despite the latter's erotic advances) or Wilkie and Barbie, and leaves the characters happily rearranged in looser imaginary communities and families, outside the sociobiological paradigm. All the characters benefit from leaving the "pair bond", the bedrock of sociobiology, behind them in favour of less archaic models. Elective communities - created culturally – have replaced so-called natural ones. The heterosexual story is moved to the margins as the plot engineers the deconstruction of the pair bond in favour of extended or invented kinship structures.

It is perhaps Leonard Zimmern who has the last word. Leonard has mellowed only slightly, to the extent of showing photographs of his grandchildren to his cousin, Lee. As he comments, at his age "you start thinking about your family ... Where do we come from, Who are we, Where are we going?" (p.248). Yet Leonard is in Key West to speak at a conference on "Nature and Anti-Nature." "I'm Anti-Nature," he announces (p.249), treating Lee to an example of his debunking anecdotes about the heroes of the environmentalist movement. Though Leonard is gleefully playing the role of agent provocateur in exaggerated terms, he is perfectly serious when he describes nature as "what civilisation was invented to get away from" (p.248). Even Wilkie finally recognises that it is not the survival of his genes (as represented by a bossy daughter and ineffectual son) which interests him. "It was the survival of his work that he cared about, not some random, rather unsatisfactory collection of DNA like the two he and Jenny had already produced." (p.232). Euphoric at his escape (at least for the moment) from the Grim Reaper Wilkie rewrites the ending of his latest work, *The Copper Beech*, a biography of a famous tree. Throughout the novel the progress of this work has been stalled as Wilkie debated its ending. Although the actual tree is in its prime, Wilkie believes that for good didactic and dramatic purposes, the book must end like all great biographies with the death of its subject – whether from lingering and pathetic disease, hostile human forces, or a natural disaster. He is sufficiently self-aware to see that the book is his own story – the king of the forest fallen – and that a tragic accident would suit both man and tree best. At the close of the novel however he revises his views, recasts the final chapter in the future conditional and posits several possible futures. The pathos of Wilkie's previous depiction of Salty, with its opening description of a lonely rodent in a zoo, the last survivor of the species, a mouse Last of the Mohicans gazing out through the bars, had actually had the effect of hastening the extinction of the mouse, presenting its fate as determined, unavoidable. By offering different possible futures Wilkie demonstrates the possibility that nature may yet imitate culture, life imitate art, that culture may be more influential on the evolution and the survival of the species than the sociobiologist imagines. Culture invents nature – but it may invent it in different ways and with different effects – ranging from Wilkie's anthropomorphism to Gerry's pastoral primitivism or the exotic orchids which Jacko buys for his gardening business. Wilkie is by no means a completely reformed character (he is planning a new book on Manny the Manatee and his mate Annie, with associated spin-off soft toys) but he has shed the determinism of his earlier beliefs. The lesson is a general one, as an exchange between Molly and Jacko demonstrates. The pair have just dug up a large bougainvillea and are in almost equal states of collapse:

> "I felt so dizzy and weak, as if I was dying. Well, of course in a way I am dying." She laughed unhappily. (p.41).

Jacko responds:

> "If you look at it that way, you're dying and I'm dying. But at the moment we're alive. So are we living or are we dying or both?... The way I figure it, everyone is living, everyone is dying." (241).

The new form of the biography suggests an unlikely agreement between Wilkie and Lee, who remembers reading that as you get older you have a choice: "you can live in the fading past, or, like children do, in the bright full present" (p.253). The novel leaves its characters right there. It is a moral which also strikes sociobiology, monopolised by the belief that all the significant things in human nature were decided in some distant past, right out of the picture. As a result Lurie's novel ends in a fashion which manages to function both as the demonstration of an intellectual position, and as the culmination of a profoundly humane work of imagination.

Bibliography

Novels

Love and Friendship. London: Heinemann, and New York: Macmillan, 1962.
The Nowhere City. London: Heinemann, 1965, and New York: Coward McCann, 1966.
Imaginary Friends. London: Heinemann and New York: Coward McCann, 1967.
Real People. New York: Random House, 1969, and London: Heinemann, 1970.
The War Between the Tates. New York: Random House and London: Heinemann, 1974.
Only Children. New York: Random House and London: Heinemann, 1979.
Foreign Affairs. New York: Random House, 1984, and London: Joseph, 1985.
The Truth About Lorin Jones. Boston: Little Brown and London: Joseph, 1988.
The Last Resort. New York: Henry Holt and London: Chatto and Windus, 1998.

Short Stories

"A Story of Women." *Commentary* 11, 4 (October, 1946): 336-8.
"Hansel and Gretel." *New Story* 2 (1951): 15-30.
"Not Wanted On Voyage." *Shenandoah* 34, 4 (1983): 3-25. (Excerpt from *Foreign Affairs*).
"Charades." *Vanity Fair* September 1984: 82-5, 121, 130-135. (Excerpt from *Foreign Affairs*).
"Excerpt from *The Truth About Lorin Jones.*" *The Key West Reader.* Ed. George Murphy. Key West: Tortugas, 1989. 143-171.
"Fat People." *Vogue* 179 (October 1989): 438-9, 466-70, and *Good Housekeeping*, 137, 5 (May 1990): 155, 158-60, 164-5, 170-171.
"Ilse's House." *New York Woman* April 1990: 110-116, and *Cosmopolitan* October 1990: 252-259.
"A Curious Haunting." *Redbook* October 1990: 40-52.
"The Pool People." *Vogue* August 1991: 250-3, 314-6.
Women and Ghosts. New York: Doubleday and London: Heinemann, 1994.

"The Highboy." *The Oxford Book of Twentieth Century Ghost Stories*. Ed. Michael Cox. Oxford: Oxford University Press, 1996. 390-402.

Poetry

"The Graveyard." *The Harvard Wake* 1, 3 (March 1945): 25.
"The Archer With His Arrow." *Poetry* 70, 3 (June 1947): 126.
"In A Good Year." *Poetry* 70, 3 (June 1947): 127.
"Trees Being Neighbours." *Poetry* 70, 3 (June 1947): 127-8.

Children's Literature

Classics of Children's Literature 1621-1932. Selected and arranged by Alison Lurie and Justin G. Schiller. New York: Garland, 1976-8.
The Heavenly Zoo: Legends and Tales of the Stars. London: Eel Pie, 1979, and New York: Farrar Straus, 1980.
Clever Gretchen and Other Forgotten Folktales. New York: Crowell, and London: Heinemann, 1980.
Fabulous Beasts. New York: Farrar Straus, and London: Cape, 1981.
Ed. *The Oxford Book of Modern Fairy Tales*. Oxford: Oxford University Press, 1993.

Non-fiction

"Realism and Sociology." *Commentary*, IV, 2 (August 1947): 199-200.
"The Unwon Victory." *Commentary*, IV, 3 (September 1947): 298-99.
V. R. Lang: A Memoir. Privately printed, 1959. *Poems and Plays* by V. R. Lang. New York: Random House, and London: Heinemann, 1975: 3-71.
"Early Powell." *New York Review of Books*, May 1963: 24.
"Consumers' Report." *New York Review of Books* 9 December 1965: 37-40.
"Intellect and Non-Violence." *New York Review of Books* 15 December 1966: 27-30.
"The View From the Moon." *New Statesman* 10 July 1970: 19.
"Some of our best friends are witches." *Nova* August 1970: 52-7.
"Up Jenkins." *Summary* 1, 1 (October 1970): 82-83.

"The Happy Extremists." *Sunday Times Magazine* 18 October 1970: 68-80.

"Fairy Tale Liberation." *New York Review of Books* XV, 11 (17 December 1970): 42-44.

"Orpheus in the Book World." *Daily Telegraph* 18 February 1971: 6.

"War of the Worlds." *Observer* 13 June 1971: 28.

"Witches and Fairies: Fitzgerald to Updike." *New York Review of Books* XVII, 9 (2 December 1971): 6-10.

"The Career that Self-Destructs." *Life* 72, 8 (3 March 1972): 16.

"The Enemy Within." *Observer* 18 June 1972: 32.

"Good Children's Books." *New York Review of Books* 14 December 1972: 40-41.

"Feminine Sensibility: A Forum." *Harvard Advocate* CVI, 2/3 (March 1973): 14.

"Back to Pooh Corner." *Children's Literature*, II (1973): 11-17. Rpt. in *Reflections on Literature for Children*. Ed. Francelia Butler and Richard Rotert. Hamden, Connecticut: Shoestring Press, 1984. 32-38.

"Wise-Women." *New York Review of Books* 14 June 1973: 18-19.

"Secondary Considerations." *New Statesman* 15 June 1973: 889-890.

"Review of *The Juniper Tree and Other Tales From Grimm*." *New York Times Book Review* 78, 44 (4 November 1973): 25-26.

"The Fate of the Munchkins." *New York Review of Books* XXI, 6 (18 April 1974): 24-25.

"Out of the Sack." *New Statesman* 26 April 1974: 591.

"What Happened in Hamlet." *New Review* 1, 2 (May, 1974): 33-42.

"Happy Endings." *New Statesman* 31 May 1974: 769-70.

"-------------." *New York Review of Books* 28 November 1974: 39-41.

"Beatrix Potter in Paper." *New York Times Book Review* LXXIX, 49 (8 December 1974): 38-39.

"The Boy Who Couldn't Grow Up." *New York Review of Books* XXII, 1 (6 February 1975): 11-15.

"The Life and Death of Bunny Lang." *New Review* 2, 15 (1975): 9-33.

"A Nonconformist Falls in Line." *Psychology Today* April, 1975: 16, 21, 96.

"The Power of Smokey." *New York Review of Books* XXII, 10 (12 June 1975): 34-35. (See also Letter from Graham Greene in response, *New York Review of Books*, 22 (18 September 1975): 60.)

"*The Drac: French Tales of Dragons and Demons*." *New York Times Book Review* LXXX, 46 (16 November 1975): 29, 38.

"Lost Women: V. R. Lang." *Ms. Magazine* December, 1975: 118-124.

"A Tail of Terror." *New York Review of Books* XXII, 20 (11 December 1975): 26-8.

"The Haunted Wood." *Harper's* June 1976: 94-97.

"Now We Are Fifty." *New York Times Book Review* 81, 46 (14 November 1976): 27.

"The Dress Code." *New York Review of Books* XXIII, 19 (25 November 1976): 17-20.

"---------------." *New Society* 9 December 1976: 520-2.

"Preface." *Holiday House* by Catherine Sinclair. *Classics of Children's Literature 1621-1932*. Vol. 24. New York: Garland, 1976, v-viii.

"Preface." *Lob Lie-by-the-Fire, Jackanapes* and *Daddy Darwin's Dovecot. Classics of Children's Literature 1621-1932*. Vol. 41. New York: Garland, 1976-8, v-vii.

"Preface." *Anyhow Stories* by Mrs Clifford. *Classics of Children's Literature 1621-1932*. Vol. 49. New York: Garland, 1976-8, v-x.

"Fairy Tales for a Liberated Age." *Horizon* XIX, 4 (July 1977): 80-85.

"Lost Women: Beatrix Potter: More Than Just Peter Rabbit." *Ms. Magazine* September 1977: 41, 43, 45.

"The Classics Remain." *New York Times Book Review* 82 (46) (13 November 1977): 31, 60.

"The Round Table in Ruins." *New York Review of Books* XXIV, 19 (24 November 1977): 3-4.

"To the Sideshow." *New York Review of Books* XXV, 4 (23 March 1978): 22-24.

"Of Pigs and Men." *Observer* 11 June 1978: 11.

"The Language of Fashion." *Observer Magazine* 24 September, 1978: 38-41.

"From Rags to Rags." *New York Review of Books* XXV, 19 (7 December 1978): 25-29.

"Braking for Elves." *New York Review of Books* XXVI, 3 (8 March 1979): 16-19.

"Vulgar, Coarse and Grotesque: Subversive Books for Kids." *Harper's* 259 (December 1979): 66-69. Rpt. as "On the Subversive Side," *Times Literary Supplement*, 28 March 1980: 353-4.

"Return of the Ship of Fools." *New Republic* 30 August 1980: 17-18, 20-21.

"Ford Madox Ford's Fairy Tales." *Children's Literature* 8 (1980): 7-21. Rpt. in *The Presence of Ford Madox Ford.* Ed. Sondra J. Stang. Philadelphia: University of Pennsylvania Press, 1981: 130-142.

"Sex and Fashion." *New York Review of Books* XXVIII, 16 (22 October 1981): 38-46.

The Language of Clothes. New York, Random House, 1981 and London, Heinemann, 1982. Rpt. London: Bloomsbury, 1992.

"The World of the Pied Piper." *New York Review of Books* XXIX, 4 (18 March 1982): 15-18.

"Mizilca, a Folk Tale." *Short Story International*, 2, 6 (1982).

"No One Asked Me To Write A Novel." *New York Times Book Review* 87, 23 (6 June 1982): 13, 46-8.

"Their Harvard." *My Harvard, My Yale.* Ed. Diana Dubois. New York: Random House, 1982: 34-45.

"My Name or Yours?" *Observer* 20 February 1983: 27.

"Skin Deep." *New York Review of Books* XXX, 9 (2 June 1983): 20-22.

"The Steamy Side of Paradise." *House and Garden*, June 1983: 30, 32, 38-40.

"Key West: Neverland with Palms." *New York Times Magazine* 9 October 1983: 38-39.

"From the Bottom Out-of-Sights On Up." *New York Times Book Review* 88, 46 (13 November 1983): 7.

"The Benevolent Tower." *House and Garden* 156, 9 (September 1984): 174-5, 226, 229.

"Class." *New York Times Book Review* 7 October 1984: 38.

"Riding the Wave of the Future." *New York Review of Books* 25 October 1984: 19-22.

"Prince Myshkin, Gigi and Dr Johnson." *New York Times* 2 December 1984: 43.

"Arts Fair." *Vanity Fair* December 1984: 108.

"Shock of Recognition." *Evening Standard* 6 February 1985: 19.

"Love in the Afternoon." *Vanity Fair* May 1985: 88-9.

"Poetry and its Smallest Audience." *New York Times Book Review* 5 May 1985: 16.

"On the Road to Timbuktu." *House and Garden* 157, 9 (September, 1985): 46-60.

"Life's Greatest Hits." *New York Review of Books* XXXII, 16 (24 October 1985): 35-6.

"Does Politeness Lead to Virtue?" *New York Times Book Review* 10 November 1985: 13.

"Bad Housekeeping." *New York Review of Books*, XXXII, 20 (19 December 1985): 8-10. Rpt. in *Critical Views: Doris Lessing*, New York: Chelsea House, 1986.

"Petals Personified." *Art and Antiques* Summer 1986: 63-65.

"To the Manner Born." *New York Times Magazine* 24 August 1986: 151, 186.

"Roly-poly Fun and Feasting." *New York Times Book Review* XCI, 45 (9 November 1986): 37, 61.

"Afterword." *Peter Pan* by J. M. Barrie. New York: Signet Classics, 1987: 193-200.

"True Confessions." *New York Review of Books* 11 June 1987: 19-20.

"Folklore and Literature." *Halcyon: A Journal of the Humanities* 1988: 1-12.

"Plain Tales from a Garrison Town." *Observer Magazine* 24 January 1988: 22-25.

"Love is on the Cards." *Observer Magazine* 7 February 1988: 48.

"Underground Artist." *New York Review of Books* 18 February 1988: 11-13. Rpt. as "William Mayne." *Children and their Books: A Celebration of the Work of Iona and Peter Opie.* Ed. Gillian Avery and Julia Briggs. Oxford: Clarendon Press, 1989: 369-379.

"A Moody Retreat Under Italy's Alps." *New York Times* 3 April 1988: 13.

"The Woman Who Rode Away." *New York Review of Books* 12 May 1988: 3-4.

"The Politics of Fashion." *Fame* June 1988.

"The Frog Prince." *New York Review of Books* 24 November 1988: 33-4.

"Books of the Year." *Observer* 4 December 1988: 65.

"Armies Marched on Hand-Knit Socks." *New York Times Book Review* 4 December, 1988: 17.

"Introduction." *Artflyer.* By Steve Poleskie. Southampton, England: Hansard Gallery, The University, 1989: N.pag.

"The Mean Years." *Ms. Magazine* March 1989: 38-41.

"Battling to the bitter end." *The Observer* 29 October 1989: 47.

"Love With the Perfect Dog." *New York Times Book Review* 12 November 1989: 12.

"A Dictionary for Deconstructors." *New York Review of Books* XXXVI, 18 (23 November, 1989): 49-50.

"A Child's Garden of Subversion." *New York Times Book Review* 25 February 1990: 1, 34.

Don't Tell the Grown-ups: Subversive Children's Literature. Boston: Little, Brown, and London: Bloomsbury, 1990.

"Another Dangerous Story from Salman Rushdie." *New York Times Book Review* 11 November 1990: 1, 59.

"Notes on the Language of Poststructuralism." *The State of the Language.* Ed. Christopher Ricks and Leonard Michaels. London: Faber, 1990: 289-295.

"The Cabinet of Dr Seuss." *New York Review of Books* 20 December 1990: 50-52.

"A Fine Romance." *New York Review of Books* XXXVIII, 8 (25 April 1991): 23-4. Rpt. as "Introduction." *The Bostonians.* By Henry James. New York: Vintage, 1991.

"A Philosopher In The Alps." *New York Times Book Review* 5 January 1992: 10-11.

"I Saw Esau." *New York Times Book Review* 17 May 1992: 23.

"Hanging Out With Hogarth." *New York Times Book Review* 11 October 1992: 7.

"An Edward Sorel Christmas." *New York Times Book Review* 6 December 1992: 16-20.

"Undiscovered Country." *New York Review of Books* 17 December 1992: 16-20.

"Love Has Its Consequences." *New York Times Book Review* 8 August 1993: 1, 25.

"Cootie Power." *New York Review of Books* XL (16 December 1993): 31-33.

"Leaving the Door Ajar." *New York Review of Books* 7 April 1994: 21-23.

"On James Merrill, 1926-1995." *New York Review of Books* 23 March 1995: 9.

"Moo." *New York Times Book Review* 2 April 1995: 1.

"She Had It All." *New York Review of Books* 42, 4, 1995: 3-5.

"Opening the Box of Delights." *New York Review of Books* XLII, 20 (12 December 1995): 48-53.

"Preface." *American fairy tales: from Rip Van Winkle to the Rootabaga Stories.* By Neil Philip. New York: Hyperion, 1996.

"Winter's Tales." *New York Times Book Review* 19 May 1996: 11.

"Bothered and Bewildered." *New York Review of Books* XLIV, 16 (23 October 1997): 48-53.

"Reading At Escape Velocity." *New York Times Book Review,* 17 May 1998: p.51.

"The Sound Of Trumpets." *New York Times Book Review* 28 March 1999: p.30.

Recordings

"Novel Marriages." Audiotape. J. Norton, The Avid Reader, 1975.
"The War Between the Tates." Videorecording. Producer, David Susskind. Time Life Video, New York, 1980.
"Alison Lurie Interview with Kay Bonetti." Audiotape. American Audio Prose Library, Columbia, Missouri, 1980.
"Alison Lurie Reads excerpts from *Only Children*." Audiotape. American Audio Prose Library, 1981.
"Writers in Conversation: Alison Lurie in conversation with Malcolm Bradbury." I.C.A. Video, 1986.

Interviews

Bannon, Barbara A. "Alison Lurie." *Publishers' Weekly*, 206, 8 (19 August, 1974): 6.
Barber, Michael. "Unlike you we don't have many serious women novelists." *The Guardian* 8 July 1974: 8.
Blades, John. "Seeing Spectres." *Chicago Tribune* 31 October 1994: 5.
Chambers, Andrea. "In Winter, U.S. Writing Talent Pools On The Sensual, Timeless Port Of Key West." *People Weekly* 23 February 1981: 24-29.
Chunn, Louise. "When being naughty can be fun." *The Guardian*, 30 May 1990: 17.
Edmonds, Dale. "The World Seemed So Empty To Me If I Wasn't Writing." *Negative Capability* 6, 4 (1986): 152-9.
Ellis, Abby. "Making Her Mark: An Interview with Alison Lurie." *Bloomsbury Review*, 10 (March/April 1990): 11, 18.
Ferrell, S. "Research for A Love Affair." *New York Times Book Review* September 1988: 3.
Hallet, Lucy Hughes. "The Deadly Accurate Miss Alison Lurie." *Good Housekeeping* February, 1985: 48.
Hite, Milly. "Belles Lettres Interview." *Belles Lettres* 2 (July-August 1987): 9.
Jackson, David. "An Interview with Alison Lurie." *Shenandoah* 31, iv (1980): 15-27.
Kaufelt, Lynn Mitsuko, *Key West Writers and Their Houses*. Englewood and Fort Lauderdale, Florida: Pineapple and Omnigraphics, 1986: 132-3.
Langton, James. "In the Court of 'Queen Herod'." *Sunday Telegraph* 3 May 1996: 3.

Lear, Liz. "Alison Lurie: An Interview." *Key West Review* 1, 1 (Spring 1988): 42-52.

Lehman, David. "A Kind of Witchery." *New York* 24 September 1984: 97.

Morris, James McGrath. "Pulitzer Winner Alison Lurie: Still 'Driven to Writing'." *Washington Post* 15 October 1985: B. 12.

Mitgang, Herbert. "Out of War, Into Love." *New York Times* 20 May 1979: 63.

Neustatter, Angela. "Inspired Laughter." *Observer* 22 April 1979: 42.

Parini, Jay. "The Novelist at Sixty." *Horizon* March 1986: 21-22.

Pearlman, Mickey and Katherine U. Henderson. *Inter/view: talks with America's writing women*. Lexington: University Press of Kentucky, 1990.

Satz, Martha. "A Kind of Detachment: An Interview with Alison Lurie." *Southwest Review*, 71 (1986): 194-202.

Stickney, J. "A Novelist Studies Fashion." *People Weekly* 16 (30 November 1981): 95-100.

Todd, Janet (ed.). *Women Writers Talking*. New York: Holmes and Meier, 1983: 81-95.

Tookey, Christopher. "The witch guide to literary London." *Books and Bookmen* 352 (January 1985): 24-25.

Watts, Janet. "American Attitudes." *The Observer* (Magazine Section), 20 January, 1985.

Secondary Criticism

Abbott, H. Porter. *Diary Fiction*. Ithaca: Cornell University Press, 1984: 40-53.

Aldridge, John W. "How Good Is Alison Lurie?" *Commentary* January 1975: 79-81.

Aldridge, John W. *The American Novel and the Way We Live Now*. Oxford University Press, 1983: 84-92.

Anon. *Current Biography*. 47 (February 1986): 26-30.

Barasch, F. K. "Faculty Images In Recent American Fiction." *College Literature* 10 (1983): 28-37.

Barber, Michael. "English Flavours." *Books and Bookmen* February 1986: 30.

Bradbury, Malcolm. "Paleface Professor." *Times* 19 January 1985: 6.

Clarke, Graham (ed.). *The American City*. New York: St. Martin's, 1988: 126-128.

Cloutier, Candace. "Alison Lurie." *Contemporary Authors*, New Revision Series. Vol. 17: 275-279.

Commire, Anne. *Something About the Author*. Vol. 46. Gale: Detroit, 1987: 130-134.

Cornwell, Tim. "Catcher of the Wry." *Times Higher Education Supplement* 1221 (29 March 1996): 19.

Costa, Richard Hauer. *Alison Lurie*. New York: Twayne, 1992.

de Grandpré, Chantal. "Les universitaires d'Alison Lurie." *Liberté* 30 (1988): 102-7.

Gunton, Sharon R. (ed.). *Contemporary Literary Criticism*. Vol. 18. Detroit: Gale, 1981.

Gussow, Mel. "Comedies of Manners, laced with morals." *New York Times Biographical Service* 29, 9 (September 1988): 1427-8.

Hall, Sharon K. (ed.). *Contemporary Literary Criticism*. Vol. 39. Detroit: Gale, 1986.

Helfand, Michael S. "The Dialectic of Self and Community in Alison Lurie's *The War Between the Tates"* Perspectives on Contemporary Literature* 3, 2 (November 1977): 65-70.

Helterman, Jeffrey and Richard Layman (ed.). *Dictionary of Literary Biography*. Vol. 2. *American Novelists Since World War II*. Detroit: Gale, 1978.

Henderson, Lesley (ed.). *Contemporary Novelists*. London and Chicago: St. James Press, 1991: 574-5.

Kapp, Isa. "Oh Mom, Poor Mom!" *American Scholar* 49 (1980): 357-371.

Kirkpatrick, D. L. (ed.). *Contemporary Novelists*. London and Chicago: St. James Press, 1986: 547-9.

Kruse, Horst. "Extended Wars in Alison Lurie's *The War Between the Tates."* Literatur in Wissenschaft und Unterricht* (University of Kiel), 25, 1 (1992): 3-12.

Kruse, Horst. "Museums and Manners: The Novels of Alison Lurie." *Anglia*, 111, 3-4 (1993): 410-38.

La Belle, Jenijoy. *Herself Beheld: The Literature of the Looking Glass*. Ithaca and London: Cornell University Press, 1988: 93-99.

Lohrey, Amanda. "The Liberated Heroine: New Varieties of Defeat." *Meanjin*, 38 (1979): 294-304.

Maury, Pierre. "Alison Lurie, ses universitaires et leurs amours." *Le soir (Bruxelles)* 7 January 1988: 27.

Millar, Dan. "Californian Graffiti." *Sight and Sound* 48 (1980): 18-21.

Newman, Judie. "The Revenge of the Trance Maiden: Intertextuality and Alison Lurie." *Plotting Change: Contemporary Women's Fiction.* Ed. L. Anderson. London: Edward Arnold, 1990: 112-127.
Newman, Judie. "Sexual and Civil Conflicts: George F. Kennan and *The War Between the Tates.*" *University Fiction.* Ed. David Bevan. Amsterdam and Atlanta, Georgia: Rodopi, 1990: 102-122.
Newman, Judie. "Alison Lurie." in *Postwar Literatures in English.* Ed. Hans Bertens, Theo Dihaen, Joris Duytschaever, Richard Todd. Groningen: Wolters Noordhoff, 1990: 1-14, A1, B1.
Newman, Judie. "Telling a Woman's Story: Fiction as Biography and Biography as Fiction in Mary Gordon's *Men and Angels* and Alison Lurie's *The Truth About Lorin Jones.*" *Neo-Realism in Contemporary American Fiction.* Ed. Kristiaan Versluys. Amsterdam: Rodopi and Antwerpen: Restant, 1992: 171-192.
Newman, Judie. "Alison Lurie: A Bibliography, 1945-1989." *Bulletin of Bibliography* 49, 2 (June 1992): 109-114.
Newman, Judie. "Paleface into Redskin: Cultural Transformation in Alison Lurie's *Foreign Affairs.*" *Forked Tongues? Comparing Twentieth-Century British and American Literature.* Ed. Ann Massa and Alistair Stead. London: Longman, 1994: 188-205.
Newman, Judie. "Solitary Sojourners in Nature: Revisionary Transcendentalism in Alison Lurie's *Love and Friendship* and Marilynne Robinson's *Housekeeping.*" *The Insular Dream: Obsession and Resistance.* Ed. Kristiaan Versluys. Amsterdam: Free University Press, 1995: 303-323.
Olderman, Raymond M. "American Fiction 1974-1976: The People Who Fell to Earth." *Contemporary Literature* XIX, 4 (1978): 497-530.
Rogers, Katharine M. "The Uses of Adultery." *American Women Writing Fiction.* Ed. Mickey Pearlman. Lexington: University Press of Kentucky, 1989: 115-134.
Riley, Carolyn (ed.). *Contemporary Literary Criticism.* Vol. 4. Detroit: Gale, 1975.
Riley, Carolyn and Phyllis Carmel Mendelson (ed.). *Contemporary Literary Criticism.* Vol. 5. Detroit: Gale, 1976.
Shapiro. H. "*Foreign Affairs* Earns Novelist Alison Lurie Acclaim And A Place beside Henry James." *People Weekly* 3 December 1984: 73-76.
Smith, Godfry. "Paperback Writer." *Sunday Times Magazine* 20 April, 1980: 97.
Stark, John. "Alison Lurie's Career." *Hollins Critic* 26, 1 (February 1989): 1-8.

Trilling, Diana. "The Liberated Heroine." *Partisan Review* 45 (1978): 501-22.

Wakeman, John (ed.). *World Authors.* New York: H. W. Wilson, 1980.

Reviews

Love and Friendship

Book World. 16 (10 August 1986): 12.
Encounter. XX, 2 (February 1963): 90. (Kathleen Nott).
New York Times Book Review 1 April 1962: 41. (Frank H. Lyell).
New York Times Book Review 6 July 1986: 24.
Times Literary Supplement 23 November 1962: 885.

The Nowhere City

Books and Bookmen February 1986: 30.
Hudson Review 19, 1 (Spring 1966): 124-134. (Roger Sale).
Observer 9 February 1986: 26.
Punch 248 (17 February 1965): 258. (R. G. G. Price).
Times Literary Supplement 4 February 1965: 81.

Imaginary Friends

Hudson Review 20, 4 (Winter 1967-8): 666-674. (Roger Sale).
Los Angeles Times Book Review 25 May 1986: 10.
New Statesman 27 March 1987: 36 (Maggie Gee).
New York Review of Books IX, 10 (7 December 1967): 23. (Denis Donoghue).
New York Times Book Review 15 October 1967: 56. (Martin Levin).
New York Times Book Review 6 July 1986: 24.
Punch 253 (19 July 1967): 108. (John Raymond).
Times Literary Supplement 6 July 1967: 593.

Real People

Books and Bookmen April 1970: 25. (Roger Baker).
Commentary 48, 2 (August 1969): 60-62. (Elizabeth Dalton).
London Magazine 10, 3 (June 1970): 87-8. (Michael Field).
New Yorker 11 October, 1969: 199-200.
Times Literary Supplement 19 February 1970: 193.

The War Between the Tates

Atlantic September 1974: 103.
Booklist 71, 15 September, 1974.
Book World – The Washington Post 11 August 1974: 3. (Doris Grumbach).
Journal of Higher Education 47, 1 (Jan/Feb 1976): 107-12. (P. G. Altbach).
The Listener 20 June 1974: 808. (Derwent May).
London Magazine 14, 5 (December 1974/January 1975): 125-9. (Julian Jebb).
Ms. January 1975: 41-2. (Rachel B. Cowan).
New Republic 171, no. 6 and 7 (10 and 17 August 1974): 24-5. (John Leonard).
New Review 1, 4 (1974): 75-77. (Marigold Johnson).
Newsweek 5 August 1974: 64. (Walter Clemons).
New York Review of Books XXI, 13 (8 August 1974): 32-33.
New York Times Book Review LXXIX, 30 (28 July 1974): 1-2. (Sara Sanborn).
New York Times Book Review 30 March 1986: 28. (Patricia T. O'Connor).
Spectator 29 June 1974: 807. (Peter Ackroyd).
Times Literary Supplement 21 June 1974: 657.
Village Voice 8 August 1974: 27. (Martin Washburn).

Only Children

Atlantic May, 1979: 4.
Booklist 75 (15 March 1979): 1132.
Book World – The Washington Post 29 April, 1979: M.5. (Victoria Glendinning).
Christian Science Monitor 14 May 1979: B.4. (J. Domowitz).
Chronicle of Higher Education 18 (16 April 1978): 12. (Doris Grumbach).
Encounter LIII, 2 (August 1979): 51-8. (Tom Paulin).
Harper's July 1979: 78. (Jeffrey Burke).
Kirkus Reviews 47 (1 March 1979): 286.
Library Journal 104 (15 April 1979): 976. (V. W. Marr).
Listener 19 April 1979: 559-60. (Gabriele Annan).
Los Angeles Times Book Review 27 May 1990: 10.
National Review 31 (7 December 1979): 1576 + 1579. (Thomas Bridges).

New Republic 180 (12 May 1979): 37-8. (Ann Hulbert).
New Statesman 20 April 1979: 563. (Jeremy Treglown).
Newsweek 93 (23 April 1979): 98. (Jack Kroll).
New York Review of Books XXVI, 10 (14 June 1979): 31-2. (Mary Gordon).
New York Times 9 April 1979: C. 17. (Christopher Lehmann-Haupt).
New York Times 11 May 1980: 47.
New York Times Book Review 84 (22 April 1979): 7, 27. (Joyce Carol Oates).
New Yorker 55 (1979): 174.
The Progressive 43, 9 (September 1979): 60.
Punch 276 (25 April 1979): 742. (Claire Tomalin).
Saturday Review 6 (1979): 61-2. (Lynn Sharon Schwartz).
Time 113 (11 June 1979): 72 and 74. (John Skow).
Times Literary Supplement 4001 (23 November 1979): 41. (Rosemary Dinnage).
Yale Review LXIX, 1 (Autumn 1979): 89-103. (Edith Milton).

The Heavenly Zoo

Booklist 76 (15 July 1980): 1676. (D. M. Wilms).
Book World – The Washington Post 13 July 1980: 8-9. (E. Merriam).
British Book News Children's Spring Supplement, 1980: 12. (G. Williams).
Center for Children's Books Bulletin 34 (October 1980): 36.
Junior Bookshelf 44 (April 1980): 70. (A. T.)
Kirkus Reviews 48 (1 July 1980): 840.
Publishers' Weekly 217 (6 June 1980): 82.
School Library Journal 27 (September 1980): 75. (P. Dooley).

Clever Gretchen

Booklist 76 (15 March 1980): 1060. (D. M. Wilms).
Book World – The Washington Post 13 July 1980: 8-9. (E. Merriam).
Center for Children's Books Bulletin 33 (June 1980): 195.
Christian Science Monitor 12 May 1980: B.8. (Alexandra Johnson).
Horn Book 56 (April 1980): 180-1. (E. L. Heins).
Junior Bookshelf 44 (December 1980): 292-3.
Junior Bookshelf 54 (April 1990): 87-88.
Kirkus Reviews 48 (1 April 1980): 441.
New Statesman 100 (14 November 1980): 20. (Rosemary Stones).

New York Times Book Review 85, 17 (27 April 1980): 62. (Selma G. Lanes).
Publishers' Weekly 217 (29 February 1980): 93.
School Library Journal 26 (April 1980): 96. (George Shannon).
School Library Journal 29 (January 1983): 31. (Elizabeth Segel).
Times Literary Supplement 4034 (18 July 1980): 808. (Brigid Brophy).
W.E.A. Women's Studies Newsletter 8 (March 1988): 21-22.

The Language of Clothes

Architectural Review CLXXIII, 1032 (February 1983): 73. (Alistair Best).
Atlantic 248 (December 1981): 92. (P-L Adams).
Booklist 78 (15 October 1981): 272. (J. M. Ehresman).
Choice 19 (February 1982): 792.
Cosmopolitan december 1981: p.22.
Glamour February 1983: 213.
Journal of Interdisciplinary History XIII, 2 (August 1982): 311-15. (Lois Banner).
Kirkus Reviews 49 (15 September 1981): 1209-10.
Library Journal 106 (15 November 1981): 2230. (M. Miller).
Listener 6 May 1979: 24-5. (Stephen Gardiner).
Mademoiselle February 1982: 46-8. (Jane Howard).
Nation 233 (21 November 1981): 541-5. (E. Fox-Genovese).
New Directions for Women 11 (March-Aapril 1982): 14. (Ann Ilan Alter).
New Republic 185 (23 December 1981): 32. (Anne Tyler).
New Society 60 (23 April 1982): 145-6. (Sheila MacLeod).
New Statesman 103 (7 May 1982): 22-3. (Marion Glastonbury).
New York 14 (14 December 1981): 100-102. (Rhoda Koenig).
New York Review of Books 29, 6 (1982): 38-41. (Anne Hollander).
New York Times Book Review 87, 3 (17 January 1982): 16. (Walter Goodman).
Publishers' Weekly 220 (9 October 1981): 58. (Genevieve Stuttaford).
Punch 282 (14 April 1982): 630-1. (Stanley Reynolds).
Saturday Review November 1981: 80-82. (Anna Shapiro).
Time 118 (30 November 1981): 56-8. (J. D. Reed).
Times Literary Supplement 14 May 1982: 525. (Lorna Sage).
Weightwatchers May 1982: 12-13.

Fabulous Beasts

Booklist 79 (1 June 1983): 1283.
Center for Children's Books Bulletin 35 (April 1982): 153.
Horn Book 58 (April 1982): 182. (A. A. Flowers).
Junior Bookshelf 46 (February 1982): 18. (M.C.).
Kirkus Reviews 50 (15 February 1982): 204.
McCalls November 1981: V 18.
Newsweek 7 December 1981: 101. (Walter Clemons).
School Library Journal 28 (January 1982): 79. (P. Dooley).
School Librarian 30 (June 1982): 133. (M. Meek).
Times Literary Supplement 1981: 1358.

American Audio Prose Recordings (1984)

Library Journal 110 (1 October 1985): 89. (Bruce Connolly).

Foreign Affairs

America 152 (4 May 1985): 379. (Ronald Wendling).
Booklist 80 (August 1984): 1571.
Books May 1987: 9.
The Bookseller 26 January 1985: 329. (Quentin Oates).
Book World – The Washington Post 14 (30 September 1984): 6. (Joel Conarroe).
Book World – The Washington Post 15 (1 December 1985): 12.
Christian Science Monitor 76 (19 October 1984): 24. (James Kaufmann).
Cosmopolitan (U.S. Edition) October 1984: 42. (Carol E. Rinzler).
Encounter 65, 2 (July-August 1985): 48-9. (James Lasdun).
Hudson Review 38, 1 (1985): 127-30. (W. H. Pritchard).
Illustrated London News March 1985: 65. (Sally Emerson).
Kirkus Reviews 52 (15 July 1984): 644.
Le Monde 16 January 1987: 20. (Nicole Zand).
Library Journal 109 (August 1984): 1468. (Anneliese Schwarzer).
Library Journal 110 (January 1985): 52.
Listener 113 (17 January 1985): 21. (D. J. Enright).
London Review of Books 7 (21 February 1985): 5.
Los Angeles Times Book Review 21 October 1984: 1, 12. (Charles Champlin).
Mademoiselle November 1984: p.86.
Ms. 13 (October 1984): 142. (Barbara Fisher Williamson).

New Republic 3638 (8 October 1984): 34-36. (Dorothy Wickenden).
New Statesman 109 (25 January 1985): 31. (Liz Heron).
Newsweek 104 (24 September 1984): 80. (Walter Clemons).
New York 24 September 1984: 97. (Rhoda Koenig).
New Yorker 60 (5 November 1984): 170.
New York Review of Books 11 October 1984: 37-8. (Gabrriele Annan).
New York Times 133 (13 September 1984): 23. (Christopher Lehmann-Haupt).
New York Times Book Review LXXXIX, 38 (16 September 1984): 9. (Anne Bernays).
New York Times Book Review XC (17 November 1985): 50. (C. Gerald Fraser).
Observer 2 December 1984: 19. (Mary McCarthy).
Observer 20 January 1985: 46.
People Weekly 22 (5 November 1984): 18-19.
Philadelphia Magazine July 1985: 89. (Constance Adler).
Publishers' Weekly 226 (20 July 1984): 71.
Punch 288 (23 January 1985): 52.
Saturday Review 10 (November 1984): 80. (Jay Parini).
School Librarian 33 (September 1985): 284. (Margaret Meek).
Spectator 254 (26 January 1985): 23-24. (Ferdinand Mount).
Sunday Times 20 January 1985: 44.
Time 124 (15 October 1984): 64-5. (R. Z. Sheppard).
Times Literary Supplement 4270 (1 February 1985): 109. (Lorna Sage).
U.S.A. Today 2 (7 September 1984): 3 D.
U.S.A. Today 3 (14 September 1984): 3 D.
Village Voice Literary Supplement October 1984: 5. (Maureen Corrigan).
Vogue 174 (September 1984): 570.
Wall Street Journal (Eastern Edition) 204 (10 October 1984): 30. (Margaret Peters).
West Coast Review of Books 11 (January 1985): 34. (D.S.).

The Truth About Lorin Jones

Antioch Review 47, 1 (1989): 106.
Belles Lettres 4 (Spring 1989): 8. (Barbara Griffith Furst).
Booklist 84 (July 1988): 1755.
Books (July 1988): 16. (Mary Flanagan).
Books 3 (August 1989): 19.

Book World – The Washington Post 18 (4 September 1988): 3 + 9. (Clark Blaise).

City Limits July 14-21 1988: 87.

Commonweal 115 (16 December 1988): 690. (Barbara A. Bannon).

Glasgow Herald 9 July 1988: 14. (Alan Taylor).

Guardian 8 July 1988: 25. (Norman Shrapnel).

Guardian Weekly 141 (13 August 1989): 29.

Harpers and Queen July 1988: 26, 30. (Virginia Llewellyn Smith).

Hudson Review XLII, 1 (Spring 1989): 137-8. (Dean Flower).

Kirkus Reviews 56 (1 July 1988): 924.

Library Journal 113 (1 September 1988): 183.

Listener 120 (28 July 1988): 29. (Scott Bradfield).

Literary Review July 1988: 22-3. (Laura Cummings).

London Review of Books 10 (1 September 1988): 24. (Anthony Thwaite).

Los Angeles Times Book Review 20 May 1990: 14.

Macleans 101 (10 October 1988): 48. (Darlene James).

Massachusetts Review XXX, 1 (1988): 107-9. (Edith Milton).

Ms. 17 (October 1988): 88-89. (Annette Williams Jaffe).

Nation 247 (21 November 1988): 540-542. (Brina Caplan).

New Directions for Women 18 (January 1989): 21. (Susan E. Davis).

New Statesman and Society 1 (8 July 1988): 39. (Sara Maitland).

Newsweek 112 (10 October 1988): 74.

New York Times 137 (8 July 1988): 39.

New York Times 12 September 1988: C. 18. (Christopher Lehmann-Haupt).

New York Times Book Review 93 (4 September 1988): 3. (Edmund White).

Observer 10 July 1988: 42. (Claire Tomalin).

Observer 17 July 1988: 42.

Observer 16 July 1989: 42.

People Weekly 30 (7 November 1988): 38-9. (Joanne Kaufman).

Publishers' Weekly 234 (8 July 1988): 39.

Publishers' Weekly 237 (6 April 1990): 113.

Punch 295 (22 July 1988): 52-3. (Paul Taylor).

Scotsman 23 July 1988: viii. (Tom Adair).

Spectator 261 (16 July 1988): 31-2. (Francis King).

Spectator 261 (3 December 1988): 32. (Anne Chisholm).

Sunday Times 10 July 1988: G. 5. (Peter Kemp).

Time 132 (19 September 1988): 95. (John Skow).

Times 7 July 1988: 14. (Victoria Glendinning).

Times Educational Supplement 5 August 1988: 17. (Frances Spalding).
Times Educational Supplement 23 December 1988: 9 (Andrew Davies).
Times Literary Supplement 8 July 1988: 759. (Austin MacCurtain).
Vogue August 1988: 24. (David Sexton).
Wall Street Journal 212 (11 October 1988): A. 20. (Donna Rifkind).
West Coast Review of Books 14, 4 (1989): 25.
West Coast Review of Books 14, 5 (1989): 22.
Women's Review of Books VI, 5 (February 1989): 11. (Emily Toth).

Don't Tell the Grown-ups

Antioch Review 48 (Fall 1990): 541. (Irwin H. Inman).
Booklist 86 (15 March 1990): 1411. (Bill Ott).
Bloomsbury Review 10 (March/April 1990): 11.
Book World 20 (8 April 1990): 8. (Michael Dirda).
Books For Keeps 65 (November 1990): 3.
Boston Review 15 (October 1990): 26-7.
Children's Book Review Service 19 (December 1990): p.47.
Horn Book Magazine 66 (May 1990): 364-5. (Robert D. Hale).
Kirkus Reviews 58 (1 January 1990): 32.
Library Journal 115 (15 February 1990): 186. (Patricia Dooley).
Library Talk 3 (May 1990): 9.
Listener 123 (31 May 1990): 20. (Adam Thorpe).
London Magazine 30, 5-6 (August-September, 1990): 119-120. (Ann Thwaite).
Los Angeles Times Book Review 11 March 1990: 6. (Sonja Bolle).
New Leader 73, 16 (16 April 1990): 20-21. (Joseph E. Illick).
New Statesman and Society 3 (25 May 1990): 32.
New York Review of Books 37 (26 April 1990): 45. (Janet Adam Smith).
New York Times Book Review 95 (11 March 1990): 13-14. (R. Brown).
New York Times (Late Edition) 139 (27 February 1990): 17. (Michiko Kakutani).
New Yorker 66 (7 May 1990): 110.
Observer 20 May 1990: 39. (Edward Blishen).
Observer 27 May 1990: 65.
Publishers' Weekly 237 (26 January 1990): 408.
Publishers' Weekly 237 (9 February 1990): 28. (Molly McQuade).
School Library Journal 36 (December 1990): 32. (Betty Carter).

Spectator 264 (16 June 1990): 30-31. (Juliet Townsend).
Times Educational Supplement 8 June 1990: B. 10.
Times Literary Supplement 8-14 June 1990: 607-8. (Humphrey Carpenter).
Tribune Books 4 March 1990: 6. (Liz Rosenberg).
Utne Reader July/August 1990: 107-8. (Deborah Vajda).
Village Voice May 1990: 41. (Polly Shulman).

The Oxford Book of Modern Fairy Tales

Booklist 89 (1 May 1993): 1572. (Ray Olson).
Los Angeles Times 3 October 1993: 1. (Frederick Busch).
New Republic 209, 20 (1993): 39-41. (Maria Tatar).
New Statesman and Society 6 (28 May 1993): 40. (Janet Barron).
New York Times 19 August 1993: 15. (Janet Maslin).
Studies in Short Fiction 32, 2 (1995): 267-8. (M. Hallissy).
Times Literary Supplement 4713 (1993): 7. (M. Warner).

Women And Ghosts

Booklist 91 (1 September 1994): 24. (Alice Joyce).
Boston Globe 11 September 1994: 21. (Amanda Heller).
Chicago Tribune 15 November 1994: 4. (Terry Irwin).
Daily Telegraph 11 June 1994.
Guardian 13 July 1994: 8. (Claire Messud).
Houston Chronicle 18 December 1994: 31. (Richard Hauer Costa).
Independent 25 June 1994.
L'Express 4 August 1984.
Library Journal 119 (July 1994): 131. (Andrea Caron Kempf).
Los Angeles Times 11 September 1994: 6. (Susan Salter Reynolds).
Los Angeles Times 28 October 1994: 4. (Elaine Kendall).
New Statesman and Society 7 (17 June 1994): 38. (Kathryn Hughes).
New York Review of Books 42 (2 February 1995): 25. (John Banville).
New York Times 3 October 1994: 14. (Christopher Lehmann-Haupt).
New York Times Book Review 18 September 1994: 12. (David Leavitt).
San Francisco Chronicle 9 October 1994: 5. (Tessa De Carlo).
Sunday Telegraph 19 June 1994.
Sunday Times 12 June 1994.
Times Literary Supplement 4759 (17 June 1994): 23. (Alex Clark).